Psyche-Soul-ology:

An Inspirational Approach to Appreciating
and Understanding Troubled Kids

David L. Roberts, BA, MS, MS, PhD

Psyche-Soul-ology:
An Inspirational Approach to Appreciating
and Understanding Troubled Kids
2nd Edition

iUniverse books may be ordered through booksellers or by contacting:

iUniverse
1663 Liberty Drive
Bloomington, IN 47403
www.iuniverse.com
1-800-Authors (1-800-288-4677)

Because of the dynamic nature of the Internet, any web addresses or links contained in this book may have changed since publication and may no longer be valid. The views expressed in this work are solely those of the author and do not necessarily reflect the views of the publisher, and the publisher hereby disclaims any responsibility for them.

Any people depicted in stock imagery provided by Thinkstock are models, and such images are being used for illustrative purposes only.

Certain stock imagery © Thinkstock.

ISBN: 978-1-4759-1618-8 (sc)
ISBN: 978-1-4759-1619-5 (hc)
ISBN: 978-1-4759-1620-1 (e)

Library of Congress Control Number: 2012907273

Print information available on the last page.

iUniverse rev. date: 08/03/2015

This book is dedicated to those who are currently serving troubled kids, and to those who plan to work with troubled kids in the future. Our dedication to be the best we can be in the respective roles we play in the lives of these kids must be based in a sense of Calling; and carried out with respect, understanding, appreciation, inspiration, and compassion.

Contents

Preface

E very day when I go to work I am reminded all over again of the awesome responsibility I have to be the best I can be for myself and for the kids I serve. My work is my passion and I take very seriously the role I play in the lives of my clients. This current text contains many ideas and examples of how to work effectively with troubled, high-risk or at-risk youth with the intention of helping adults, within all roles pertaining to kids, match their efforts with their desired outcomes and goals. As I continue my career I am always amazed at how biased and ineffective many adults are relative to the roles we all play in the lives of kids. With this book I hope to give people the tools needed to actually produce favorable outcomes through appropriate interactions, relationships and associations we have with the kids in our charge either personally and/or professionally.

My first book, At the Mercy of Externals: Righting Wrongs and Protecting Kids, 2ⁿᵈ Edition, raises and addresses many issues faced by adults and kids in various situations and contexts. It has been revised and is now offered as a companion text to this book. The title suggests a two-step approach to the problems families, kids and professionals face relative to successfully guiding kids into adulthood. The concept of "righting wrongs" suggests the need to intervene with adults in an effort to improve effectiveness through an ongoing process of open and honest self-evaluation and self-assessment. "Protecting kids" suggests that when adults conquer our own unresolved issues from the past, the kids in our care can be protected to a large extent from abuse and victimization which comes in many forms and occurs within different contexts. Awareness of unresolved issues comes through understanding the Roberts FLAGS (RFLAGS) Model which graphically explains how we tend to act out emotion-based anxiety rather than face the issues from the past often fueling our negative emotions of **F**ear, **L**oneliness, **A**nger, **G**uilt and **S**hame. The intensity and severity of the negative emotions is directly related to the degree of abuse and victimization we experience during childhood. These ineffective and damaging patterns of interaction are then passed down to the kids with whom we have contact and for whom we have responsibility.

At the Mercy of Externals: Righting Wrongs and Protecting Kids, 2nd Edition, clearly goes hand-in-hand as a companion text with the current work Psyche-Soul-ology: An Inspirational Approach to Appreciating and Understanding Troubled Kids. I recently entered a contest for self-published writers and received a critique of my first book. The critic liked the overall concepts and the material's content and quality. Commentary from numerous readers, including college students, parents, and professionals, supports my belief in its effectiveness relative to providing insight into issues faced and seldom understood by people outside the real life situations of troubled kids. Through this, my second book, I intend to step up to the challenge and offer the means for identifying, correcting, and resolving the issues and concerns I raise. What makes my approaches different from many other professionals is my foundation of a purely spiritual, non-religious perspective which supersedes many views and beliefs of organized religions. I see my career as both my calling and passion in life, and consider my role as a licensed clinical psychologist to also be a ministry - without any religious affiliation - which reaches out to society's throwaway kids and their families. As a very important part of my job and my thinking I constantly seek out spiritual guidance as I work and continue my own process of open and honest self-evaluation and self-assessment relative to personal and professional growth and development. The term and title of this book, Psyche-Soul-ology, focuses on both the mind of those I serve and on their soul which I explain to them as "the energy that is you is God or Spirit in you." My kids get this and understand they do not have to change into someone else. They need only to work differently with who they already are.

In March 1996 I moved from Los Angeles to the desert around Palm Springs, CA to take a job with the Riverside County Department of Mental Health. This book was started in 2004 and not finished until 2007 originally. It is being revised now as a second edition and covers a few additional details relative to my experiences in LA, through the move back to Mobile, Alabama in December 2004 and beyond into early 2012. The subject matter of this text originated while in Riverside County, through my present day activities with my private practice now in Mobile. My experiences with low income kids and families now encompasses the range or kids from as young as three years old all the way to nineteen. My practice is 99% based in services to low income kids and families now back in my hometown. The racial mix is different here in Alabama with services being primarily provided to both low income European and African American families and kids. Occasionally I have Spanish-speaking clients, but no more than three families to date here in Alabama. This is a very big change in target populations compared to my experiences in California. The theories and practice approaches I formulated and perfected in California work equally as well here in Mobile with the populations I now serve.

Through the current text I will reintroduce some of the topics and perspectives from At the Mercy of Externals: Righting Wrongs and Protecting Kids, 2nd Edition as they apply to the issues and subjects introduced within this material. Because I am a practicing psychologist who specializes in the population of troubled, at-risk, and high-risk kids I will be able to offer appropriate and specific case examples to help validate some of the points I will raise. All names and other specific details of each case example have been changed to protect personal privacy and confidentiality. As you read you will encounter everything from myths to misperceptions relative to issues of psychological development, sexuality, addiction, criminality, and intelligence, all mixed with tried and proven approaches which maximize efforts to reach and guide kids successfully into their respective and subjective futures. The RFLAGS Model will be revisited and connected to all of this as a very important frame of reference.

As you read you will be able to see how this book takes kids and adults out of the bondage to external factors and gives them the internal perspective needed to successfully move forward in life. Of utmost importance is the willingness on the part of the reader to look openly and honestly at your own beliefs and techniques used while interacting with kids. From there it will be equally as important to make internal and external changes and adjustments as needed which will ultimately lead to effectiveness and successful outcomes regardless of the roles we play in kid's lives.

New to this text will be the introduction of codes of ethics, codes of conduct, and the concept of moral development and responsibilities which need to shape our value systems and the way we prioritize things in our lives. Be sure to look again at the Oath to Children I proposed at the end of chapter six in my first book and keep in mind the significance of this as a place to start for all adults. I will also introduce and share the basic spiritual beliefs I use as a constant guide in my work with kids and even in my interactions with my own daughter and my grandchildren. I believe that through this book we can begin to agree upon some basic standards and building blocks which will improve the overall conditions of people within all of the contexts of home/family, school, community, society, politics, and religion. You will have the opportunity to see troubled kids through my eyes and will learn to see them for whom they really are rather than judge them for and by what they do and say. These are critically important changes in perspective and reference which need to occur within each of us and within all settings and contexts in which kids live and learn. This entire book represents a significant part of my entire 'author bio'.

1

Myths and Misperceptions

Many people today talk a lot about "those kids", using various labels and phrases which do nothing to identify and assist the kids behind the labels they attach. However, very few people talk about "those adults" who are ineffective in their attempts to reach this misunderstood and mistreated group of kids. I am always amazed at the inappropriate and damaging techniques often used during interactions with kids in general, not only within the home/family context, but in various settings outside this context and by professionals who have supposedly been trained to teach, guide, or otherwise supervise kids. Some kids are actually more traumatized by adults outside their home/family environment than they are within it. I believe one of the main reasons for these mistakes is based in the unwillingness of many professionals to learn about other people, cultures and realities as part of their professional training. One of the most arrogant, ignorant, and damaging attitudes held by many adults, often referred to as "do-gooders", is the belief that: *I already know enough, based on my own life experiences, to know how to assist every other group.'* Or, even worse, are those adults who think everyone should see things their way and through their often biased and subjective ways of looking at life and the world. Furthermore, I am certain one of the main reasons for my effectiveness with troubled, high-risk kids is based in the fact I did everything I could to learn both from my past and from the realities many families face daily by literally going into those environments. I did so with the desire to learn about the people I wanted to serve before I ever tried to imagine how I could be of assistance to them on any level. This is part of what makes my professional life so rewarding and satisfying.

There is never a work day when I think 'I really don't want to go to work today'. Sure there are times when I think about getting a few extra hours of sleep, but that's never enough to make me call in sick or dread my day. I consider myself to be one of the luckiest people anywhere simply because I love my job – literally everything about my job, except of course some of the paperwork. My work as a licensed clinical psychologist is truly my calling in life and that aspect about which I am the most passionate. All of this is due to the fact I get to work with some of the most wonderful and incredible kids in the world. The kids I am referring to are those at risk of having the greatest number of problems and getting into the most trouble because of numerous complicating factors, poor judgment, and lack of self-control. Webster's defines passion as an "intense, driving or overmastering feeling". It is associated with "ardent affection" and "a strong liking for or devotion to some activity, object, or concept." The affection I feel for my kids is that of simply pouring my heart into my work with them. When they succeed, fail, get injured, or die I am easily moved to tears because I have an emotional investment in them which exceeds my professional requirements. One of my co-workers said this is because "you give them your heart." My satisfaction comes through their success and the awareness I had at least some part in helping that happen.

In my first book At the Mercy of Externals: Righting Wrongs and Protecting Kids, 2nd Edition, I give some of the history of how I found my niche in the field of psychology. Because I'm sure you have already read that text I won't go into the historical aspects of my decision. However, I will go into the reasons I chose this population as the major focus of my professional efforts. Keep in mind that I grew up in the so-called "Deep South" and moved to Los Angeles in 1989 to begin my Ph.D. program in clinical psychology. As a European American I grew up surrounded by religious extremism and hatred based in the rawest forms of bigotry and prejudice. My introduction into the culture which is California was a bit of a shock at first, but I quickly learned to appreciate my surroundings and the people and diversity I encountered. In spite of having grown up in Alabama during the entire civil rights movement of the 1950's,- 60's and -70's I never bought into any of the racism. However, I didn't fully understand the horrors of discrimination and prejudice until I moved to Los Angeles. I am so grateful for the awakening I experienced through my graduate training, especially the experiences I had in and around East Los Angeles and Upper South Central Los Angeles.

My training with this population of kids labeled as at-risk, high-risk or troubled youth began in September 1992 as a predoctoral psychological intern in a gang prevention task force program literally located behind the Los Angeles County, University of Southern California (LACUSC) Medical Center. This is the hospital featured at the opening credits of "General Hospital", an old, but popular daytime soap opera from the past. I was working in Murchison Street Elementary School and the area of Ramona Gardens Housing Project, home of the Hazard Gang named for Hazard Park in the same area. The movie "American Me", filmed in the early 1990's, was shot in this specific area of East Los Angeles. I was working in a Family Service Center at the school with families and children primarily living in and around Ramona Gardens. I went into this area knowing I knew nothing about the culture of East LA, rather than thinking I knew everything I needed to know because of my graduate training toward my Ph.D. and previous degrees and life experiences and perspectives. Thank goodness I had already learned of the arrogance most European Americans exhibit in various respective fields when working with so-called minority populations. My ignorance and the awareness of my ignorance allowed me to be fully accepted by the people who lived within this community.

I remember the first few weeks of driving into an area most people were afraid to enter. In the mornings the gang members were still sleeping, but in the afternoons they would be hanging out on the street corners and would 'dog' me (stare at me) when I drove by. There was a four-way stop at the bottom of the hill where I would have to come to a complete stop. I could feel them staring at me and was always uncomfortable, but knew they had to be wondering who I was and what I was doing in their neighborhood. This continued until one afternoon when I stopped at a convenience store at one of the two entrances into the area. As I got out of my car I was approached by two obvious gang members who asked me for money. I told them I didn't give out money and walked into the store.

While inside the store I thought about the possibility of this being an opportunity to introduce myself to them and tell them who I am. It made sense and, while I didn't have the money to spare as a graduate student, I decided to give both of them $5.00 each. I called them over to me in the parking lot and offered them my hand in friendship after giving them the money, telling them my name and describing my training as a graduate student in psychology working at the school site as part of an internship. After assuring them I was not involved in law enforcement or any kind of undercover work with immigration (as was often their assumption), I explained the nature of my training as that of providing assistance to kids in the area, some of whom were probably even related to these two guys. I asked them to remember my face and my car, asking them to also tell their friends who I am. They agreed and assured me I would have no problems in the area because of the way I had talked to them. This was my first experience of gaining respect from a group hated by most people and judged as worthless throwaways because of their behaviors. I understand this perspective of outsiders and have learned not to make the same mistake, realizing that these guys are human beings too and deserve respect as such even if I can't respect the criminal activity in which they involve themselves. From that day on I never had anyone stare at me as I drove in or out of the area. I learned about the communication network within the gangs and the importance of understanding and learning how to use that to my advantage so I could work with them more effectively and without being viewed with suspicion.

My decision to accept this internship in East Los Angeles was made in February 1992 for the beginning of the next school year which would start in September. This would be my last predoctoral training program before I completed the requirements for my Ph.D. in clinical psychology. There was a list of other possible training sites, but no one in my school was signing up for this one. Realizing that the group of kids known as troubled youth was about the only population I had not worked with during any of my previous trainings, I decided to give it a shot. So, I applied for the opportunity and was hired by the school staff after an interview. The program at the elementary school was funded through a Healthy Start Grant offered at that time by the state of California. Murchison Street Elementary School was one of the first schools in the state to receive the so-called "seed money". The Family Service Center would have to be self-supporting by the end of the third year. My internship was called a Gang Prevention Task Force which ultimately became a force of only one from my graduate program, with other students choosing trainings in different areas of the city.

Just two weeks after accepting the September 1992 internship position for the 1992-93 school years, I got mugged in February 1992 by three gang members only two blocks from my apartment. I had decided to get out of my apartment and go for a walk to a local park one afternoon at about 4:00 PM. The walk to the park took me through the gang territory of "Avenues", but along a major street which I had walked many times before and only during the daytime hours. In the past I had a habit of walking and looking down, usually deep in thought about any number of things running intensely through my head. Therefore, I didn't hear or see these kids running up to me. Suddenly I was startled as they grabbed me, with one on each side holding weapons against my ribs - one had a knife and the other was holding a sharpened screw driver. I couldn't tell if the one behind me was armed as he was the one who immediately started going into my pockets.

I had tried to imagine such a scene several times in the past, trying also to imagine how I might actually react to such an event. To my surprise, rather than being frightened, I was enraged. From my mouth came a whole string of obscenities clearly reflecting my extreme displeasure at what was happening. It was obvious to me these kids realized they had probably grabbed the wrong guy. I had sense enough not to overreact in a way that would get me stabbed or cut. However, I reacted enough to let them know I wasn't going down lightly. Because I was watching the weapons, constantly waiting for either of them to draw back to stab me, not even once did I see their faces. My thoughts told me I would fight back rather than get stabbed, but not carry this to the point of them thinking that stabbing me was their only choice for their own protection. They kept telling me to "shut the fuck up" and I kept yelling that back to them wanting to know why they were doing this to me and repeating many of their own words back to them. In hindsight I believe they were thinking I must be crazy not to be afraid and finally pushed me forward telling me to walk ahead, pick up my wallet, and not look back. As they ran away they yelled out "we know where you live". I yelled back "fuck you – you don't know where I live".

In the process of all of this I lost $35.00 cash which I needed for gas and food for the week, along with two gold rings which couldn't be replaced. My keys were thrown into a very large patch of ivy. I never found those primarily because I was too afraid of the rats known to live in that stuff to even venture very far into it. I walked back to my apartment still fuming about all of this. As I got to my building I had to ask the manager to let me into my apartment, explaining to him what had happened in case he needed to re-key the outside doors. Fortunately I had duplicate keys for my apartment and my car, but lost several other keys which had to be replaced.

As I thought about all of this I began to realize how lucky I was not to have been hurt or killed. I was also upset that no one on this busy street stopped to help me. As time passed over the next few days I became quite paranoid for about two months, jumping whenever I heard noises as I walked from my car into the building. It took a while for me to get over blaming myself and simply accept the fact I had been a victim of a crime. I never called the police because I couldn't give them a description of anything but the clothing of the kids. This is how I came to understand the importance of all gang members dressing and looking exactly alike in order to make it more difficult to identify them. I told all of this to my neighbor across the hall in my apartment building who was a member of this gang. Despite my protests he insisted this would be taken care of because I was his friend. I have no idea what happened to these kids after that encounter with my neighbor who I knew and trusted. In a remarkable manner my neighbor always looked out for me. He was older than the kids who robbed me and always told me he respected the work I was doing with gang kids.

As I'm sorting through all aspects of having been mugged, a feeling of dread begins to seep in as I think about the internship in East LA I had just accepted two weeks earlier. It was absolutely too late to change it and I looked toward September with a sense of uncertainty relative to what I was getting myself into within what could turn out to be a completely hostile environment. The only good thing about the mugging experience is that I still use it today to let kids know how bad it feels to be a victim of what they do. Kids always tell me "I would never do that to you Dr. Roberts." I tell them "of course not, you know me. But if you saw me walking down your street wouldn't it go through your mind that I might be an easy victim with money if you didn't know me?" They readily agree, giving me a chance to tell them how messed up it is for them to think that kind of behavior is okay under any circumstances. I can use it to try and get them to imagine the life situations of any victim and what impact such a robbery might have on that person and their family. They always discuss this with me and learn something from the discussion. Fortunately this was the only time anything even close to this has ever happened to me. The lesson I learned is to always pay attention to things going on around me, especially in a large city like LA. Growing up in the South this kind of thinking wasn't necessary. What a hell of a way to learn this lesson. I am glad now that I had something for them to steal because kids usually agree with me these guys would likely have stabbed me out of anger for not getting anything of value from me.

* *

One of the most amazing things for me about my journey to Los Angeles and graduate school at the California School of Professional Psychology, LA campus and now part of Alliant International University, was my exposure to cultural diversity even within the student body which included students literally from around the world. Through these kinds of experiences I began to see that differences between people are based more in socioeconomic and cultural differences than in racial differences. The so-called "races" aren't as clearly divided today as in the past and people of the very same race are often quite diverse when they have different cultural backgrounds. This awareness is the basis for my beliefs in the need to move away from race as a dominant distinction and focus more on cultural/social aspects and poverty as the true differences and indications of diversity. Even for me, the cultural differences in the South were mild when compared to the cultural differences found in California. Imagine the level of culture shock I experienced. I had even considered myself to be rather advanced in my thinking and beliefs compared to others in the South, but soon found I had a lot more to learn.

The people who taught me the most about possible differences between race as a perspective and culture as a perspective were the people from different Spanish-speaking countries and from African Americans I encountered through several different settings. Most associations with African Americans were within professional contexts in California, and more as friends while still living previously in the South. However my personal connections outside of my school environment to those from different Spanish-speaking countries and cultures were more on a friendship basis. At first I couldn't figure out why my level of comfort was so high, especially with people from different parts of Mexico, Cuba and El Salvador until I began to see the similarities between these cultures and the culture in the South. One evening, while visiting the family of one of my Salvadorian friends, it occurred to me that gatherings within these cultures as in the South, center around family, food, and special occasions. Even though at that time I couldn't speak a work of Spanish, I felt like I knew these people and could relate to the familiarity I associated between them and my own cultural background. The other most prominent (though unfavorable) factors were that both cultures were generally male dominated, with a huge significance placed on extreme conservative religious views. Through close friends I had many such experiences and opportunities to learn about different aspects of the respective heritages, traditions and lifestyles.

I also had an opportunity to see Hispanic people as some of the most genuine people I had ever met, especially if they were immigrants from their countries of origin. Very few of those I met were taking advantage of the American welfare system or disability, with probably 99% being gainfully employed in jobs most Americans wouldn't want because of the feeling that as Americans we are above many of the menial jobs requiring hard labor or tasks considered to be boring and meaningless. Even if I didn't like or agree with some of their customs I always knew where they were coming from with regards to our interactions. They didn't try to hide or pretend like a lot of Americans do in order to look better than we really are. I also had the opportunity to understand how hard their lives had been in their countries of origin. It always amazed me to see how some of these immigrants lived, finding it hard to believe that things in this country could actually be better for them than what they left behind. It wasn't until December 1993 when I had a chance to visit with a friend of mine deep into Mexico in the state of Nayarit that I had a chance to see true hardship for myself on a scale which would have been impossible for me to imagine. I have never seen such poverty in my life and, after a two week stay, came back to the US with a different perspective of the realities many Hispanic immigrants try to escape by coming to America.

The single most amazing experience I had in Los Angeles was with a very close friend of mine who lived in the same apartment building with me. His name was Adan Lopez (Adam in English) and he was included in the dedication of my first book along with my grandmother, my daughter, and Susan. Adan became a tremendously important part of my life and my experiences in California. Much of my perspective and many of my beliefs are based on the things I learned through and with him. He was an undocumented immigrant who was diagnosed with a terminal illness at the age of twenty-seven. He had lived and worked in this country for about seven years paying income taxes and money into our social security system which he couldn't recover or claim. He died at the age of twenty-eight, only eighteen months after his diagnosis. I became a significant and important person in his life as well, taking it upon myself to help him get the healthcare and other assistance he so desperately needed. His decision to stay in this country was based on the reality that medical care was better here than it would have been in his hometown in Mexico. Even though he had one sister in the area and a number of friends from his "little town" none of them knew how to access the services he would need in an effort to fight his illness, or for the additional help he needed as he reached the end of his life.

As Adan neared his death he began to use me somewhat like his confessor, telling me that I was the only one who knew "both of his faces" – not in the sense of being two-faced, but in the sense of having two very separate and distinct lives and personalities. He revealed many things to me about his past as a child which included an extreme history of abuse and neglect in Mexico. Domestic violence and alcoholism were the only relationship dynamics he had ever known and he found himself in the streets at the age of eight trying to support himself and his family any way he could. As a result he became involved in a great deal of illegal activity in Mexico which continued through his adolescence until, with the help of his friends, he had the opportunity at twenty years of age to come to Los Angeles and begin working in a factory. This allowed him to support himself and even send money to his mom and siblings back in Mexico. It is easy to see in Mexico the families who have relatives sending them money from the US compared to those who have to exist on what they can earn in Mexico alone. The contrast is shocking and extremely sad.

Adan had a really difficult time trying to work out the issues related to his past, believing, according to religious doctrine, that he was destined to spend an eternity in hell because of his involvement in criminal activity during his childhood years. Together we explored different spiritual perspectives which gave him the peace he needed before his death on February 20, 1992. Through our efforts to make some sense out of his life we were able to learn a lot from each other, all of which served both of us well. There is no doubt in my mind we met so I could help him die with dignity, and so that through his death I could learn to live and to be of service to people in ways I could never have imagined. Eventually

I was able to give Adan's mother the peace she needed as well. I had the privilege of meeting her and his siblings with a friend I knew through Adan during our trip to Mexico nearly two years after Adan's death. His mother was so grateful that I and others could send her son home for burial with the generous donations from friends and coworkers who knew him and loved him. He was a good person with a beautiful soul. His true character had nothing to do with many of the choices he had to make in his life just to survive as a child. Unfortunately Adan's need to survive overshadowed the goodness in him for many years. Two of my most prized possessions were given to me by his mom and oldest sister during my visit and in appreciation for my efforts to help their son and brother. While in Mexico my final gift to Adan and his family was providing a beautiful monument for his grave. These very wonderful people, and especially Adan, touched my life in ways I could have never imagined. I will be forever indebted to Adan and his family for this. Not only did they accept me as a "gabacho" (white American outsider), they saw me as a friend and brother, welcoming me into their lives and into their families. These are the kinds of experiences I had while in Los Angeles and in Mexico that literally changed me forever and clearly influence and impact the way I still see and interpret things today.

The single most important bit of wisdom I gained from all of this is the reality that people will do things as a result of lives based in hardship and chaos which they would never do under other circumstances and conditions. It became very obvious to me how wrong we are, especially here in the United States, and especially as European Americans, when we arrogantly judge and label those individuals and groups we don't know much about or understand. Not only do European Americans judge and misjudge, so do those from the different cultures and backgrounds who become successful in this country and turn their noses up to those who haven't yet "conformed" and who seemingly cause them to be ashamed of their own heritages and roots.

Because of these aforementioned experiences, I have been given the opportunity to know with certainty that behaviors, especially of kids, do not necessarily represent the true character or souls of people. There is a very big difference between making an observation and being judgmental. Judgments literally become personal because we tend to assign labels and descriptions to a person's character. Observations are nothing more than an acknowledgement of what is visible and obvious on the outside relative to behaviors, characteristics, and words. Ignorance simply means that someone doesn't know. Arrogance is when the individual knows they don't know and are actually proud of it, with no desire to change their frame of reference or learn something which could change their minds and increase their understanding. The *arrogantly ignorant* are the ones who do the most harm especially when they put themselves in positions of power and authority over those judged as being less than they are. These are all too often the people who take on roles and responsibilities relative to kids and others easily identified as underdogs and throwaways; and these individuals are without any doubt the most dangerous. Those considered as underdogs and throwaways in society are those who are the most vulnerable and those with the least abilities and means to defend themselves from abuse and victimization.

* *

In my work as a psychologist I have to deal with the aftermath of injustices which can be caused by life circumstances, uncontrollable situations and factors, and by people who are directly responsible for the development and well-being of children. This is what is meant by the phrase "at the mercy of externals" – those factors over which we have very little if any real or perceived ability to effect or change. Because there can be so many things beyond our control, everyone should be extra careful to control those things which we are able to direct and influence. This is extremely important for adults who are in control of the lives and outcomes of kids of all ages. I am constantly shocked with the reality of how ineffective people are in actually directing and redirecting the lives of kids, and even more so when the kids in question are the troubled kids referred to in the title of this book.

As I began my second predoctoral internship in September 1992 at Murchison Street Elementary School I started asking all kinds of questions about the area, the kids, their families and the overall environments in which they lived. I was appalled to learn that each family had a basic plan of what to do to protect themselves when gunfire erupted at any given moment and on a daily basis in the housing project and in the neighborhood around the school. In getting to know each one of the kids and their families I was assigned to serve I would always ask about this and would ask what this experience was like for them. Needless to say the artwork drawn by these K through 6th grade kids was very dark and depicted a lot of violence and death. Generally speaking, I was dealing with single mom's whose kids were the offspring of active members of the Hazard Gang. Even if families weren't directly associated with the gang activity they were all affected tremendously by the violence and criminal activity associated with it.

I spent so much of my time just trying to help these kids and families deal with their emotional distress and daily realities of horrific experiences and events. Every kid I met had either seen someone dead on the streets or had witnessed a shooting of a friend or family member. They had to deal with extreme family problems which included domestic violence and serious alcohol and drug use within their homes and in the area, not to mention all of the gang and criminal activity. It was very common for kids to find used syringes on the sidewalks and in the shrubbery, especially in the housing project. These kids literally lived within a war zone with no way to make peace for themselves, and in many cases with no way to escape from the area by moving. Where could they go but to other areas that were equally as dangerous! A trip to a store was a major outing and many of these kids had never even seen the Pacific Ocean which was no more than about 10 miles from where they lived. Their entertainment consisted primarily of video games and movie rentals, with many parents afraid to let them play outside for obvious reasons including trying to protect them from being recruited into the local gang.

I was given most of my cases either directly from teachers and other school staff or by simply sitting in the front office and getting to know the kids who were seemingly always in trouble. These were usually boys. As a result of the extreme violence in the area and even on the school campus I developed a program called "K.I.T. Cadets: Kids In Touch against

Violence" (included in my third book – ProKids, Inc.: The Message and The Movement; A guide for Parents and Professionals – available through www.createspace.com/3526148). Each group lasted for six weeks, consisted of eight to ten kids from the third or fourth grade and up, and included group discussions and skits. During each weekly group the kids could participate in safety as they discussed and acted out roles and experiences very real in their lives outside the school. It was a very effective program. At the end of each six week group each kid was given a certificate and was graduated as a "K.I.T. Cadet" and charged with the responsibility of trying to make and keep the peace at school as Ambassadors of Peace. Every Monday morning at this school site the principal held a general assembly for the entire student body and staff. He and other staff made announcements and took care of school related business. It was during these assemblies that my K.I.T. Cadets were graduated and presented with their certificates. Each time I explained the purpose of the program to all of the students, telling the other kids to watch and see if these "cadets" were living up to their assigned mission. The program was so popular some kids were actually offended when I told them I had to limit it to the kids who got into the most trouble. One kid even told me he would start getting into trouble if that was the only way to get into my group. As a result I gave him the "special privilege" of working with me on a one-to-one basis for a relatively short period of time.

I liked the experience at Murchison Elementary School so much I volunteered to do one of my postdoctoral internships at this site for the second year – 1993-1994. The biggest success story I had during my two year internship was a kid by the name of Ricardo who I met when he was in the fifth grade, about half way through the school year. He was always in the office and was disliked by virtually every teacher and staff person in the school. He fortunately came from a stable two-parent family, and in spite of his parents' efforts Ricardo just wouldn't calm down. He was extremely intelligent and had a strong desire to be gang involved someday, always acting tough on and off campus. I recruited him into my group and into private therapy. He very reluctantly agreed and found my role as his therapist to be very different from his experiences with adults in other roles in his life. We had fun together and he looked forward to the time we spent during the sessions at school. I got to know his family really well and they were amazed at the changes in their son which became apparent very quickly both at home and at school. When he graduated as a "K.I.T. Cadet" he was very proud of his accomplishment and took his roles as a peacekeeper and a peacemaker very seriously and very appropriately. Everyone was thrilled at the progress and the changes in every aspect of his life, including his academic performance. At the beginning of Ricardo's sixth grade year he was elected as president of the student council and served in that role all year. At the end of the year and during his graduation he was given an award for excellence and achievement. Everyone in the audience cheered and his parents and I welled up with tears of joy. I asked Ricardo once what made him change his direction and behavior. He replied, "All I could see when I wanted to fight was your face, and I just couldn't do it. I knew you would be disappointed in me."

During this graduation I was given the opportunity to be the guest speaker, unanimously voted on by the parents who regularly attended and supported activities and events in the Parent Center which was part of the Family Services Center on campus. This was one of my proudest moments ever and yet one of the most humbling experiences in my life both before and since. Their invitation represented a great deal of acceptance and appreciation for my two year involvement in their lives and in their community. I had started learning Spanish and wanted to give my commencement address in both English and Spanish. At the last minute I chickened out and asked Arturo, the center director, to translate my speech and then read it with me paragraph after paragraph, side by side. I thanked the people in the audience for everything they had taught me and for the level of trust they developed for me in spite of the fact I was so clearly an outsider to their world and experiences. I urged them to take a good look at themselves with the purpose of continuing to try and improve their lives and life conditions and situations. As I spoke I could see some of the women elbowing their husbands and boyfriends to get them to listen to what I had to say. I assured them I would never forget the experiences and opportunities they had given me to know them and to learn from them. I specifically thanked all of the kids, and especially Ricardo for giving me the most incredible memories and moments anyone could ever hope to have, assuring them I would never forget any of them either. From these experiences I gained a very solid basis from which to begin what became my career of working almost exclusively with troubled kids who live in and through some of the most horrendous hardships and conditions imaginable.

* *

My training in and around the Los Angeles area also included: three years at Lincoln Alternative Education Community School in San Gabriel just outside of LA; nine months through the Los Angeles Learning Centers/ Los Angeles Educational Partnership at Elizabeth Street Learning Center in Cudahay, and at Foshay Learning Center in Upper South Central Los Angeles; and at Orange County Community Hospital in the City of Orange. All four of my training experiences overlapped at different times giving me a great deal of exposure to different communities and populations within Los Angeles and within the LA unified School District and the San Gabriel Unified School District. There was no better training ground than Los Angeles for the work I continued to do in the California desert around Palm Springs, known as the Coachella Valley, until December 2004.

Lincoln Alternative Ed. was a sixteen week program provided through LA County Department of Education to middle school kids who were identified as high risk kids for gang involvement and criminal activity. These kids were given an opportunity to work informally with a probation officer and also catch up on their academic skills. Each school-based internship program I trained in, including this one, were model programs in the area and in the state of California. It was during my training at this site that I had the opportunity to develop my own interview format (summarized at the end of Chapter 10) which I still use to this day when interviewing kids for the first time. This was also my first exposure to the population of middle school kids who were acting out in their respective school environments. In all of these settings I had opportunities to work with kids from very large and very well-known Hispanic, African American and Asian gangs. This was also the first setting in which I worked almost exclusively with kids and not their entire families. I found this to be equally effective with this population, believing in the Murray Bowen approach to Family Therapy of self-differentiation whereby changes in one family member can effectively change the entire family system. Many times I would have parents contact me to ask exactly what I was doing with their kid that was helping them to make desired changes in their lives.

One client who really stands out in my mind was a girl by the name of Monique. I would call her "Sneaky Moniquey" because she was always finding ways to get into trouble without getting caught. However, some of her activities put her at a high risk of getting into serious trouble. Initially she hated the name I gave her, but in time would actually joke with me about it. I have a plaque in my kitchen that has a very nice "thank you" message on the front given to me by Sneaky and her mom when I ended my work with her. My success with kids at this school and at Murchison Street Elementary School earned me a great deal of recognition and positive feedback to my supervisors. This eventually landed me an invitation to present my "K.I.T. Cadets Program" at the International Congress of Applied Psychology in Madrid, Spain in the summer of 1994. It was also during these years that I began to receive other opportunities to talk about the work I was doing and still do with this population.

My job as Change Facilitator through the Los Angeles Learning Centers/Los Angeles Educational Partnership allowed me to work at school sites in and around the LA area at learning centers. These centers provided non-traditional services to kids and their families actually on site at each school for kids in grades K through 12. This was a project, rather than an internship, privately funded through the Wellness Foundation and based on a model developed by Howard Edelman, Ph.D., a well-known professor from UCLA. As a change facilitator I had the responsibility of assisting teachers and administrative staff in changing their approaches to addressing students' needs on all levels. This was a very big project with the ultimate goal of increasing academic performance and excellence by meeting all needs of the kids and their families in a non-threatening environment.

This setting eliminated the stigma often associated with going to county agency buildings for assistance. Each agency usually involved in the lives of low income families would provide services to families at the school site, actually increasing the likelihood of families seeking out and utilizing the services they so desperately needed. This approach "enabled" (a term used by Dr. Edelman as one of the components of his model) the family in order to increase their stability and success in different areas of their lives.

The Learning Centers offered me opportunities to get to know even more professionals and people from different walks of life and to understand the problems and obstacles people often face through no fault of their own. It is easy to see within these settings how difficult life can be for many people - circumstances often beyond their control and beyond their abilities to influence and affect without assistance. The model worked, but I was amazed at how much resistance we got from teachers and other school staff primarily because of union and contract issues. It was shocking to see how many educators were unwilling to go the extra mile to assist families who were in the greatest need of help and guidance. It was also frustrating to see how many of those who resisted and protested the most were European American and working in schools with student populations composed almost entirely of different ethnic minorities.

My last training experience was at the Orange County Community Hospital in the City of Orange. This was a private psychiatric hospital where I worked as a psycho-educational instructor and group facilitator. The population with which I worked at this hospital was a group of dual diagnosis patients who had serious addiction problems along with other psychological disorders. My job on the unit at this hospital was extremely beneficial to me because this is the setting where I originated my RFLAGS Model. I was given the responsibility of leading psycho-educational groups related to abuse, grief and loss, anger management, and dysfunctional family histories. Having never led groups like this I had to come up with program formats for each of these groups. It was through these efforts that everything from my graduate research (beginning in 1986) relative to grief and loss associated with losses from dysfunctional backgrounds really gelled. By using these patients as test groups for my model I was able to put together a program format for each of these groups that eventually became the formats I use in my workshops, classes and in my first book At the Mercy of Externals: Righting Wrongs and Protecting Kids, 2nd Edition.

The only other training experiences I had in the Los Angeles area were a nine month practicum at Hollywood Sunset Community Clinic and a nine-month internship at Glendale Family Service Association. These were significant experiences, but were less directly responsible for the work I now do as my specialty with the population of troubled kids. Probably the single most important factor on a personal level was my involvement in therapy for over 5 years as a client with a wonderful therapist in North Hollywood. My therapy began as a requirement for my graduate program and continued during most of my training experiences and education. It is impossible to be an effective professional, especially a therapist, if we haven't been on the couch, so to speak, to understand the perspective of a client and to work out all of our own issues and problems. Too many people are good at problem identification and no good at problem resolution simply because they have never figured out how to face and deal with their own problems. These are the people who do the most harm in spite of their intentions, especially if they hold positions of power and authority over kids.

When I said I used patients and clients as test groups or even as individual test subjects, what I mean is that I practiced on these people as a group facilitator with the intention of learning everything I could about my craft as a psychologist. As I worked very intensely through my own therapy to understand myself and my past, I took what I was learning back to my clients as offerings which might help them as well. Also, as I encountered issues and experiences from clients I didn't know how to address, I took these back to my therapist. Together we figured out how to address these issues and experiences for the clients and oftentimes for myself. The most difficult issues for me to address with clients were the ones that hit a little too close to home relative to my own personal life experiences. All of these efforts together helped me to work on and work out many of my issues and insecurities in order to be the best therapist I could possibly be for my clients. At the same time I was able to begin and facilitate my own personal and spiritual growth which I will talk about throughout this book.

I have to admit that from all of my experiences and training I have developed a serious lack of patience and regard for arrogant adults who work with kids and families regardless of their role. It's bad enough when parents are unprepared and ineffective, but for professionals who *choose* their careers there are no excuses. This factor is especially evident within my field of psychology and with therapists of all levels and professional degrees; within all academic settings and institutions; and within all areas of law enforcement, to include juvenile halls and placement programs. The thing I hate the most is the labeling of kids relative to their behaviors and other outward signs of acting out. Included in the list of labels are terms and phrases such as: incorrigibles, bad kids, trolls, little demons, problem children, losers, lost causes, unreachables, undesirable elements, evil, delinquents, deviants, worthless beings, menaces to society, dregs of society, brats, nuisances, etc. All of these terms are quite damaging to the kids to whom they are applied, clearly reflecting an outward bias against each so-labeled kid.

Labeling, in my opinion, reflects a tremendous amount of ignorance and insensitivity, and clearly reflects serious issues and problems within the person who applies these labels to kids. I also think adults who have no children of their own are at greater risk for judging and misjudging kids because of their lack of any direct parental perspective. There are many things in life which cannot be understand unless they are experienced personally and subjectively, and I firmly believe the experience of being a parent is one of those experiences. That is not to say that people who have no children of their own can't learn to be effective. It simply means they have to try harder to understand and realize their lack of personal perspective as a potential obstacle to their intentions and outcome goals. This would be the same as me saying I know how it feels to be a juvenile offender or a gang member. My lack of direct awareness means I have had to work very hard to learn what their perspective is even though I can't tell them I know exactly how it feels to be one of them. My lack of direct awareness doesn't mean I can't try to find other ways of attempting to understand their subjective experiences. For instance because of my history of abuse described in my first book, I do know how bad it feels to feel bad as a kid. From there it is possible for me to *imagine* what they might be experiencing; generally acknowledging that their sense of feeling bad is likely much worse than anything I could ever know. But at least they can see I have something personal to which I can compare their experiences of life and the world. I can also assure them I have been working with this population long enough to have a very good idea at least about what life is probably like for them without insulting them by saying "I know exactly how you feel." What an incredibly arrogant, ignorant, and insulting thing to say to virtually anyone if we haven't walked in their shoes.

Labeling is the same as categorizing and stereotyping and as such ignores and diminishes the uniqueness of each and every individual. That is why it is important to label only the *behaviors* of both kids and adults rather than use the behaviors as ways of defining every aspect of a person's character and personality. For example think of the kid who *does* bad things, the child *with* problems, or the kid who *exhibits* deviant behaviors. It is also important to understand that arrogant, ignorant adults say things to kids they would never say to another adult, or allow another adult to say to them. Kids today are too sophisticated to accept that level of disrespect and disregard without reacting negatively and defiantly to it. As adults we have no respect for other adults who aren't respectable, so why should we expect any different perspective from kids.

Arrogant people who are in positions of power and authority are especially dangerous and threatening to kids. It is alarming for me to see how many teachers, social workers, probation officers, juvenile hall staff, youth placement staff, and officers within the different law enforcement divisions who think they have the right to label and thereby discard kids whose actions and lives don't meet with their approval. In my own experiences of observing and overhearing adults in positions of power and authority over kids, I am appalled at how little effort is put into helping these kids redirect their lives, as opposed to simply making their lives a living hell. There is no doubt kids have to be held accountable for their actions. However, such accountability should not be in the form of abuse, victimization, or disregard for the kid behind the labels and the behaviors. Kids are reachable and can be redirected with the right guidance by helping them see what is in their own best interest. Those kids who don't take advantage of the opportunities to learn from people who are effective in their efforts to reach and assist will simply pay a price for their refusal or inability to learn from their mistakes and bad behaviors. However, they will at least know the difference between what is appropriate and what is not.

In addition to labeling, another big concern I have is related to adults who lie and exaggerate events in order to make things worse for kids. I have heard several cops make the statement that "I won't write up any offense I can't make stick." There are incidents where probation officers and teachers will write false reports to insure that kids "will get what's coming to them". Some police officers often seem to feel they don't care if a kid is dead or incarcerated simply because either way the kid is "off my streets". One cop a few years ago was openly talking in juvenile hall and in front of me about one of my kids. However, he did not know who I was or about my association with the kid he was trashing. He made the statement to juvenile hall staff that "this kid's a lifer. It's just a matter of time before I will be able to get him through the juvenile justice system and on to prison for good. Even if he gets killed before then, he's still of my streets." The juvenile hall staff interrupted the cop and introduced him to me identifying me as the kid's psychologist. The cop was shocked and I assured him I would make my client aware of everything I heard the cop say about him.

Fortunately (and I believe as an act of Karma) that cop was later relieved of his duties because of alleged sexual misconduct with underage girls at a local high school. Rather than do prison time he was allowed to simply vanish into the woodwork so to speak. He was the resource officer actually assigned to that particular high school campus at the time of the incidents. This conversation about my kid is just one of many examples I can't back up with actual proof, but only because I don't have access to the juvenile records. I spend a great deal of my time with kids and their families trying to empower them to stand up and defend themselves from these abusers. The kids and families targeted the most by law enforcement agencies and educational systems are generally those with the least abilities, means, and opportunities to defend themselves. I am amazed these kinds of injustices go undetected by the so-called monitoring systems supposedly in place to keep people in these positions of power and authority in check.

I wish I didn't need to write a book of this nature, but I feel I have an obligation to be open and honest about what I see, hear, and know even if I can't prove it with hard evidence. The mentality of many adults today is that of only getting upset when they get caught doing something wrong. Until then everything is okay as along as no one finds out. This very message is given to kids in juvenile justice settings, including placements, every time an official falsifies documents and records; turns their back to a situation after encouraging one minor to "take care of" another minor for them; covering up incidents to protect themselves and their jobs even at the expense of some kid getting serious consequences for something actually sanctioned by staff as okay; or simply breaking the rules and then telling kids to keep quiet about it or "don't tell Dr. Roberts". All of these kinds of behaviors and attitudes only reinforce the same behaviors and thinking in the kids. It is no wonder to me kids do the things they do since many around them are doing the same kinds of things in all arenas and contexts of society.

Even within school settings kids and families are told certain kinds of educational support services aren't available to them simply because school districts don't want to pay for such services. This happens quite often and throughout this country. There are other instances when parents are told that school staff members are acting in the best interest of their kid when it is clear to everyone else the decision only benefits the school. A good example of this is what some schools call an "opportunity transfer". This occurs when a school decides it can no longer deal with the behaviors of a kid and decides to literally dump him or her on another school. On more than one occasion I have been in school-based meetings where this is the decision, only to shoot them down by openly revealing the true intent behind their deception. The really bad thing about all of these kinds of examples is that quite often supervisors and administrators know about and are in on the deceptions in a number of different settings. This is no less true for corporate officials and politicians who line their own pockets at the expense of others, or religious officials and institutions who cover up the misconduct of their clergy. It is shocking to see how far reaching these conditions are within all arenas of society. Is it any wonder why kids act and think the way they do? There are far too many angry adults who have little or no compassion working with kids, often acting like kids themselves complete with defiance, temper tantrums, and breaking rules while hoping not to get caught.

Before I leave this chapter I want to propose a set of ethical principles and standards which need to be adopted, implemented and applied to adults in all positions of power and authority over kids. As a psychologist I am required by law, by the American Psychological Association, and by the California and Alabama Boards of Psychology to comply with a set of very specific and rigid ethical principles and standards in order to do my job and keep my license. My opportunity even to become licensed depended upon my clear and specific understanding and acceptance of these mandates before I could even get through the licensing process. In my opinion no one working with kids should be held to any standards lower than these exact kinds of conditions if they are to be employed to work within any context, and with children of any ages. Furthermore, systems supposedly in place to monitor people and contexts should be very active and vigilant in enforcing the acceptance and utilization of these conditions on an ongoing basis. Such monitoring should occur for people to even be hired and to keep their jobs related to working with kids if they are in violation of these guidelines. The frightening thing is many of these monitoring boards and groups look the other way rather than enforce the rules needed to protect kids and their families, often using the excuse of being overloaded with cases and paperwork. If everyone was forced to understand and sign a statement of acceptance of such principles and standards, and was monitored accordingly by neutral independent parties, kids would be much safer and professionally assisted rather than victimized. My proposed principles and standards follow. I have formulated these guidelines and suggested mandates based on those established by the American Psychological Association for practicing and licensed psychologists as my model of reference.

Ethics Regarding People Employed or Volunteering in Positions of Power and Authority over Children Through Late Adolescence and Into Early Adulthood

Principles

I. Competence

A. Achieve an appropriate level of training and education to understand the psychological, developmental and emotional needs of children through late adolescence and into early adulthood.

B. Be aware of limits and boundaries pertaining to professional roles relative to teaching, guiding, and directing. Never blur limits and boundaries through inappropriate social relationships.

C. Understand all aspects of diversity, being aware of and in control of any personal prejudices and biases you may have.

D. Participate in continuous education and training to insure compliance with these guidelines.

E. Be fully aware of complicating factors which contribute to the likelihood of kids or young adults engaging in negative and destructive behaviors, always separating what they do from who they are meant to be and meant to become.

II. Integrity

A. Integrity is defined as a strong set of professional and personal values based in honesty, fairness and respect.

B. Never engage in false, misleading, or deceptive practices which would create a dishonest or deceptive interaction or association.

C. Be aware of your own belief systems and never allow these factors to harm others in any way.

D. Be completely specific and honest with children and young adults about your professional role and responsibilities in their lives within all contexts.

E. Avoid dual relationships such as social interaction or trying to be a friend when such associations are not part of your professional role or in the best interest of the child or young adult.

III. Professional Responsibilities

A. Do not attempt to provide services for which you are not fully trained to provide.

B. Recognize limitations on your abilities to help, console, teach, or assist, and seek assistance from other professionals as needed and appropriate.

C. Work closely with professionals from other fields and disciplines as this applies to the best interest of the child or young adult.

D. Be aware of and concerned about the ethical compliance of others. Never allow misconduct to go unreported.

E. Do not use your professional role as a means of meeting your own personal unmet needs beyond a simple and reasonable amount of job satisfaction, especially the needs to be liked, needed, accepted, and especially the needs to control, dominate, punish, shame, or humiliate.

IV. Respect for Rights and Dignity

A. Recognize and honor the value within every child and young adult regardless of your personal belief systems and biases.

B. Never engage in harassment, discrimination, or coercion of any kind.

C. Appropriate peer pressure can be effective in compliance with rules as long as illegal measures, shame, and humiliation are never used.

D. Disciplinary instruction and actions as sanctioned by program, institutional, and organizational guidelines should be given and applied fairly, consistently and on a one-to-one basis away from other staff (when possible), children and young adults.

E. Always teach and guide by example through consistent right actions, behaviors, and choices. Always maintain self-control and self-restraint, never interacting with a child or young adult when you as the adult are emotionally charged or out of control.

V. Concern for the Welfare of Others

A. Determine what is in the best interest of a child or young adult and utilize appropriate and effective techniques to address the individual's needs and issues.

B. Always avoid and minimize harm to others. As dictated by the context or setting, efforts to control and maintain control should be minimal and efficient. Once control is established or restored, move beyond control as an issue and back to an appropriate routine as quickly as possible.

C. Consequences should be reasonable and fair if harm to others is to be avoided and minimized.

D. Always work to de-escalate rather than instigate or inflame any situation. Take only those necessary measures required to ensure safety and welfare to self and to others.

VI. Social Responsibility

A. Never seek only to punish. Find ways to allow consequences and learning opportunities to exist side by side. This will facilitate a transference of learned skills to other settings as well.

B. Always seek to redirect, educate, support, console, understand, guide, and/or rehabilitate in an effort to increase awareness of social responsibility and appropriateness as a treatment or academic goal for the child or young adult.

C. Never replicate or recreate negative social or street standards through misconduct, especially the idea that it is okay to break the rules as long as you do not get caught.

D. Recognize and appreciate the need for an interdisciplinary team approach for the purpose of teaching, guiding, redirecting, supporting, and/or rehabilitating a child or young adult.

Standards

- Establish and post reasonable rules and guidelines of conduct for both staff, children, and young adults which are contextually specific (school, law enforcement agencies and institutions, detention facilities, placement programs, etc.) Make certain through discussion and ongoing training that all rules are understood and accepted by *all* concerned and at *all* times.

- Always provide and allow for appropriate grievance methods and investigations without any threat of retaliation against children and young adults from staff.

- Never use shame or humiliation privately or publicly as a form of discipline. Always find appropriate and effective measures for correcting and addressing conduct. Be sure to take into account individual differences relative to learning abilities, psychological/mental health issues, level of maturity, and coping skills, always allowing adequate time for recovery and correction.

- Never use deceptive or false and misleading information with children and young adults or when providing verbal or written reports to others relative to incidents of misconduct.

- Always follow rules established which clearly define roles, limits, and boundaries relative to appropriate actions and interaction with children and young adults. Avoid horseplay, cover ups, dual relationships (trying to be their friend or socializing), false representations of roles (intentional or unintentional), favoritism, deception, ineffective efforts to control or maintain control, provoking and instigating. Remember that unless you are related to a child or young adult you are likely in some position of power and authority over them making a completely causal and open relationship virtually impossible depending on your professional roles and responsibilities.

- If any actions (verbal or behavioral) escalate or otherwise worsen the emotional state or actions of a child or young adult the staff member involved should examine carefully their approaches, personal emotional state, and motivations. Such an increase in the negative behavior or emotional state of the child or young adult usually indicates ineffective, inappropriate, and incorrect actions on the part of the adult staff member.

- Recognize limitations relative to your ability to understand and assist. Call in support from other professionals specifically trained to address the issues. This could include, but is not limited to: social services, mental health professionals, child protective services, and medical professionals. In this day and time working with children and young adults often includes the role of case manager and team member. Never presume to know more than professionals trained in specific disciplines or try to override or undermine proven practices and approaches. Diagnoses and treatment plans should be carefully understood and followed without question except where dire or adverse reactions are evident. Appropriate staff and personnel should be notified immediately. Never humiliate or shame children or young adults based on your knowledge of their academic standing, medications, developmental issues, family or life circumstances, personal issues, and/or diagnoses. Accept and respect all professional limits and boundaries.

- Never seek to meet or serve your own unmet and/or inappropriate needs through any professional associations with children and young adults. Interactions should always remain neutral, non-personal, fair/just, unbiased, and in the best interest of the child or young adult.

- Children and young adults should never be punished or reprimanded based on the history of their parents, family members, or legal guardians. Furthermore, records of other people should never be reviewed in front of a child or young adult given the reality that some information should never be shared by anyone but the adult relative and only at their discretion.

- Deception, dishonesty and fraud should never be used in any professional role with children or young adults. This includes law enforcement agents who should always recognize and respect the legal rights of minors and young adults. Never take advantage of any lack of knowledge or awareness on the part of children, young adults, or their families. Follow mandated policies and procedures regardless of the situation at hand relative to protecting and assisting children, young adults, and their families.

- Monitoring systems should always be in place, with requirements for constant scrutiny and examination of actions, records, and grievances/complaints related to adult staff regardless of context or setting.

- Senior staff, supervisors, and administrators should never simply assume their respective systems are working. Professional roles related to children and young adults often attract people who are abusive and irresponsible in different ways and considerations, and who may be seeking opportunities based solely in the needs for power, control, and punishment. This is especially true in juvenile justice related contexts. Every prospective employee should be screened for and warned about such practices *before* they are hired.

- Programs, institutions, agencies, and organizations should never exist and thrive solely by preying on those groups of people and individuals who are the least likely and capable of defending themselves and standing up for their rights.

- All policies, services, and procedures should be fully enforced, explained, and offered to all who qualify based on needs and circumstances. Organizational needs should never take priority over the needs of the people for whom they exist to provide necessary services.

- Existing programs and services should be constantly monitored and evaluated for success, effectiveness, appropriateness, efficiency, and usefulness relative to money allocated to service provision. Those programs found to fall short of established goals should be restructured to provide services which would put available funding to use where it is needed the most. No organization should be allowed to exist solely because of its political power to maintain itself. This often applies to law enforcement divisions, educational programs, long standing institutions and agencies, and government waste.

- Carefully and periodically review and reemphasize the Ethical Principles and Standards with all employees at least on an annual review basis. Require signed acceptance statements relative to all policies and procedures outlined within these guidelines and standards.

- Every organization, agency, institution, and all associated staff should be held fully accountable for its performance and compliance with ethical principles and standards by a neutral regulatory panel or board.

2

Nature vs. Nurture: Developmental Issues

In almost every undergraduate psychology course there is a discussion of the nature versus nurture debate. Questions usually include the importance of hereditary and genetic factors (nature) as compared to environmental or contextual factors (nurture). The argument is about the degree of influence of how either or both of these considerations play into determining personality characteristics and behaviors throughout lifespan development. Emphasis is always placed on the importance of these factors especially during the early years. The conflict is now always resolved with an understanding of the importance of both sources of input and impact relative to growth and development and to future outcomes either of effectiveness or complication and maladjustment.

I cannot stress enough the importance of the home/family context relative to determining both current and future outcomes. There exists sufficient evidence within all psychological literature and research to indicate a clear interaction between both nature and nurture. There is no accepted way to date of changing basic biological/genetic foundations which determine physical appearance and predispositions to many other aspects of other characteristics relative to personality and temperament.

On the other hand is the reality of the many ways in which we *can* control and influence many of the environmental factors we face every day of our lives. There will always be certain things in addition to physical aspects of our being we cannot control as associated with such life circumstances as the parents we have, the time at which we are born, many of the conditions into which we are born, the makeup of our family constellation, etc. However the one thing adults can control is the home/family environment into which children are born and raised. The single most important element is the quality of care and interaction between parents and children.

Further evidence indicates the importance of the first five or six years of every child's life since this period of development includes such rapid and extreme changes both on a physical level and on a psychological/emotional level. One of the most profound cases I have ever had involved a thirteen-year-old boy named Ricky who had a very serious and obvious jagged scar on his left arm. The scar looked like some type of extreme injury that went untreated for quite some time and covered about a six to eight inch section including the areas just above and below his left elbow. I asked him how this happened and to my amazement he told me he didn't know. This encounter was our first meeting and I was doing an intake evaluation with him to determine his needs and an appropriate treatment plan. Because of the seriousness and prominence of this scar I urged him to go home and ask his maternal grandmother, who was his legal guardian, how this happened. I suspected it somehow involved his mother because of information Ricky supplied indicating he was taken from his mother and adopted by his grandmother when he was six months old.

The next day I called Ricky back into my office at the school site and asked what he had discovered. Immediately he started crying, telling me that after pushing his grandmother for the information she finally told him the whole story. Grandma pulled out a picture of him at six months of age showing him with both arms and both legs in casts. She told him his mother had broken all four of his limbs in some sort of substance induced rage. Apparently this was not discovered for a few days. Grandma wasn't sure how the authorities were notified, but after a temporary period of being in a foster home Ricky was permanently placed in the custody of his maternal grandmother. This boy cried as he told every horrifying detail of his story, identifying the new rage he now felt toward his mother who was actually part of his life at this point. He told me he could now understand why he wasn't able to watch any kind of violence without becoming very panic stricken and overwhelmed. Because of this information he was also able to understand a recurrent dream he had of his mother's hand reaching down to grab him. Just before she grabbed him he always woke up terrified.

The significance of this incident to me is the apparent evidence that even before we have the verbal and intellectual processing skills to encode memories which are easily retrieved and explained, memories can be encoded both physically and emotionally based on the visual and tactile experiences in early infancy. Ricky was able to tell me about these associations without any prompting from me. At the age of thirteen he had already started acting out in some very serious ways, serious enough to get him removed from a public school setting and placed in an alternative school. The single most unfortunate aspect of my interaction with this kid was his removal from this alternative school for defiance only a few days later, so I never had the chance to work with him on any kind of long term basis to help him resolve the extreme emotions which fueled his extreme behaviors. Once he was removed I had only one additional contact with his grandmother. At that time I gave her a referral and encouraged her to get him into therapy with someone qualified to deal with this kind of abuse and trauma. I can only hope she did as I suggested. Since that time I have had no way of following up with this boy to know how things eventually went for him. If no one intervened successfully after my initial contact he very likely got into more trouble as he got older, possibly acting out rage he now understood, but without any reasonable means to resolve. This is one of the unfortunate aspects of many of the systems which are in place to help kids face and cope with the negative aspects of their lives. As kids get moved around from setting to setting there is often no consistent or appropriate follow up with needed services to assist with mental health issues.

Imagine the importance of having completed the appropriate level of training needed just to begin working with a kid as damaged as Ricky was.

This is only one example of the need for implementation and enforcement of the Ethical Principles and Standards I presented in Chapter I relative to limits and boundaries associated with the professional ability to work with kids on different issues and from different professional disciplines. It was very hard for me to believe no one had ever told Ricky the truth about what happened. Furthermore, it was difficult to believe he had never asked about the scar before I met him. My basic professional beliefs include the idea of dealing with rather that ignoring the obvious. There was a statement I heard repeatedly in graduate school indicating "if it's in the room you have to deal with it." This means as professionals we must address everything we observe as being significant or even potentially significant. Development of needed skills and approaches takes practice and time. Care must always be taken to "at least do no harm" in any situation involving interactions between people, especially between adults and kids.

The factors which fuel and even create negative emotions and behaviors can be present at any stage of childhood development. The earlier the traumas through any form of abuse and victimization, the stronger the negative reactions are likely to be in the long run. In my professional experiences I have discovered most serious acting out behaviors begin toward the end of elementary school or right after the transition into middle school. The unfortunate reality is the likelihood of previous indications of damage which go unnoticed in school until the child begins to act out by engaging in negative behaviors. Because girls are less likely to act out behaviorally the need for intervention with them often goes unnoticed as long as they are quiet, even if quiet means withdrawn and depressed. Boys generally externalize their negative emotions while girls often internalize them. However, I believe this previous trend is changing as more and more girls refuse to buy into the stereotypes of the well-mannered, "sugar and spice" images of the past. In the majority of cases girls still tend to act out less violently than boys, but I believe that factor is also beginning to change. Because I have worked in so many school settings and on several high school and middle school campuses I am noticing an increase in violent and physically aggressive behaviors between girls as well and at times toward boys. Assaults from girls toward boys often are overlooked and unpunished compared to the boys who almost always have to face sometimes severe consequences. The assumption of female to male aggression is that of the male having done something to deserve the abuse. Males are less likely to report abuse from female partners for fear of damage to their concept of masculinity. There is very little doubt in my mind females know this and take advantage of this factor.

Also accepted as a rather well known observation is the reality that when kids are exposed to abuse and victimization in the home/family context they are likely to act out first in their school context. From there their acting out behaviors begin to filter out into the streets, especially since virtually all schools now have zero tolerance policies for things such as violence on school grounds. As soon as negative behaviors are observed, especially if there are recurring incidences, it is critical at that point to not only give consequences, but to also begin some form of intervention and even investigation into other possible contributing factors present in the kid's life outside of the school setting. Such efforts, when accompanied by appropriate referrals to other professionals in other fields outside the school environment, could be effective in discovering complicating and contributing factors for the purpose of avoiding any further escalation in frequency or severity of acting out behaviors.

Let's look for a moment at some of the most common complicating and contributing factors present in the lives of troubled kids. Most of these kids come from very chaotic and conflicted homes where families, if together, are often dealing with a great deal of marital strife and a great deal of financial hardship. When the mix includes substance use and domestic violence then the conditions are more likely to cause extreme trauma to the kids living within this environment. Quite often if there are incidents of domestic violence there are also incidents of abuse toward the kids. Even repeated exposure to domestic violence is enough to cause extreme emotional damage to the children who are generally helpless when it comes to intervening or preventing the violent acts. One of the most destructive factors relative to chaotic and conflicted family situations is the inability to prevent the violence. It is easy to know what will eventually happen, especially if there are patterns and cycles of violence. However, the most uncertain factor is the inability to predict exactly when these things will again erupt. In some cases the incidents are frequent with only short periods of time between them. In other cases kids will often do everything in their power to try and keep peace in the family only to realize that no matter what they do there is no way to prevent or control what eventually becomes an inevitable and unavoidable experience. In these kinds of environments kids often blame themselves for the violence especially when they are unable to control it or even more importantly are unable to protect themselves or their moms, or in more and more cases to protect their dads.

Even more traumatic than the above examples are those settings where there is only a single mom with any number of kids, and the single mom continues to act out and make very bad choices in the relationships she has with men. I had a fifteen year old client once by the name of Randy who would literally stand outside the bedroom door of his mother's room while she was in there having sex with someone who was a virtual stranger. While in the hallway he would be holding a knife in case he had to go into the room and rescue his mom from being hurt. There were numerous occasions when he had to act on his fears and rush in, threaten the guy with the knife until he stopped assaulting the kid's mom and left. The first time Randy found the courage to finally take action was at the age of ten when he decided he was probably big enough physically to protect himself if necessary. He said usually the guys would leave once he entered the room rather than get into a scuffle with a kid. Because of the nature of what he described I had to report his mom to Child Protective Services which meant Randy and his siblings got removed from the home and eventually placed with their maternal grandmother. Rather than see her part in all of this the mom blamed me for destroying her family and refused to allow me to continue working with her kids. In time Randy ended up on probation and in a community school where I was assigned to his case by probation. With time he was able to understand I did what I had to do to help him and his siblings and we made quite a bit of progress in helping him deal with his past. This is just one example of many I could give with similar or equal circumstances.

The result for kids in these kinds of environments is the tendency to internalize their rage – not anger, rage. This is especially true for boys and especially for the oldest boy in the household who usually feels the greatest degree of responsibility to protect his mom and his younger brothers and sisters. I believe in every one of these cases kids develop rage fantasies because of their inability at younger ages to actually do anything to intervene and to actually make a difference. This rage is coupled with an extreme amount of fear which only fuels the rage because of their feelings of helplessness and hopelessness. In these fantasies kids will spend a great deal of time acting out in their heads what they would like to do in reality. Depending on their environment and the awareness of violent acts, or their exposure at young ages to violent movies and video games, these enraged, frightened, helpless, hopeless kids will concoct an almost unbelievable scenario of revenge which includes acts of torture and ultimately ends in the death of the perpetrator of the violence.

This is also true for kids who are direct victims of the violence and other forms of abuse. At times the rage fantasy might even include revenge toward the adult or adults who continually expose the child to violence and abuse. As the child grows up physically the rage continues until the child has their first opportunity to unleash the rage on someone else. At that moment the child will usually experience a strong feeling of relief at finally stopping and controlling their victimization and fear. Also, at this moment this child realizes fear and victimization can be eliminated or at least significantly reduced through violent acts against others which they can actually control. This moment of acting on and acting out their rage reinforces both the rage and the need to act out, often setting the kid up for a future of violence which they then create in order to never feel vulnerable or 'at the mercy of externals' ever again. This is the cycle of violence initiated by the adults in a kid's life which gets perpetuated and carried down to the next generation in some form, even if it isn't exactly the same as the violence to which they were exposed as kids. Rather than domestic violence it may take the form of bullying other kids; open and active defiance of any form of authority which feels the same as the abuse they originally experienced; or even worse in the form of street related crimes and acts of violence played out through gang rivalry and competition set up by law enforcement officials and other agencies. The ineffectiveness and inappropriate actions taken by educators, law enforcement, probation, courts, judges, district attorneys, juvenile hall, and various other placement staff, not to mention the virtually useless concept of state youth facilities, only make the rage of kids stronger. This occurs as kids again experience the abuse from people who should help them rather than offer them the same kinds of abuse, violence and disregard they have experienced as young children within their home/family environment.

It is not uncommon to find the content of rage fantasies to be so much stronger than the violence these kids learn to perpetrate on others. Thank goodness this is generally the case, because the content of rage fantasies generally reflects the degree of rage and fear they experienced during the violent and abusive acts. During milder forms of rage fantasies kids may actually turn the violence on themselves by imagining their own deaths even by suicide, with the hope those who are supposed to love and protect them would perhaps love them and want them once they were no longer alive. The essence of revenge in these kids is based in the act of punishing the adults who caused them harm by creating intense feelings of guilt and regret which would then last for a lifetime. What a horrible waste of energy and creativity bound up in hatred and resentment about which and with which they can do nothing. When adults in positions of power and authority over kids create any form of disrespect or disregard toward kids, at that moment they provoke the rage boiling within these kids just below the surface. It is important to understand anyone who is filled with rage always has some degree of rage available to fuel them into an extreme overreaction to any situation which feels threatening in any way. Adults and children alike who hold onto this kind of rage never go from zero up. They start at whatever level of rage is churning within them and go up from there. Because it is impossible, without some amount of investigation, for any adult to know the stories behind a child's need to act out, extra care should be taken not to provoke any child to anger while trying to address negative behaviors.

I believe virtually every overreaction exhibited by a child during any type of interaction or exchange with an adult is usually the fault of the adult who acts or reacts arrogantly, thoughtlessly, and carelessly. This is equivalent in the child's unconscious experience of actually blaming the child for everything which has ever gone wrong in that child's life. To the child this adult is just like every other adult in his or her life who fails to see there are many circumstances in the kid's life they not only did not create, but also could not stop or prevent. This type of interaction further frustrates the kid who probably doesn't know why she or he just did what they just did, much less how to correct it. The failure to see an overreaction as an indication of serious underlying conditions and factors reflects a very strong disregard for this kid's well-being. Emotional overreactions from a child almost always indicate a history of trauma which has likely gone unaddressed or unnoticed throughout the child's life. To further abuse and victimize only worsens the turmoil they feel inside and fuels their need to act out even more in order to protect themselves from a perceived threat. There are some cases when a child, who has been correctly diagnosed with an impulse control disorder such as Attention Deficit Hyperactivity Disorder (ADHD), acts out solely because of an inability or difficulty to control impulsive behaviors with the disorder being the primary cause. However, kids with temperaments which are difficult to deal with are also more likely to have been the victims of abuse as a result of the frustration their behaviors can create for the adults in their lives. Abuse coupled with impulse control problems creates an even more dangerous circumstance relative to rage and rage fantasies.

Perhaps the single most important factor of childhood development, in addition to their level of intelligence, is the level of emotional maturity a child has achieved as compared to their chronological age. Environments or contexts which expose any child to abuse and victimization through acts of violence or exposure to violence will also limit and distort their emotional development. This result is due primarily to the lack of appropriate modeling of emotions by adults, and by the child's lack of opportunities to learn how to deal with and express their emotions in appropriate ways. It is not unusual to encounter a kid who is still amazingly immature at sixteen or seventeen. A significant lack of emotional or psychological maturity limits the success of interventions with kids of any age. Quite often kids under the age of sixteen do not yet possess enough maturity, which includes a certain level of reasoning and understanding, to be able to understand or grasp the idea of what is in their best interest.

In my experience the most effective and long-lasting interventions are based in a kid's ability to recognize certain kinds of behaviors and reactions as acceptable, with negative behaviors and reactions only further complicating their lives. It is only at the moment when a kid can understand this perspective she or he can benefit from attempts to address and correct maladaptive actions and reactions. Because of this it is extremely important for adults to avoid the need to compete with any kid to be the one who is right. Kids, especially adolescents, often don't care what adults think unless they can see how it fits into their realm of possible benefits. This represents the need for adults inside and outside the home/family context to choose their battles carefully based in some sense of the level of risk of unfortunate outcomes and consequences to the kid if they fail to learn from and correct their maladaptive behaviors. I believe for interventions to be effective they must provide not only consequences, but also an opportunity to learn from the mistakes made which led to negative outcomes. Any exercises offering the opportunity to learn will always be more beneficial to the kid and thereby increase the speed with which they are able to see things for themselves relative to their own best interest.

Another factor preventing or impeding appropriate emotional development and maturity is a lack of effective parenting. This is especially true with parents who are overindulgent. These parents often give kids anything and everything they want and rarely try to set limits and boundaries. Parents in lower income brackets will try to make up for the lack of material things by going overboard in other areas; while parents in middle and upper income brackets just simply do too much perhaps to make up for their lack of direct involvement in their children's lives. In either scenario these are kids who also never learn to soothe themselves or calm themselves down because parents are always trying to fix things and overprotect them. I believe it is extremely unfortunate when parents treat their kids like they are little princes and princesses, giving them the impression they are more special than anyone else in the world. Kids who are overindulged and overprotected by their parents are in for a rude awakening when they eventually realize no one else in the world will give them the same kind of preferential treatment.

I had an occasion once at a local ice cream shop to encounter such a kid. I was out with a friend and got up from my seat to get our ice cream. When I returned a little girl about nine or ten years old was sitting in my chair. Her mom was there and was clearly aware her daughter had taken my chair and yet made no effort to make her get up. I politely asked the girl to move so I could sit down and she ignored my request. After my second attempt to get her to move, knowing her mom heard my request I literally told the child "obviously someone has given you the idea you are more special than you really are. Now get out of my seat." Both the little girl and her mom were clearly shocked, but the child got up and moved not only away from me but to the other side of her mom. My friend and I laughed at the looks of surprise mom and daughter displayed. Mom looked away indignantly when I proclaimed to my friend "I hope the little girl and her mom both learned something." This is not my usual means of interacting with kids. However, I was really annoyed because the mother did nothing to make her daughter move as I would have done with my daughter when she was a child. To this day I still get a feeling of satisfaction out of thinking about and telling this story. As you might imagine they were European Americans who were totally oblivious to the realities of life. I felt I had a duty to inform and I did so. You can be sure neither of them ever forgot the experience, even if it was to remember me as some kind of smart ass. At least I tried.

Virtually any kid will try to pull adults into an argument. By doing so kids are able to often shift the focus away from the real issues to something entirely different such as you don't trust me, love me, or care about me. In such interactions it is important for the adult to be more mature than the kid. However, all too often I see or hear adults engage in exchanges with kids in which no other adult would willingly participate. How ignorant and arrogant for adults to think they can treat kids with any less respect and appropriateness than they would be able to treat other adults. Kids truly are too sophisticated in their level of awareness about fairness and mutual respect to ever allow adults to get away with such futile and foolish attempts to intervene and redirect. The reasons adults get away with such things is often due to the backup they receive from colleagues within the same environment, often insisting kids are lying about abuse or inappropriate behavior the kid experiences from the adults, when in fact the kid is telling the truth. This is especially evident in school settings and in agencies associated with so-called law enforcement and juvenile justice. Unfortunately many parents side with the officials who insist they are only trying to do what is in the best interest of their child; or they comply out of fear that to do otherwise would only create more negative outcomes for their child and thereby for their family. Many adults do not want to believe or even entertain the possibility of another adult, especially someone in a position of power and authority, lying to them about their child. This reflects the assumption and hope many people have of adults in professional roles and contexts being trusted to act in an unquestionably respectful, ethical, and professional manner at all times. The assumption is adults in such positions should and do honor the implied and specified ethics of the professional role they have chosen which associates these adults directly with children.

The most shocking reality associated with this issue often occurs behind closed doors within various settings where other adults are not present. Or, the other possibility is the adults who are present are working equally as ineffectively and inappropriately in the same setting or context. Many times I have overheard deans, principals, probation officers, and law enforcement officials interacting one way with kids and in another entirely different manner when parents or adults outside that particular system are present. It is not uncommon for the kid present to be expected to endure unbelievable verbal abuse simply because of the power differential. Whenever such competition exists certainly the adults will 'win', but in reality everyone loses, especially the kid involved. This kind of exchange only further enrages and provokes kids to act out even more aggressively, blocking their ability to see or even care about what might or might not be in their own best interest. Giving in at this point and under these conditions leaves the kid feeling like she or he has lost and the only way out is through compliance. This form of surrender on the kid's behalf feels like they are in effect kissing some adult's ass who can only win because of the power they have over a kid to make their lives a living hell. The fact so many officials back each other up and cover up the injustices only makes this kind of behavior even more reprehensible and abhorrent. I wouldn't respond favorably to such an approach. Why should any kid be expected to do so?

So much of my work with troubled kids includes having to help them learn to deal with adults in their lives that are abusing and disrespecting them on different levels outside their home/family. This goes on in virtually every different context where I work with kids. Because I cannot change the adults causing the damage, I am left to try and get a kid to understand how to deal with these kinds of realities in ways which won't further complicate their lives. If a kid is at least fifteen or sixteen, and depending on their level of emotional and psychological maturity, I can usually accomplish this. When I explain things in terms of the best interest of the kid they are usually able to understand that taking care of themselves relative to certain realities is not the same thing as kissing someone's ass.

As I mentioned in the principles and standards, different fields which involve working with and or supervising kids often attract adults who have a number of unmet needs or even worse inappropriate needs to abuse/ victimize, control, humiliate and shame kids. Quite often kids are helpless in defending themselves from such abuse simply because other adults are often reluctant to believe adult staff or professionals would actually commit such acts against kids. I have known of several kids who went to placement facilities only to return more enraged or even more addicted to alcohol and drugs than when they left. So often staff members within different settings are willing to break the rules sometimes out of a need to simply hang out and be accepted by the very groups they are hired to assist and supervise. There are also incidents inside juvenile detention facilities where staff members approach kids with the intention of getting one kid to "take care of" another kid disliked by staff. One kid even told me once he was offered $200.00 and a weapon to take another kid out. Fortunately this kid refused realizing staff would never back him up if he got caught. This was not something I could prove since the kid would not give me a name, telling me he would deny everything if I told anyone about what he had told me. Plus I wasn't willing to put my life on the line in any situation like this.

Less serious offenses on the part of adults involve only the need to provoke anger in a kid. In so many cases I literally see adults who are as emotionally and psychologically immature as kids in their charge. I have even had staff members from different programs with which I collaborated attend my Adolescent Psychology class at a local community college. Back on the job I realized in many cases they had not learned anything from my presentation of these concepts about themselves and their ineffectiveness. People like this are generally so narcissistic they are unable to even entertain the possibility they might need to do some open and honest self-assessment to look for areas where improvement is needed. Both adult men and women seek to control and provoke kids almost equally, even if in different ways. I try to get staff members to understand if any kid walks away from them more enraged and out of control than they were before the interaction started, then the adult or adults involved in that situation likely did something inappropriate.

The truly tragic reality is many times these adults actually believe they are doing the right thing and in the right manner. I often wonder how dysfunctional their families are and how damaging their own personal backgrounds probably were as well. It is not uncommon for adults to model what they were exposed to as kids unless they possess the ability to transcend and rise above, and the resiliency needed to bounce back from their own hardship of abuse and victimization. The only good thing which can come out of these kinds of errors is the chance I have to help kids learn how to deal effectively and realistically with these kinds of staff. This gives the kids an opportunity to learn how to avoid such people when they are in settings and circumstances where these kinds of people are present. It also gives them a chance to learn how to keep such people from pulling the kid into the adult's need to provoke and then punish. I can't even begin to understand what kind of satisfaction adults get out of this kind of interaction. I think such approaches clearly reflect specific biases against certain populations of kids deemed to be somehow undeserving of support, respect and consideration.

Some of the most infuriating situations kids have to endure are the cover ups by cohorts and colleagues who support and accept the injustices committed against kids. In most instances these adults know they are wrong and in some cases are actually breaking the law and violating basic human rights. Even law enforcement officials often act like immature adolescents as they compete with these kids to control the streets and bust kids, rather than use appropriate measures to try and assist or intervene in order to effect change and help them avoid entry into the adult criminal systems. Street gangs already enjoy the competition they sense from breaking the law and trying to get away with their offenses. In many instances they are actually mimicking the actions and tactics utilized and exhibited by law enforcement. It is obvious to me law enforcement agencies and staff often prey upon those with the least abilities and means of defending themselves from being targeted. This again reflects the immature thinking of these adults when it comes to trying to be effective in their jobs. So many agencies exist based on the game of money and numbers which equals job security, often creating false situations to justify their efforts to detain and otherwise supervise minors. All of these types of mistreatment and maltreatment clearly exist as complicating factors for kids and their families who are targeted in this manner. I fully believe kids have to be held accountable for their behaviors and misconduct. However, the important distinction between older adult offenders and juvenile and young adult offenders is that kids can still be redirected; whereas for many adults it is often too late because of the more permanent nature of their maladaptive ways of viewing and dealing with life.

This brings me to the issues of money/funding and the need to make sure available grant and foundation funds are used in the most effective, efficient and beneficial ways for nurturing and assisting kids in need of the services being provided. This is why I suggest that no program, institution, agency or organization be allowed to continue solely because of it has the political power and influence needed to maintain itself. This is equally true for educational contexts as it is for other public or private agencies and institutions. The importance of early interventions with the hope of preventing future problems is especially applicable within the educational systems. It seems kids who often need the most assistance are the least likely to get what they need because of the misuse and ineffective use of funding. This is especially true if a child exhibits a serious lack of self-control along with learning disabilities or difficulties. I can imagine everyone, including a teacher, who decides to devote their lives to serving kids and meeting the needs of those in their charge entering their respective field with the optimistic goal of making a difference. Reality quickly sets in, even for therapists, as we try to implement theoretical paradigms and techniques or treatment plans we were told in school would be effective in reaching virtually every child. What our professors failed to tell us is there will always be a few kids who don't readily fit into any of the molds, profiles or models we were told to use in order to be effective.

As a result and over a period of time our levels of frustration and confusion begin to build to levels of anger and annoyance relative to the unexpected difficulties we have encountered and yet were not warned about sufficiently. The only way to avoid burn out at this point is to develop the ability and willingness to adapt and adjust as we go along. Learning how to better serve those who need greater attention and assistance is a requirement of educational systems and issues related to special needs. Even then there will always be the challenge of assisting regardless of our personal feelings toward any kid. When it becomes personal each of us needs to recognize our limited willingness or ability to intervene and try to find others who are better trained and/or equipped to work effectively with the child who now only frustrates and angers us. Collaboration, rather than removal of kids and denial of needed services, is essential at this point. Each of us has an obvious ethical and moral obligation to do everything in the best interest of each and every child. This reality must be embraced and honored to the maximum level possible, especially as related to ethical, legislated, and efficient uses of funding.

When it comes to funding relative to educational settings clearly a significant amount of money and effort should be concentrated on efforts to reach kids from the very beginning of preschool. By doing so every child then has a much greater chance of being successful at the higher grades and on into their adult lives. When any child fails to thrive within any context specific efforts need to be made to identify those factors serving as obstacles and barriers. Referrals should then be made to appropriate sources where those deficiencies, disadvantages, and needs can be addressed and remedied or at least contained and improved. This is also one of our unquestionable ethical and moral obligations to do whatever it takes to provide children and their families with any and all assistance necessary for children to learn and achieve. It is under these conditions and circumstances where the concept of team work and interdisciplinary efforts come into play. Money spent appropriately at younger ages, to include work with parents in helping them understand and improve their respective roles and responsibilities, will greatly reduce spending later in a child's development and academic years.

Of tremendous importance, and as part of the nurturing process, is the need to teach children to dream and then give them the confidence and means to achieve those dreams and goals. This was done in earnest when I was a child. I never imagined any other option than going to college or otherwise seeking out some level of advanced job or vocational training. Quite often when I ask a troubled kid what they want or wanted to be when they grow up they look at me as though dreaming about their future is a foreign and unfamiliar concept to them. How tragic to think a kid in middle or late adolescence has never been given an opportunity to think about or dream about their future careers and the kind of life they would like to have as an adult. Clearly this is one area where we as professionals fail to do our jobs as effectively and thoroughly as we should relative to our obligation to nurture kids in our charge.

A serious amount of effort needs to be invested in teaching parents how to parent and nurture effectively and appropriately. I firmly believe parenting roles and responsibilities should be taught in each and every high school in this country. This is especially true for teen parents who should be required to take classes which would provide them with the most basic skills needed to effectively conduct their own open and honest self-evaluations and assessments. The goal would be to give them at least a place to start in being able to make improvements within themselves in order to be effective in providing appropriate guidance for their children. Awareness of their own experience of being nurtured as a child - or the lack thereof - would be essential as part of their process of self-assessment and even personal inventory. This, I think, is a major shortcoming of many parenting programs being utilized today. The basic assumption of many parenting classes is people having a rapport of mutual respect and regard between them and their children which just needs to be repaired and improved. In reality many people referred to parenting classes lack the skills to take care of and provide for themselves on many levels, much less be effective in guiding their children. My RFLAGS Model presented in my first book is equivalent to what I call "Parenting 101". It helps adults examine their own issues before they can ever be effective in their roles and responsibilities as parents. How can any individual be good at parenting if their own lives are in conflict and chaos because of their inabilities or difficulties making appropriate choices in their own lives? If they cannot control and direct their own futures and destinies successfully how can they possibly nurture their children effectively?

The concept of self-improvement through honest self-assessment is one of the main aspects of my model and theories making them a more effective and powerful learning tool in improving the lives of both adults and kids. The concept of *righting wrongs* proposed in the title of my first book addresses the need for intervention with all adults in the hope of *protecting kids* as an effort to prevent problems in their lives now and into the future. The beauty of my approaches to parenting lies in the reality they can be used equally and as effectively with adults and kids. I love getting kids to identify the roles and responsibilities of adults in any role and watch them as they begin to realize the extreme shortcomings of many of the adults involved in their lives within different contexts and environments. The awareness of these deficits on the part of adults helps kids understand why their lives are so complicated in various areas and aspects. Once they realize what needs to be done, kids can at least take an active role in improving their chances of being successful as adults. This is especially true when compared to the lack of achievement and growth missing in the lives of adults who play vital roles in their lives. Furthermore, this is essential for kids who are in middle to late adolescence as this is their last chance before entering adulthood. The importance of spending considerable amounts of money with this population is critical. Such an investment in this age range will greatly improve their chances of success as adults.

One of our main responsibilities as parents is that of nurturing and raising our children to be independent, high functioning, responsible adults, with the intention of them ultimately and successfully leaving us to start their own adult lives and experiences. This doesn't mean severing ties and connections with them. It simply means we have given them the means to take care of themselves in a world offering many obstacles and challenges. The success of future adults depends deeply on the effectiveness of adults in each and every role which is part of a kid's growing up experience within all settings outside the home/family context. If any one of us fails to maximize our efforts to meet the needs of kids in our charge then we miss an opportunity to provide something of value to that child's development - something you or I, and only you or I could have given them which might have proven useful to them at some important moment, or during a critical process of problem identification, problem solving and decision making. How senseless and easily avoidable it is to miss the chance to create this missed opportunity by simply doing what is right and in the best interest of everyone involved. The art of effective nurturing leads to optimization of the potential of every child's inherited nature.

3

Abuse and Victimization of Kids

As of June 14, 2004 I was permanently banned from the Indio Juvenile Hall facility, and the Dessert Youth Academy placement program. This event was a major turning point in my entire career while in California. Because I had to file a 'Suspected Child Abuse Report" with Child Protective Services against Mr. Allen, a senior probation officer (SPO) within the institution, my career in Riverside County as I had known it ended. Since 1996 I had been allowed full access to this facility for over eight years by this point, and yet was told I would be arrested on sight for trespassing if I ever tried to step foot back in the facility. This reaction resulted from a demand made by Brian Casier - my supervisor at Riverside County Department of Mental Health - that I owed Candice Collins, the director of Indio Juvenile Hall, a "professional courtesy". I was ordered to tell her about the suspected abuse report. These kinds of reports are generally reported confidentially in order to protect the mandated reporter, but my supervisor insisted that this provision was not applicable in this situation. He had worked very directly with juvenile probation for many years and was always more loyal to them than to the staff at mental health he should have protected. The previous supervisor who, retired the year before and facilitated every aspect of my work with Riverside County Departments of Probation and Mental Health, would never have made this demand.

I walked across the county complex from my office, went into Ms. Collins' office and told her I was going to file the report as a mandated reporter, telling her I had every reason to believe the assault against the kid had probably occurred. She became extremely enraged and yelled at me, "You have just become a threat to the institution". She further stated, "Everyone knows that you are pro kids and you always take the side of the kids". Her biggest concern was that "now that you have filed the report, it will go public. This incident has already been investigated and handled internally." This, of course, told me the incident had actually occurred as reported to me by the kid who was horribly assaulted a few weeks earlier in an isolation room within the facility by the SPO. Furthermore she told me: "if you're going to believe everything these kids tell you and report everything you see around here, then we will have nothing but problems with you." She even agreed with my defense that I had no choice but to file the report given the fact I am a mandated reporter, again raising her voice and yelling at me: "then go back to your office and do what you have to do!"

Needless to say I was hurt, astounded, and shocked by both her overreaction and her lack of professionalism. In all of the eight plus years I had served this population of kids, I had never before been put in a position of having to report something this horrific. I immediately went back to my supervisor and told him "she's really pissed". By this time I was really angry with my supervisor. He dropped everything he was doing and went straight to juvenile hall to try and reason with her. This all started about 2:30 PM on a Thursday afternoon. When I left at 6:00.PM my supervisor had not returned from juvenile hall. The main reason for Ms. Collins overreaction was that my office was in the process of reassigning me to juvenile hall full-time in order to shield me from other reassignments related to the budget problems we were experiencing at both the county and state levels in California. I would have worked half-time in the juvenile units doing crisis interventions and medication monitoring with the kids, also serving as liaison between the kids and our psychiatrists. The other half-time position would have been my continuation as staff psychologist for the Desert Youth Academy lock-in placement program located within the facility, a job I had volunteered for some eighteen months earlier. Until the day of this experience with the director of Indio Juvenile Hall, I had served as a therapist and assessment specialist for the institution since I started with Riverside County Department of Mental Health in March 1996. This suspected child abuse report was the first I had ever made against juvenile hall staff in over eight years. I worked with all twenty of the placement minors in Desert Youth Academy, and always saw other minors assigned to me on the outs when they were locked up in juvenile hall. Everyone, including the previous and current directors, had *always* told me how much they appreciated my assistance and presence in the facility, telling me and my supervisors they had the utmost respect for me and my work as a psychologist. I was given a lot of credit for the success of the countywide DYA program through my work with the kids as their psychologist.

It wasn't until the following morning I went into my supervisor's office to find out what had happened between him and the director. To my utter dismay and disbelief the director had refused to budge. She had called in her regional director for the entire Riverside County Department of Probation which oversaw the operations of Indio Juvenile Hall. My supervisor had to call in our regional manager for the department of mental health. Both the director of juvenile hall and the director of probation reportedly said nothing but good things about me to my supervisors. They even told them about me being favorably "pro kids" and "always taking the side of the kids" – with a different twist on that line than when I was in her office. They both fully understood I had no choice but to file the suspected child abuse report, and even understood this was the only time in over eight years I had found it necessary to take such action. Furthermore, they understood that because of the budget problems it was "Dr. Roberts or nothing" and still refused, stating over and over again I was now a "threat to their institution". Even the police officer who came to my office the following week to interview me about the incident I had reported told me he tried to get the director to understand I was only doing my job. He couldn't get her to change her mind either.

The obvious reality which came out of this is that the staff at juvenile hall and staff within the entire department of juvenile probation apparently have much to hide. This condition of cover up and deception had been building since the 9/11 attacks in New York City and Washington DC. Clearly their level of paranoia must be grounded in the perception there is a lot wrong with their system. This is something I have always suspected, being constantly aware of the blatant mistreatment (in the sense of abuses of power and authority) of kids at all levels of probation and incarceration. Some years ago I was investigating, with the help of two reputable probation officers, an apparent injustice against a kid who was being sentenced to the California Youth Authority (state prison for kids). He was being prosecuted for stabbing an adult gang member from Los Angeles as this kid and his older brother and cousin tried to protect themselves from being assaulted by the entire group of five LA gang members. Even the family of the gang members came forward to defend the kid and his brother and cousin. None of this was allowed in court and the kid was sent to CYA for three years without any prior history of arrests or any history of gang involvement. The knife was a tiny pocket knife the kid carried around with him, and the man he stabbed was only superficially injured. The three young men were on their way to a Posada, a very popular Christmas event celebrated within the different Spanish-speaking cultures.

To make this even worse, the kid was told by police if he would cooperate and tell them everything, nothing would happen to him. Instead, and according to a direct account to me about all of this from the kid, he was charged with assault with a deadly weapon and coerced into pleading guilty to a serious felony. The police report I read was a serious exaggeration and misrepresentation of the incident and the truth as reported to me by the kid. Even the two probation officers told me they didn't believe a word of the report and believed the kid was telling the truth. The one probation officer who had recommended CYA was actually told by the supervisor of juvenile probation he *had* to do so and do it without questioning. I spoke with this kid's father by phone, urging him to get a private attorney for his son. He cried as he told me "as a poor man I have to choose which one of my sons I can help. Because my older son is facing prison I feel I have to get an attorney for him. I feel bad having to make such a choice, but this is all I can do." This is a translation from the words he said to me in Spanish. The older son pleaded guilty to less serious charges and got out on probation only, but with an adult record.

This was one of the crisis cases I was called in by juvenile hall staff to work on with the hope of helping this kid, a victim of the juvenile justice system, through this unbelievable ordeal. When Debbie Waddell, the supervisor of Indio Juvenile Probation at that time, found out I was working on this with her probation officers they were apparently seriously reprimanded. I was given a message from their supervisor that if I continued to investigate this case I would be banned from probation. That was nearly five or six years before the outrage of June 14, 2004, and nothing has changed since then either with probation or law enforcement and related organizations and agencies. If anything, these agencies and institutions have gotten worse around this entire country, including the Mobile, Alabama area where I now live and practice. The supervisor in charge of juvenile probation at that time was one of those who openly spoke out against kids, using many of the labels I have mentioned to describe them. She hated the fact I would dare to oppose her and her efforts to get kids off the streets at any and all costs, even if done unjustly and illegally. This supervisor was, of course, white.

There were other incidents over the years I knew about, but wasn't obligated to report because they didn't involve direct physical, emotional, sexual abuse, or neglect. I realize the idea of emotional abuse is questionable, but because these kinds of events are perpetrated upon kids by law enforcement officers, officers of the court, and probation staff there is no way to investigate the situations. This is clearly one of the problems with the so-called juvenile justice system when their power and authority goes unmonitored and uncontrolled. The reality of juvenile records being protected, because the kids are underage minors, only gives law enforcement and related personnel more opportunities to get away with unimaginable injustices against kids and families who are the least likely and least able to defend themselves. Another major problem is the reality in juvenile courts of there being no jury. Kids are, therefore, convicted and sentenced based on reports filed by law enforcement and probation staff only. Even to this day cops openly brag about not writing up any report against a minor they can't make stick, so they generally give outrageous charges forcing the kid to plead down to lesser charges. The minor is given the impression by public defenders that they will lose if they fight the case, and will then get extremely severe consequences. As a result kids generally accept the plea bargain, sometimes pleading guilty to things they didn't even do. This never happens for kids who can afford private attorneys and the court officials and participants all know this.

My removal from the juvenile justice system is a clear reflection of the likely cover-ups taking place regularly behind the "blue curtain" nationwide, including where I now live and work in Mobile, Alabama. My supervisors were even told by the director of juvenile hall the incident I reported to Child Protective Services "had already been investigated and handle internally." In my mind this means it was covered up given the fact the only one removed from the setting was me and not the senior probation officer who allegedly assaulted the kid. Furthermore, the kid for whom I reported the alleged abuse probably had no idea this would be something I would have to report, so I never detected any feelings of revenge on the part of the victim. The kid knew too much information about the incident for me to doubt his honesty and account of the situation. Included in his account were the indications the assault was caught on tape, witnessed by staff to include the person watching the monitors in the control room, and commented on by staff to the kid about 'how messed up it was', further stating 'we now know what this guy is all about'. SPO Waddell was white and the kid was Hispanic.

My account of these matters is not about revenge, because I can and have moved on. I am simply and literally telling this to bring attention to the abuse and victimization of kids within this particular context so-called the 'juvenile justice system'. Even though this was a local event I firmly believe it represents realities for juveniles around the country. Similar acts of abuse and victimization occur within other contexts such as schools, religious institutions, political arenas and ideologies, and social levels and perspectives. All of these are outside the home/family context I talk a lot about in my first book. They don't even include the injustices and other circumstances existing within the communities where kids must deal with all kinds of issues about which they either can do nothing or very little. The irony of me being distinguished from those within all areas connected to juvenile justice by the label of "pro kids" is absolutely absurd! As I recounted this story to one of the field probation officers recently I made this very point with her, further explaining their perception of "always being on the side of the kids" is not accurate as they are trying to imply. The last implied part of that phrase which is deliberately omitted when presented to me and to the staff at mental health is that I am on the kids' side 'against probation'. I told her I firmly believe kids have to be held accountable for what they do. However, with the consequences kids face, they should be given very effective and appropriate opportunities to learn from their actions. They should be supported by everyone involved in their lives at that point to facilitate their chances to redirect their lives and energy. Instead they often receive serious maltreatment and harassment, both of which only make them more enraged, increasing their need to act out without caring about themselves or others because of this form of abuse and victimization from authority figures.

The ultimate irony for probation and law enforcement is they can only keep their jobs relative to juvenile offenders if there are juvenile offenders around. When law enforcement officials do their jobs effectively (even if inappropriately), the number of juvenile offenders drops and these personnel become afraid of losing their jobs which can only be justified through numbers which guarantee funding. The broader issues of funding will be addressed in a later chapter. All too often I have seen kids placed and/or kept on probation or in certain programs just to keep numbers up and justify the existence of the programs and jobs of related staff with no regard for the well-being of the kids.

The only way to view abuse and victimization of kids is to understand adults are the perpetrators of the various forms of maltreatment and are the only ones who can prevent such injustices. Furthermore, because many of the people within the general population only want their streets safe no matter what the cost to kids, these injustices are allowed to go unchecked and unmonitored as long as private citizens feel protected. The serious misperceptions of many adults reflect their false sense of safety and security which are easily and laughably violated by the kids. It is extremely important to realize that the more kids are mistreated the more they are going to act out. As their rage increases so does their desire to act out on members of society who are perceived by the kids to have 'everything' compared to the realities of the kids who feel they have nothing. While not completely justifiable, their thinking is an understandable reality.

All too often the messages given to kids and the behaviors modeled for kids from adults within all contexts is that everything is okay as long as we don't get caught. There is no doubt in my mind kids are taught this every day and in every setting imaginable. This is no less true relative to political, corporate, and religious scandals which are common knowledge and unfortunately rather common occurrences. It seems apparent to me when kids are caught up in any system which only provokes and feeds their rage, they simply get deeper into the system because of their inability and unwillingness to care about themselves or others. They firmly believe there is no reason to care since no one seems to care about them. Within school settings kids who are mistreated and neglected become so frustrated and discouraged they give up, drop out, and otherwise stop trying to better themselves educationally. Kids generally cannot respond to negativity in any other manner given their lack of psychological and emotional maturity. Many adults are no better at problem solving than kids appear to be when the kids are denied opportunities to learn, by people who treat them with disrespect, and who seemingly care nothing about them.

The single most important factor within this text is that the kids who are abused and victimized the most represent the troubled youth identified and addressed in this book as society's underdogs and throwaways. These kids and their families are always the least likely and least able to defend themselves from most injustices. This lack of defense against offensive actions and realities represents different considerations. For many there is the sense of hopelessness and helplessness which may have developed as a result of life circumstances about which people believe they can do nothing. For others there is the fear of going up against authority figures based in the belief things will only get worse if they even try to defend themselves or stand up for their rights. Another reason lies in the lack of knowledge and awareness many people have relative to what their rights really are, and how to go about guaranteeing themselves the consideration and opportunities they deserve and are actually entitled to receive.

One other reality is that some families just don't care enough to get involved in the lives of their kids to even bother protecting and defending them. I see this all too often for kids who come from extremely destructive and chaotic family environments. Sometimes adults within these kinds of family settings are struggling so hard just to survive from day to day they don't have the energy or the time to take on yet another battle. However, for some kids their parents and guardians are so selfishly involved in their own lives they actually don't care about the needs of their kids. These are the families who for me are the most difficult to work with because of my own anger toward parents who bring kids into the world with no desire or intention to give them a good life. These are the kids who often result simply as an outcome of irresponsible sexual behavior on the parts of their parents. In my first book the title deals with the concept of "righting wrongs". Represented by this phrase is nothing more or less than adults doing everything possible to make themselves better people before they even become parents, or at least after their kids are born. This is where the ideas of both intervention and prevention come into play. Parents who at least eventually work on their own issues are generally able to tear down walls between themselves and their kids. They finally establish new relationships rather than repair relationships which never worked well for the kids involved. This is the part about "protecting kids".

This is a good point at which to reintroduce my Roberts FLAGS Model presented in my first book At the Mercy of Externals: Righting Wrongs and Protecting Kids, 2nd Edition. The FLAGS are the negative emotions of **F**ear, **L**oneliness, **A**nger, **G**uilt, and **S**hame. My RFLAGS Model graphically depicts how all of us tend to act out anxiety and depression based in these five negative emotions. While these are not the only emotions, I have found and still find them to be the most destructive when these emotions become the motivations and provocations of thoughts and actions. Let me briefly review the cycle which originates in unchecked and often unconscious emotions. Kids who are damaged by histories of sexual, physical, and emotional abuse as active forms of abuse, and neglect as a passive form of abuse, will have tremendous emotional damage and open wounds, with the depth and extent of their wounds being positively correlated to the degree of abuse. The lack of conscious awareness of the negative emotions and open wounds is a direct result of the kid's lack of opportunities in the early and critical years for appropriate and proper emotional development. All too often kids are not allowed to experience emotions and generally are not given opportunities to learn the appropriate expression of emotions. This is especially true inside home/family contexts plagued with tremendous chaos, conflict and instability. On the other hand other kids only see adults who have no control over their emotions, so nothing appropriate is displayed or taught. This means quite often people are reactive as a matter of habit based in observations and experiences within extremely dysfunctional environments. The result is that of having a level of strong emotions present at all times and boiling just below the surface with little or no conscious awareness of, or regard for their presence and potential.

The imagery of a pressurized tank with a gauge on the top is a good metaphor. People with this level of raw unidentified and unaddressed emotions fail to see the needle on the gauge as usually half way to the danger zone most of the time. So for them the needle doesn't go from zero to fifty, it goes from fifty up to the point of the person (tank) exploding. As the emotions build in intensity the level of physical discomfort, annoyance, and frustration build to the point when even kids often say or think to themselves "fuck it, nobody else cares so why should I?" At this point of hopelessness and helplessness the kid or adult will begin to act out their emotion-based anxiety in ways intended to alleviate, escape, release or even resolve anxiety. A number of acting-out behaviors exist from which a person can choose, and the larger the number of inappropriate and ineffective choices made will equate exactly to the degree of complicating factors people experience in their lives. These complicating factors only lead to more distress and the need to act out until the person recognizes the necessity of trying to determine where, why and how these overreactions are generated. For kids the opportunities to seek understanding of their thoughts and behaviors are rarely if ever presented to them. Therefore their need to act out only increases.

When you put these kids into systems where they are exposed to additional abuse and victimization then the patterns are set for them to continue down a destructive path causing harm to themselves and to others. The right interventions at the right time and by the right person or persons can be extremely effective in helping kids redirect their energies through more positive and productive activities and aspirations. To do anything less is in my opinion criminal – as much so as any criminal activity in which a kid might participate. Think about how the systems often set kids up to compete with rather than learn from the very adults there who could actually help them. Instead adults all too often provoke kids and fuel their negative emotions, thereby only increasing their rage and the desire to act out rather than change their thinking and actions.

The very tragic reality is that it wouldn't take much for any adult to learn to be effective when working with troubled youth. All that is required is for adults to develop the willingness to look beyond what kids do and see them for who they are meant to be. This means looking for the piece of heart present within every kid, even the ones who are the hardest to reach. There is always goodness inside of every kid and it is extremely important to look for and nurture that goodness through kindness, non-judgmental acceptance of the kid, and with the awareness that kids who have good lives and stable homes usually don't end up complicating their lives. In too many instances adults look at kids as being bothersome nuisances, an attitude which only brings out the worst in both adult and kid. My experience indicates that by looking beyond what kids do and seeing the potential for good inside of each and every one of them, kids respond by opening up and working with, rather than competing against the adults who are part of their lives. For any kid to trust an adult it must be apparent what the parameters are relative to each and every respective role. People in positions of power and authority must be up front in every situation about what and why they have to report or otherwise act on certain bits of information. As a psychologist the sky is the limit for me in this area because I am only required to report incidents of abuse and neglect, and threats of harm to self and to others. I make this clear from the very instant we meet so there will be no misunderstandings. If a kid knows they can really trust us to tell them the truth they will open up and tell us most everything about which they need to talk.

The miracle about this approach is kids get to know up front you are there to help them, not to try and bust them. Because so many adults use deception and outright lies to get information from kids, very few kids are willing to even try, much less trust any adults who come into their lives. Kids seem to always view adults as having ulterior motives in every interaction adults set up with kids, especially in professional settings and contexts. One of the ways I gain a kid's trust is to assure her or him I don't trust many adults within certain settings any more than they do. As they hear me confirm their suspicions that adults are often out to trick them, the kid begins to think I must not be "one of them". This approach is clearly the "pro kids" part of me. I spend at least the first ten or fifteen minutes going over issues of confidentiality with them and explain carefully why and how my job is different than the jobs of many people in their lives, especially within school and juvenile justice-related systems. I swear to them in any manner necessary to get them to at least try and believe I am being totally honest with them. In effect I am bashing other adults based in the reality that I know what I am saying is true relative to the tactics often used to set kids up and trick them into trusting long enough for the adult to get the information needed to use against them. Adults are shameless in these kinds of tactics and feel perfectly justified in betraying a kid's trust rather than getting to know a kid in ways which could foster growth and change. Because of my approach kids see me as an ally rather than as the enemy and they begin to open up more and more as they see and accept the fact I am for real.

Because I went into East Los Angeles in September 1992 knowing I knew nothing about the people and their environments, they were able to see my sincere desire to learn *from* them, not just *about* them. This gave me an opportunity to look into their world without any assumptions or prejudices. By very genuinely using this approach I learned a lot about what it is like to live in areas where there are very few positive opportunities and factors, but with an overabundance of negative circumstances and realities. What I found was a very sincere desire on their parts to both teach me about themselves and their environments, and to *then* use what I had learned in school as we worked together to try and make life better for them. I firmly believe they also wanted me to learn as much as I possibly could from them so I could continue to help others in different areas, but with the same kinds of life situations of stress and distress. This to me is where the idea of spiritual psychology comes into the picture.

In my first book you read that I am not a religious person at all. However I do consider myself to be a very spiritual man whose beliefs include: the concept of one Source; innate goodness in everyone; being altruistic and non-judgmental; unconditional acceptance and regard as a form of love; and karma, in the sense of what goes around comes around. The innate goodness is the eternal Soul of each person. Being altruistic means doing something for nothing to help others, which also requires some degree of work and sacrifice on the part of the doer. The concept of karma has to do with the idea that whatever we put into motion – positive or negative – is what comes back to us. I do not believe in the concept of love as spoken about during the hippie era of "free love"; rather in the concept of love as consideration and respect for people as spiritual beings regardless of what we observe about them. This doesn't mean we have to join with them or even like what they do. It simply means we must look beyond what we see, and understand each of us is going through our own personal process which no one can control or redirect except as acts of personal and very individual conscious and unconscious choices and actions. I believe the concepts of being non-judgmental and practicing unconditional acceptance have a lot to do with recognizing the profound uniqueness of each and every person alive.

Even my RFLAGS Model is based in this kind of spiritual psychology, believing in the innate goodness and uniqueness of each individual and also explaining why these characteristics often go unnourished and underdeveloped. The model and related topics seek to explain why we do what we do strictly from a cognitive and behavioral perspective only, with negative emotions being the fuel feeding the distress and stress we try to act out rather than resolve. From a spiritual viewpoint I also feel kids are much less responsible for their actions and reactions as are their adult counterparts. This is not to say kids are not accountable for their actions and reactions; they are just not as responsible for them as kids as they will be as they get older, and after they have worked with me for a while. In other words, there are reasons why kids do what they do which explain rather than excuse what they do. This is a very simple concept and is the one most often misunderstood and misinterpreted.

The standard profile for troubled youth include a number of complicating factors, all of which are listed in my first book. A brief summary of factors includes chaos and conflict within the family which create a great deal of instability. Quite often kids are unsupervised for a number of reasons, leaving them feeling both neglected and free to experiment with many different things. Then there are the families who are so self-absorbed in daily living they have little or no time for family togetherness, resulting in a serious lack of interpersonal and intrapersonal connectedness. Some families so overindulge their kids and the kids come to expect everything about life to be easy and without meaning or merit. In so many troubled families kids experience threatening circumstances through constant open conflict which can include domestic violence and abuse toward the kids, sometimes by both parents. Within single family homes things often get more complicated with single parents struggling just to survive and provide for themselves and their kids. Unfortunately with many single parent homes there is a greater likelihood of strangers being introduced into the mix by parents who date and have live-in significant others or sexual partners. As a result in many situations there is an increase of siblings who share only one parent. The larger the family tends to be the more responsibility falls upon the older kids to take care of the younger siblings, resulting in resentment aimed in many different directions and for many different reasons toward the parent or parents. If the parent living outside of the family is also uninvolved in the family with the kids, there is further resentment and frustration, not to mention constant questioning as to why things are the way they are. All of this is made worse when alcohol and drugs are part if the mix, along with any degree of criminal activity. Parents who are incarcerated bring a sense of shame on the kids who are embarrassed to have parents who are also criminals. This is even worse when the mother is the one or one of the ones incarcerated.

One other problem is when the criminal activity in the home actually helps improve the conditions of the family, sending a very confusing message to the kids who buy into the concept it is okay to break the law as long as you don't get caught. This also adds a huge responsibility for everyone in the family to keep this as a secret about which no one can know. From there a further breakdown of the family results when kids are removed and placed into foster care situations, often made worse when they eventually have to be adopted out to strangers, who in many cases only use foster kids as sources of income. Kids who end up in this kind of circumstance often face extreme abuse and neglect and are often turned back into the system as they get into trouble and begin acting out their rage. This then becomes another abandonment issue about which they can do nothing.

Things continue to deteriorate as kids get into the juvenile justice system where they are all too often only further abused and victimized by people within every aspect of the system, including the court level. Some kids are actually never even picked up from juvenile hall or placement and have to be sent to foster care facilities until they reach the age of eighteen or older, depending on the state. Add to this the elements of hardship, hunger, poverty, homelessness, insecurity, uncertainty, Fear, Loneliness Anger, Guilt and Shame and you have a volatile mixture which constantly fuels negative thoughts and actions. These are behaviors based in negative emotions which lead to anxiety and depression, hopelessness and helplessness, and then to the need to act out that which cannot be controlled. All of this is too unimaginably complicated for adults and kids to understand or even recognize without assistance. All anyone knows in these circumstances and conditions is that life sucks and they feel like shit, believing there is nothing they can do to change things. It's like the trapped lab rat or dog in an old cognitive/behavioral experiment that eventually gives up and lies down in the cage on the electrified grid once any chance to control or escape the unimaginable situation is gone. With all of this, how can kids possibly be held completely responsible for their actions? These are factors and realities many kids live in daily. And, while these realities do not represent excuses for their actions, it is easy to see why kids do what they do given the conditions of their lives.

How can any adult fail to question and consider the needs and circumstances of the lives of troubled youth who are at extreme risk of making seriously bad decisions and choices? One of the best examples of an adult who corrected her perspectives and biases was a woman who worked in juvenile hall as a unit counselor. She had no children of her own and openly despised virtually every minor who got locked up. Eventually she was reassigned to probation as a probation officer with the responsibility of doing investigations into kid's lives, and then using these results to make recommendations to the court. I never liked anything about the way she handled kids in the hall and to my surprise she called me one afternoon in my office at the clinic. She was actually crying as she told me about a kid who really needed some help with serious problems in his life and family. I was so taken aback I found myself wondering what had happened to her, so I asked her to explain the change in her feelings toward kids. She told me she had never imagined what the lives and realities of these kids might include until she was reassigned. By going out into their homes and environments she was forced to look at how complicated their lives actually were.

During the conversation this transformed probation officer expressed deep regret for damage she had likely done to other kids, and made a verbal commitment to me insisting she would try to make up for it in the future. She was later put in charge of a day treatment program run by probation for kids on probation. At the end of about one year she was replaced because other staff felt she was too lenient with kids. However, under her supervision several kids successfully completed the program and received their diplomas. Her immediate replacement and the senior probation officer supervising the program were soon reassigned for the same reasons. The two who were in charge since that time, ran the program as though it was a lock-in program where kids could be simply detained during the day and sent home at night. Kids became extremely frustrated and angry about the lack of support they received, complaining constantly about the lack of regard the probation officers and staff had for the kids and their well-being. In so many instances these are the issues I have to help kids deal with in therapy, using the approach of validating their perception of reality and then helping them learn to deal with it without further complicating their own lives and circumstances. What a waste of my time and what a waste of resources which could and should be used more effectively and appropriately. This is one of those programs I referred to which exists only for the sake of staff keeping their jobs and not for the betterment of the kids in their charge – a money and numbers scandal at its best!

Over the years I have seen some very good probation officers leave juvenile probation and move up to adult probation simply because they no longer agreed with the way things are run. There is very little doubt in my mind these conditions are likely representative of conditions for kids around the entire country, especially with the thinking and philosophies under, and remaining since the Bush administration. One of the most outrageous deceptions of the George W. Bush administration was and still is the misuse of money to treat gang kids like terrorists. I knew nothing about this extreme injustice and complete deception to the American public until nearly a year after 9/11.

In October or November 2002 one of our therapists from the children's service department where I lived and worked in California, invited Debbie Waddell, the aforementioned senior probation officer (the very one with whom I clashed on a regular basis based on what I perceived to be her obvious hatred for juvenile offenders) to come and make a presentation to our staff during our weekly staff meeting. The SPO brought with her Anthony Villalobos, one of the assistant district attorney's so he could also talk about their work in the field with kids and their families. The program they discussed was called the Youth Accountability Team (YAT) and was an informal probation program. Parents were given the opportunity to access this program when their son or daughter got into trouble for a minor offense. That minor offense was then held over their heads for six months as a threat of prosecution if the kid did anything to violate their informal probation. These were charges that would have never been prosecuted anyway because they were petty things like fighting at school, truancy, runaway, and possession of small amounts of marijuana. During this six month period probation officers and law enforcement could show up at the minor's residence anytime they wanted and search the kid's bedroom and bathroom, and other parts of the house if people naively gave them permission to enter other rooms. If there were no violations during the six months the entire matter, including informal probation, was dropped. The charges initiating the informal probation were kept so they could be added to any new charges which might come up at a later time. The SPO explained that the purpose of the program was to keep kids out of trouble, in school, out of gangs, and away from drugs and alcohol. One additional component was that of providing support to families who were having difficulty managing the behaviors of their kid or kids. So far it sounds like a really good program except for the searches which could be conducted.

However, the SPO Waddell literally leaned forward over the table and exuberantly exclaimed: "but what we're *really* doing is using this program to get them into the system by fingerprinting and photographing them. We can search their homes anytime we want and work to obtain evidence against them so that when we can get 'em, we can really get 'em!" This is a direct quote. I don't think I will ever forget her words. The exuberance in her voice was shocking as she openly bragged about the outright deception being perpetrated upon unsuspecting families who thought the informal probation program would be there to help them, rather than something which would ultimately be used against them and their kids.

After SPO Waddell's last statement ADA Anthony Villalobos, chimed in saying with equal exuberance: "yeah, and we have more rights than ever before to invade people's privacy. We can do all kinds of surveillance, including wire taps on phones, without even having to get permission from a judge." He explained that all of this became possible after 9/11 and the US Patriot Act when the US Congress made the definition of terrorism so broad that law enforcement agents are able to list street gangs as domestic terrorist groups, and gang members as domestic terrorists. The US Patriot

Act also enhanced the power and authority of all levels of law enforcement, AND protected them with a veil of secrecy. Simply enter the terms "US Patriot Act and Domestic Terrorism" into any search engine and you will be astounded at what you will find. Since then I have learned that the Patriot Act further made *any* criminal code in the United States a potential act of domestic terrorism if such acts posed any threat to life or property. These determinations are made on a case-by-case basis and solely at the discretion of law enforcement.

I have also learned that under the laws of the Homeland Security Act and the US Patriot Act all law enforcement officials have the right to go after anyone simply *suspected* of domestic terrorist activities. Once *suspected* of terrorist activity, anyone can be detained as an enemy combatant without any rights related to due process. All of the corruption within the Bush administration trickled down through all levels of law enforcement around this country based on the examples set and sanctioned by the Bush administration and its cronies. Very few people know that large sums of money earmarked for Homeland Security have been deceptively spent by local law enforcement agencies to buy ridiculous equipment in areas where terrorist attacks are the least likely to occur. If the money had been spent as presented to the American public, all of our ports and borders would now be secure! Furthermore, billions of dollars were funneled down to local law enforcement agencies to establish such programs as the Youth Accountability Team, so-called gang prevention task forces, and probation controlled school programs. None of these programs are monitored independently by anyone or any group, which means there is no accountability or independent oversight and scrutiny.

I listened with utter amazement as the SPO Waddell continued and openly talked about "those incorrigibles" referring to all juvenile offenders as being beyond hope or help as indicated by the use of this term to describe them rather than use it as a reference to their behaviors. She used the term repeatedly talking about "those incorrigibles (this)" and "those incorrigibles (that)" until I could no longer sit quietly. The members of our staff who knew me really well and understood my feelings about kids and injustice, told me later they were surprised I let it go on for as long as it did.

I literally interrupted SPO Waddell's bravado by stating: "Excuse me! First of all I'm surprised you would say these things in front of me knowing how I feel about the way you think and talk about kids. However, this only confirms for me all over again the apparent hatred you have for kids in the system. Your use of the term incorrigibles to describe kids, rather than refer to their behavior is appalling and offensive to me. Even more appalling and offensive is the fact you would use the YAT program against kids and their families." I then looked at ADA Villalobos and told him: "by the very fact you're sitting here with her I must assume that you feel the same way as she does about kids. I find it hard to believe that you would brag openly and publicly about the fraudulent and deceptive misuse of a program. You trick parents into trusting you and probation without explaining to them that by voluntarily signing their kids into YAT, parents are actually giving you permission to use whatever means necessary to gain information against them and their kids." I then told both of them "you can be sure I will let everyone in the community know of your actions and intentions, and will encourage them not to sign their kids up for your Youth Accountability Team."

Both of these people were stunned at my confrontation, looking like two deer caught in the headlights of a car. ADA Villalobos never said another word, and SPO Waddell quickly started back peddling in an effort to save face. Immediately she began to apologize and tell me very patronizingly and insincerely, "well Dr. Roberts, you're right. I do need to watch what I say about kids. I'll have to be more careful in the future." With that the entire presentation came to a screeching halt and both of them left with their tails tucked between their legs. My supervisor and other staff later congratulated me for speaking out against them and backed me fully. SPO Waddell is the one who threatened to ban me from probation at an earlier time when I was investigating the case I mentioned earlier in this chapter.

I followed through on my promise to warn the community as much as I could. Since that time I have also tried to get this obvious misuse of money appropriated for homeland security revealed to the general public, but so far no one will break the story. However, I have had it confirmed for me consistently by political officials, law enforcement officers, and even a news reporter not only in California, but also here in Mobile, Alabama. One reporter told me the FBI participated in training local law enforcement officials how to treat kids as enemy combatants and use them for combat training by sending agents into areas where the threat of a terrorist attack is virtually nonexistent. I have talked with one TV reporter, a radio talk show host in Fargo, ND, and wrote numerous times to the Democratic National Committee and finally to the John Kerry presidential campaign headquarters in 2003, all to no avail. On the streets locally everywhere around this country there are a large number of heavily tinted black SUV's hanging out in lower income neighborhoods. Kids in California would walk up to these vehicles and to vans parked in their neighborhoods and offer those inside a beer, laughing at the fact everyone knew they were there. I have heard numerous stories from kids who are shocked to hear taped telephone conversations from their private residences played for them when they are brought in even if only for questioning. They would be detained for hours in "the white room" at the county sheriff's office in Indio, CA and released without charges and without any written record of their detention.

In my opinion kids are being used by law enforcement for entertainment and harassment purposes only. Given the fact we don't have any active terrorist groups in this country as those existing in other parts of the world (the exception being white supremacy groups and militias), the gangs and other kids are easy targets for such activities. The people being targeted are the young underage street kids and not the heads and older gang members. Probation officers and members of the gang task force show up at the homes of kids any time of the day or night to perform searches, even when the kid whose house is being searched is doing well. Gang task force members are more than willing to speak out to kids about how much federal money they are being paid because the kids are considered to be terrorists. I know of two instances in California when families were simply moving from one location to another, and the cops would show up and dump out everything the family had packed up for the move, making them have to pack everything all over again. Law enforcement officials even here in Alabama have confirmed my information. One former member of Homeland Security was absolutely shocked at the extent of information I had been given by law enforcement officials in California. This is not only a scam against disadvantaged kids, but against the entire American population who knows nothing about these secretive and underhanded misuses of power, authority, trust, and money. As I stated earlier, please go online into any search engine and enter the terms "US Patriot Act" and "domestic terrorism". You will be shocked and outraged by everything you will find. Hopefully you will then take at least some minimal action to help hold public servants accountable for these injustices.

These are other examples of how so much of my time with kids is spent trying to help them cope with these forms of abuse and victimization. I teach them to deal with these realities without giving law enforcement additional opportunities to become more deeply involved in their lives. Because of the way things are being handled kids are immature enough to see this as a challenge and as a form of competition and cops know this.. These tactics make them want only to fight more against the system rather than back down and let the system win. These kinds of abuses and injustices only fuel the rage of the kids as cops act out their own childish fantasies of again playing "cops and robbers". None of this is working in the sense of helping redirect and rehabilitate kids. More and more kids are getting locked up for serious and violent offenses committed out of rage which I believe is strengthened and intensified because of kids being incorrectly labeled and mistreated as terrorists.

With all of this going on no wonder law enforcement officials and personnel don't want caring people like me around to expose their misdeeds and misconduct. There is very little doubt in my mind that recent increases nationwide in violent crime are directly related to the harassment and socioeconomic profiling sanctioned by the federal government and passed down to the state and local communities. Because I am so outspoken about all of this I believe I am probably listed on at least a few government reports as a threat to national security. Keep in mind I did not go looking for any of this information. It was handed to me again and again as a result of the arrogance and ignorance of those given the responsibility to "keep the peace" by "serving and protecting" **_all_** of the "American people". First and foremost I am an advocate for those kids and families who are the most vulnerable in our society. This sense of personal obligation results not only from my duties as a psychologist, but also from the deep Spiritual convictions to which I subscribe. I truly hope Karma will play out against those political figures and other groups who have violated our trust and who have violated many of the rights we hold sacred in this country!

I strongly propose and support a nationwide campaign staged by low income, disadvantaged families and their supporters protesting these acts of injustice and deception. Unless people organize at a grassroots level, these kinds of injustices will only continue. In a recent live talk radio interview I did through the University of California, Irvine, I was informed that in California corruption is finally being both exposed and prosecuted. I told the attorney conducting the interview that so far this doesn't seem to have "trickled" over into other parts of the country, including places like Mobile, Alabama where the mayor reportedly won't even allow city employees to use the word "Gangs" publicly. The slogan for this grassroots campaign is:

F.A.T.E. Stops the H.A.T.E.

And

Equalizes the R.A.C.E.

Fairness		**H**arassing
Accountability	STOPS	**A**ntagonizing
Truth	THE	**T**errorizing
Ethics		**E**xploiting

And Equalizes the

Resilience, **A**ssurance, **C**ompetence, and **E**xcellence

With this approach and through community empowerment alliance programs it will be possible to peacefully unite those being targeted to make a public stand against social injustice through violations of human rights and civil liberties. In my experience these injustices are not even racially motivated in many cases. They are motivated by an apparent loathing toward *all* lower socioeconomic people frequently viewed as low class citizens. This should be a campaign emphasizing inclusion, rather than exclusion, for everyone. Rather than racial profiling, public service agencies, institutions, and organizations at all levels of government are using socioeconomic profiling as a means of sustaining their existence and securing their jobs at the expense of low income, disadvantaged families and kids. All of this is part of the money and numbers games I talk about frequently. The really alarming fact about all of this is that the "veil of secrecy" is so strongly enforced, very few people know about any of these violations of trust and civil liberties. Please help me spread the word and put a stop to all of these injustices!

4

Criminality

While I tried to edit the last chapter to reflect changes in my career and perspective in California, this chapter will explain everything which has changed since then. I find the extent of change in my life since the writing of the first three chapters in this book in the summer of 2004, and during the succeeding 18 months, to be almost beyond belief.

As I resume my writing it is now fall 2005 (Revision in 2012 as well). I have relocated permanently and officially back to my home state of Alabama after retiring from my job with Riverside County Department of Mental Health California at the age of 50 and as of February 2005. The changes detailed in chapter three left me with no choice but to leave the state of California given the reality that high risk youth were "no longer a priority" in light of serious budget problems and a lack of "evidence-based treatment" for this population within the mental health system at both the county and state levels. Keep in mind that funding for various law enforcement agencies is now almost limitless relative to changes since 9/11 and based in the misuses of the Homeland Security and US Patriot Acts. I was pulled in from my field work with the kids, even at the school sites, and reassigned to work exclusively in the clinic doing walk-in assessments. The reassignment by my office was in response to a significant loss of staff and a need to prioritize all cases based on more serious needs of intervention rather than any opportunity to provide preventative therapy for virtually any population. Without any sense of superiority I felt anyone with evaluation skills could do the job to which I was reassigned and I immediately began to rethink my professional future. The loss of professional contact with "my kids" was an almost unbearable loss given the fact by this time I had dedicated my entire career to this population of high risk, troubles kids. I also know that the probation department and law enforcement agencies were able to get back at me for speaking out so openly against them. I have to let go of, and learn from all of that rather than be destroyed by it. I am very proud of the work I did in both Los Angeles and in Riverside County.

During the time I spent in California following the changes in my job I put a great deal of thought into how I should proceed and where I should go. My family ties in Mobile, Alabama were a major deciding factor in my decision to "go home". One of the things missing in my previous work with at risk youth was the reality I had nothing else to offer this group of kids but support through my work as a psychologist. There was nothing I could offer them in exchange for their efforts and willingness to redirect their lives. The loss of contact with the kids was a devastating blow to me emotionally, and my anger and grief gave way to a determination to evolve into more than I had already become personally and professionally. I also felt very strongly the need to protect myself from agencies and institutions having the ability to shut me down with no recourse available to me to fight for my right to fulfill my calling in life. I fell very strongly that my work with troubled kids is what I am supposed to do both from a professional and spiritual perspective.

As a result of the changes in my career path I am now in the process of establishing a non-profit youth center that will give high-risk kids the opportunity to progress on all levels. The center, under the name of Liberating Youth, Inc., will offer advocacy; counseling/social services focusing on redirection and support; adult education; and on-the-job training. This project will be a freestanding private venture intent on collaborating with other organizations and institutions. This is all going well and will become a reality within the next few years. This book and my first book will both serve as the foundations of what will become a very structured program format allowing me to offer more of what these kids need in order to have a better chance of being successful. One main goal of this project is to provide the "evidence-based treatment" needed to prove that with the right approach, program format, and resources these kids can be redirected toward more positive goals.

My primary focus with this new program will be transitional age kids, ages sixteen to twenty-four, and we will seek to address all the needs of this very vulnerable group of troubled kids. While this chapter is about criminality it is important to point out that not all troubled kids are involved in criminal acts. However, it is very easy for kids in this category to fall into criminal behavior given the right combination of complicating factors and feelings of helplessness and hopelessness described earlier in this book and addressed in detail in my first book. Other groups of troubled kids besides juvenile offenders and gang kids include: gothic kids, devil worshipers, witches who practice black magic, white supremacy groups, some skaters, taggers (graffiti artists), punks, rockers, emos (kids identifying themselves as being emotionally disturbed), homeless/street kids, and substance abusers. Some kids simply want to be identified as non-conformists and nothing more, while some kids seek to organize in order to promote some type of hate-based cause. Of interest to me is the reality that each of these groups generally represents different dynamics psychologically. Some of them are driven to have fun, to stand out in a crowd, to be part of a larger group, or some out of a need to survive as is often the case with homeless kids and runaways. With each of these groups it is extremely important to approach the individual members as human beings first and foremost and then try to understand what their group affiliation represents to them.

Of critical importance is the need to avoid judging them for their appearance or actions. It is also necessary to avoid making their exterior identity a constant focus of interaction or intervention. One of the most interesting cases I ever had was with a kid by the name of Eric. He was referred to me by probation and I was warned he was dangerous because he was a devil worshipper. I chose to ignore this and was able to get to know one of the most intelligent and talented kids I have ever known. I told him up front everyone who knew him was reportedly afraid of him and his religious beliefs, assuring him I was not threatened in anyway by him or his religious practices. Eric thought it was funny that everyone was afraid of him and I simply addressed this factor as something he would have to deal with if he continued with his current practices. There were so many other aspects of his character which were much more interesting to me, so I set out from the start to get to know who Eric was deep down inside. I worked very diligently to know his soul and to identify those things in his life and past which gave him cause to hate.

We met for several times before I directly addressed his religious beliefs. By this time I had been able to determine a very high level of intelligence he possessed, and had the opportunity to read many of his thoughts expressed in some of the most profound poetry I had ever read. His use of words painted a vivid picture of what was truly in his soul – both negative and positive aspects. Eric told me his father was a very conservative fundamentalist Christian who had "forced religion down his (Eric's) throat" for many years. He said he chose to worship the devil to get back at his father. I congratulated him on his choice as having chosen the one thing his dad could never have been comfortable with for himself or for his son. We then talked about Christianity as a religion and I simply pointed out the reality of Eric buying into Christianity by worshipping their devil as the evil opposite of their concept of God. The look on his face was priceless and I knew he was intelligent enough to realize he really wanted no part of any aspect of Christian theology. Within a matter of two or three weeks Eric completely changed his manner of dress from dark to lighter colored clothing, and stopped wearing the skeleton hand necklace he always proudly sported. This was all it took for him to realize the futility of his choice against the purposes it was intended to address. We successfully concluded his therapy over a two year period as I followed him through school during his junior and senior years. His goals were to become a chef so he could support himself through college and into a career as both a writer and an actor.

This is one example of a troubled kid who chose to stand out as different and deviant, and yet never got involved in any criminal activity. He had also been into heavy substance use, but that resolved over time as he realized his own desire to protect his mind and his ability to think clearly and purposefully. The concept of deviant doesn't necessarily equate with the concept of bad or evil. To deviate simply means to fall anywhere outside the range of what is considered to be normal or average. Individuality and its appropriate expression and manifestation are extremely important in my work with kids. I try to help them deviate from the norm without drawing negative attention to themselves beyond anything they might be able to withstand. I also try to help them draw their own lines relative to how far they want to deviate away from average before the expression of their individuality becomes counterproductive. Some kids are simply average. However I have found a rather large percentage of troubled kids to be way above average on many levels. This represents a much larger percentage than for those kids who would register in any way below average as defined by whatever set of group standards you may choose.

Pro-criminality or pro-criminal thinking are two terms commonly used in current literature and discussions about juvenile offenders. These concepts are defined as a mindset whereby participants in criminal activity see absolutely nothing wrong with their choices. There is a commonly held belief among many criminals that the ends justify the means, with the ends being some gain on the part of the offender without any regard for their victim(s). As I stated in a previous chapter many kids get angry about getting caught, but feel no anger toward themselves for having committed a crime. Criminal acts are much more likely to occur in partnership with other participants from the viewpoint of strength in numbers and the loss of individual identity when part of a duo or group. I believe most of the criminal behavior in which kids engage early on is motivated by peer pressure, getting even, and getting ahead materially or in social/peer position or status. Kids rarely put themselves in the place of their victims as a way of trying to imagine how their targets might feel in response to their criminal victimization.

Jesse, one of my clients, and a group of his friends were arrested for assaulting and robbing a pizza delivery man one evening. I knew all three of the kids involved and had an opportunity to interview each of them separately. Each of these kids was angry about getting caught and as a group were motivated by their perceived need for money to spend on alcohol and marijuana. Having already established a high level of trust with these kids I was able to confront them relative to their misperception and misinterpretation of the situation. Jesse was the one who more readily saw the error of his thinking and was able to admit they wouldn't have gotten arrested if they had not done anything wrong in the first place. He was then able to see that his anger should be toward himself and his own actions and bad choices rather than against the victim who identified the kids and the police who arrested them. He also allowed me to guide him into seeing things through the perspective of the way their victim probably experienced the entire incident. All three of the kids were low income, high risk kids with numerous complicating factors present in their lives and histories. Jesse cried as he imagined the reality of the older man probably working more than one job and simply trying to provide for his wife and children. Jesse was motivated by anger fueled in part by his own abandonment and financial hardship resulting from his dad's exit from his life some years earlier. The other kids were able to see things differently as Jesse confronted them with the same approach I had used with him.

It is important to understand none of this work with Jesse and this group of kids would have been possible if I had screwed up in any way in my efforts to build a rapport of trust and mutual respect with these and all of the kids I have served over the years. My position as a psychologist rarely ever puts me in a position of authority over kids. Over the years professionals in other fields who work with kids often get jealous or even threatened by my ability to join professionally with kids in an exchange which actually results in the achievement of very positive goals. When I have worked in the field at various school sites and juvenile placement programs and facilities, it is obvious to every other adult present the kids I serve appreciate and respect me. Numerous times I have been confronted by staff members from other programs challenging my role and job with these kids, suggesting that trying to be their friend was not the answer. Actually, to some extent, that _is_ the answer in a professionally appropriate and responsible relationship between me and the kids. I have told several adults I chose my profession wisely and carefully. I get to nurture and support, rather than lord over kids in positions requiring a great deal more control relative to circumstances and context than my job requires. It has always been very clear to me that those adults who were jealous and accused me of being "pro kids" were likely frustrated I was getting greater positive results from these kids more often than these other professionals were able to achieve. The adults who worked as effectively with kids as I did were never negatively impacted by my professional relationships with my kids. Rather they worked collaboratively with me to further insure the success of the kids we shared in our respective roles.

Those who care within other professions don't seem to last very long unless they learn to reach out to and actually reach those kids they seek to serve. In reality not every kid is easy to reach. This only means it is necessary to try harder and with approaches based on a very personalized and individualized style with each kid. Unfortunately those caring professionals, within systems where kids are being confined and supervised by law enforcement staff, are often forced out. This happens as a result of the overwhelming majority of other male and female staff drawn to these environments and driven by strong agendas to break down and dominate those under their charge. Believe me, there are likely very consistent personality profiles which could be developed to identify and describe those who are the most likely to choose jobs which give them authority over troubled kids. Working with troubled kids as part of most any group setting is often quite challenging. However with the right combination of training in sensitivity, realities and circumstances present in the lives of these kids, and in ethical principles and standards, a great deal of progress could be made from which all involved would benefit.

In recent years it seems that more and more people and politicians are focused on incarcerating and punishing offenders rather than making attempts to rehabilitate as was the focus for many decades. There is nothing to be gained by this thinking or the actions taken to simply house and punish without any significant efforts being made to offer juvenile/youthful offenders and adult offenders the opportunities to redirect their lives and futures. I believe very strongly there is a very big difference between older adult offenders and juvenile/youthful offenders relative to the ease with which kids can be redirected compared to older adult populations. This is also true in general mental health populations as well. The reality with kids is that their personality characteristics are still somewhat fluid rather than fixed and rigid as they are with many adults.

After having worked successfully with literally hundreds of troubled kids since 1992 I am convinced that with the right combination of efforts and support kids will make different choices as long as they see it is in their own best interest to do so. The only lasting changes made by kids are those they make for themselves and not out of any sense of guilt or obligation to other adults in their lives. Criminal activity and pro-criminal thinking can easily become permanent ways of living and dealing with life. The incarceration of kids without opportunities to redirect their lives is in itself criminal. Every effort needs to be made to educate the public and change the focus of juvenile justice more toward addressing every aspect of their lives and personalities beyond their observable behaviors and reactions. Scientific evidence indicates that brain development and maturation continue until approximately age 25. Therefore, both juvenile and young adult offenders need redirection and support services rather than incarceration in many cases. Re-entry programs cannot undo the damage of extended confinement for crimes which do not really require such drastic consequences.

One of the biggest problems at the present time is the mentality of those in charge of these programs and the decisions as to how they will be run and staffed. I have watched over the years in Los Angeles and Riverside Counties in California, and now in Mobile, Alabama, as law enforcement agencies and institutions have fortified the blue curtain to exclude the option and need of collaborating with other agencies and professionals. Every effort should be made to expand their resources and outreach to other systems involved in the lives of these kids. Rather than reach out, most (if not all of these systems) have built walls around themselves and their programs, foolishly believing they know everything there is to know about working with offenders of any age. I firmly believe this is based in a need to guarantee and protect their own existence relative to staff, salaries and benefits. Law enforcement officials – not officers - and related staff within all environments are some of the highest paid workers in the country. They tend to be very territorial and secretive in order to protect themselves from outside scrutiny and accountability. I have said many times it is more often about money and numbers with many agencies and less about effectiveness and desirable outcomes. This is self-preservation in its ugliest and most destructive form.

At this point in our national history I also firmly believe the climate of secrecy, supremacy, domination, and an arrogant disregard for ethics and integrity allow for serious misuses of power. We have seen this clearly within politics, corporations, and religious institutions whose leaders appear to believe themselves to be above the laws and rights of people here and around the world. This is gang mentality at its worst, existing and modeled at all levels of government and business. It is no wonder kids think in the ways they do, believing it is okay to break the laws and violate the rights of others as long as they don't get caught. Even our top political figures try to cover up their misuses of power by trying to put a new spin on their original reasoning and justification which were, in many cases, outright lies as well. Criminality at any level and within any environment or context serves the same purposes and follows the same attempts at illogical justification as is found with kids and adults involved in street crime. Even officials within the so-called justice systems are often corrupt and yet protected by those who hire and supervise them as was the case in the situation I outlined in chapter three. It is time for a change if we ever want to change the thinking of our younger generations who witness these scandals and cover-ups on a profoundly frequent basis.

I think it is time for every professional in this country to be forced to attend regularly mandated classes and workshops regarding laws and ethics relative to every existing profession and religious institution. We have all lost sight of what is important in this country and in the world as evidenced by the arrogant positions exhibited even within religious organizations in this country and around the world. There is a natural progression in the development of pro-criminal thinking and it is often fueled by rampant greed and arrogance. How can we expect kids to make different choices when they see adult leaders in many settings pursuing their own personal and institutional agendas without any regard for the laws and rights of others? Everything in our culture needs to be reprioritized to match the true meaning and philosophies of democracy and freedom. There can be no positive gains when systems and individuals within our country are, or believe themselves to be above public scrutiny and accountability. There are so many disparities within our society whereby the rich make progress at the expense of the poor and those less able to defend themselves. There is no context in which this is more apparent than in our criminal justice systems, and especially at the juvenile offender level. Systems of checks and balances which are supposedly in place over any organization should be independent of those working within the systems regardless of their nature and purpose. Outside public scrutiny and accountability are essential if we are to avoid corruption and any misuses of power and authority.

The current political climate in this country which is dominated and controlled by special interest groups has given rise to the '*right*-makes-right' philosophy as a way of governing and otherwise running this country. People in the general public are misinformed and often lied to relative to realties existing in the lives of many ordinary and vulnerable people. The US Patriot Act in conjunction with the Homeland Security Act have given more authority to law enforcement agencies without any significant and effective use of independent monitoring. There is too much power in the hands of a relative few under the guise of "antiterrorism", to the point even kids suspected of street-related crimes can be treated as terrorists under the provision of the US Patriot Act. The general public has very little awareness of the level of power and secrecy provided by this legislation which opens the doors for private citizens, who have no involvement in terrorist activity, to be treated as urban terrorists. I saw this happen on an extensive scale in the last few years I worked in California as represented by the example I gave earlier in this book about the senior probation officer and the assistant district attorney. I even heard a law enforcement agent giving a talk to the kids in the lock-in placement program where I worked in juvenile hall openly bragging about the equipment purchased and the outrageous salaries paid to local law enforcement agents and agencies. He thought it was funny he had access to so many resources which could be used to fight street crime, and was using this information to let kids know they were nothing more than terrorists in his eyes if they engaged in any form of criminal activity.

The kids I talked with after this presentation were shocked at the reality of being listed as terrorists and reacted with a "we'll show them" kind of response. This kind of bravado allowed by the US Patriot Act gives law enforcement officials the opportunity to misuse their power. Furthermore, it only increases the determination of kids with a pro-criminality mindset to see this as a challenge. I witnessed an unimaginable level of the abuse of power while in California since 9/11. Kids were picked up and held for hours in secret locations without any written record of this ever occurring. The abuse of power resulted in a ridiculous show of force for even the most minor of offenses. Kids were questioned without adult or legal representation, and were detained without their parents or families having any awareness of their whereabouts. These kids were released without being charged with any crime and were sent back into the streets even more angry than before, and with an increased determination to win the war of terrorism being waged against *them*.

The same tactics were used with adult offenders, but only when they could be ultimately charged with a crime even if they had to be provoked into "resisting arrest" or "assaulting a police officer". As with the kids there was never any record of these adults being detained without probable cause. They had to appear in court to face charges which were often times dismissed or treated as misdemeanor crimes which would never have occurred without harassment from law enforcement officers. Most of these acts were targeted against African American and Hispanic individuals likely due to their vulnerability and limited ability to pay for private legal representation. The fact that juvenile offenders are not judged by a jury gives rise to unbelievable misuses of power and authority since documentation is simply the word of a kid (terrorist) against law enforcement personnel.

More care is taken with adult offenders who might have to go to trial before a jury in adult courtrooms. This is accepted, but not discussed, as common practice in the juvenile justice systems. It is a clear mirror image of the tactics being put in place and utilized by our current political administration in this country and around the world.

In Alabama the juvenile courts I have knowledge of commit kids to mental hospitals, run by the Alabama Department of Mental Health and Mental Retardation, when they cannot be legally charged and detained. Such court ordered hospitalizations are referred to as "evaluations" and last anywhere from one to two full weeks. Kids are then released to local state funded mental health clinics in many cases with erroneous diagnoses and on medications clearly not needed. Patient rights are violated and only against low income, disadvantaged families covered by Medicaid. The justification given to families is that juvenile records can be sealed. However, in reality medical records are permanent records and do not fall under this option. Kids are afraid to come forward because they do not want to face public humiliation of having been incorrectly labeled as "mentally ill". I am certain that these hospitalizations wrongly inflate statistics reported by race and socioeconomic status nationwide relative to minorities and mental illness. However, this keeps all of these related and interconnected agencies in business and fully staffed. All of this can be backed up with proof.

Major changes are needed relative to the pro-criminal mindset of our political leaders at all levels of government. The American people need an itemized account of money designated for protection against terrorists and terrorist attacks which were misappropriated and misspent around the country by local law enforcement agencies. The kinds of vehicles and surveillance equipment now owned by many relatively small town law enforcement agencies only feeds the egos of the officers and does not match the needs of these small communities or the needs of the country as a whole. The deception of fear and the cover of secrecy presented repeatedly to the American people has given people in positions of power and authority the opportunities to misuse their power and authority. These injustices trickle down from the federal level all the way to local levels. This has likely resulted in an increase in the numbers of people incarcerated with very little if any effort made to rehabilitate them. It has also likely created criminals and sentences people didn't deserve and wouldn't have received if they had not been harassed by so-called "peace officers". Based on my awareness of things said by law enforcement personnel, the idea is clearly to get as many *potential* criminals into the 'system' as possible so they can be monitored before or until they do something really big. I firmly believe these factors are responsible for our more overcrowded detention centers and prisons, and for recent increases in violent crimes nationwide. Furthermore, I firmly believe this was money MIS-spent which could have been utilized more effectively toward preventing rather than compelling and provoking crime.

With the current political and social climates in our country, the number of complicating factors for troubled youth is only rising. Very little money is being spent in any arena to provide resources needed by low and middle income families. Our educational systems are failing to meet the educational needs of kids of all ages, and represent the same kinds of closed systems as are present within governmental and legal systems. Much of this is fueled by the lack of concern and regard for others espoused by religious extremists within our own country who seek only to promote their non-mainstream agendas of supremacy and self-righteousness. Most of the so-labeled "faith-based" programs only seek to further their cause of spreading their views around the country and the globe, lacking any true sense of altruism or respect for other religious or even spiritual points of view. Their goals are to simply increase their membership numbers, rather than do anything just for the good of others, representing a high level of deception as well. People here and abroad are paying a price for this kind of arrogance and elitism.

My hope for the future is to be able to combat these realities through the nonprofit youth center I am working to establish under the name of Liberating Youth, Inc. All of these points will be made through the center to the kids and to the community to help them understand both the obvious and sometimes invisible obstacles they face every day. With the youth center I will have the opportunity to provide these kids with the skills needed to guard themselves against obstacles which can only be fought by bettering themselves in all aspects of their lives. Knowledge is power and I hope to inspire the kids we will serve to be both aware of and informed about every factor in their lives which could serve to keep them down. The only way at this point to fight the larger corrupt systems is to teach and empower kids and families how to expose them and shut them down. Once kids begin to improve the choices they make and better their chances in life then there will be less need for incarceration and involvement of law enforcement officials. The fight has to be at the community level and not just against the systems and leaders specifically. We have to teach kids to act and be smarter than those who would seek to hold them back. Education is the key to the future for all who fall into the underdog category in life. Kids would laugh when I told them they could actually shut down juvenile hall and juvenile probation if they would simply stop breaking the law and giving these agencies the opportunity to control them and their destinies. While they agreed with me and liked the idea, they couldn't see how this would ever happen. It is my goal to make this belief a reality in the future.

5

Substance Use and Addiction

Drugs and alcohol are two of the biggest obstacles kids face relative to educational success and lifestyle choices. The two biggest factors that lead to substance use are availability and peer influence more than peer pressure. It's like the old adage of "everybody's doing it." Unfortunately the contexts in which these kids live are full of opportunities for kids to drink and use. In many cases this is true both within the home context and out in the community. When you look at the temptation to drink and use, coupled with the wide variety of complicating factors present in the lives of troubled kids, it is no wonder they begin to experiment with things which will dull the harshness of many of the realities in their lives. I tell kids no one sets up a goal of becoming an alcoholic and/or a drug addict. It just happens, especially when kids and adults fail to pay attention to their increasing use of substances coupled with the emotions and circumstances motivating them to seek different forms of escape.

Kids in this day and time do not seem to be afraid to engage in many different potentially harmful experiences and activities. Early experimentation with drugs and alcohol are often quite common first choices. Not every kid who drinks will use drugs. Nor will every kid who smokes marijuana try harder substances. However, the initial choice to drink or use even tobacco opens the gate to try other things if for no other reason than curiosity. Adolescents in general have a very limited sense of danger given their abilities to convince themselves 'nothing can go wrong for me'. Because kids have very little fear about danger to themselves and their bodies and minds, fear tactics do not serve as a deterrent to risky behaviors. They see others engaging in risky activities and over time come to see such activity as simply part of the norm within their frame of reference. Boredom is one of the biggest contributing factors to ongoing substance use. There is a lot of time taken up by substance use from the efforts to obtain the substance, use it or drink it, and experience the effects induced by the substance. For kids with too much time on their hands it is very easy to fall into this cycle as a way of simply filling time and fighting boredom in many cases.

Then there is the factor of socializing with friends. Unfortunately many adults and kids come to believe substance use makes them more appealing and helps them to make accomplishments and overcome different factors only when they are under the influence of some type of substance. Shyness, social awkwardness, boredom, anxiety, and numerous other intrinsic inhibiting factors simply go away while drunk or high. These realities then become reinforcements in the desire to continue using and drinking. People in general fail to understand that the physiological effects of substance use are nothing more than the bodies reaction to the presence of something not naturally found in the body. The reaction is simply the body's attempt to fight off and contend with the invasion of something foreign and is usually experienced as a state of euphoria. The fact that in most cases the effects are pleasant only reinforces the desire to use and drink again. Because kids have trouble with limits there is a strong tendency to overindulge in many of their activities. Even if the experience ultimately makes them sick, the initial experience of the induced altered state brings them back after a period of recovery.

Addiction is also one of the biggest obstacles in reaching these kids through therapy and other attempts to help or assist them. I do not believe a kid should be expected to be completely clean and sober for someone to try to intervene on their behalf. It is completely futile to work with a kid while they are directly under the influence, but it is an unrealistic expectation that a kid will achieve and maintain sobriety, and then seek out services of assistance. Furthermore, substance use cannot be the only or even the primary focus of every interaction adults have with kids. It is important to accept it as a reality, with the awareness that as a therapist, educator, counselor, or mentor we have no control over their activities outside our offices. It is also important to see it as a byproduct of the FLAGS identified in my first book and in early chapters in this text. If we try to take a position of authority over them, kids will often see this as a challenge to their rights to make whatever choices they want to make. The process will then become more of a competition, rather than an attempted intervention of trying to deal with every aspect of a kid's nature and needs. Unfortunately, the more you tell a kid they can't do something, the more likely they are to do it if for no other reason than proving they can. How many of us as adults make this same mistake out of sheer stubbornness? As I've said before, just because we can do something doesn't mean we should.

Kids fail to see they are actually addicted to something until they are forced to face this reality. One of the best interventions is to find out exactly how many times they drink or use within a given week or month. If their use is daily then challenge them to go for one week without drinking or using. Ask them to pay attention to how hard it is to resist the temptation, and encourage them to be totally honest about their success at their next session with you. This will help make them aware of the existence of a problem which they and only they can address. Accept the fact they and only they can make the decision to address the problem and be patient with them. Help them identify both the positives and negatives related to their substance use. Openly challenge their belief of things being better when they are drunk or stoned, but do not make this a confrontation. Offer everything simply as something for them to think about and give them the option as to how to deal with it in their own way and in their own time. To make sobriety a prerequisite for treatment will cancel out the opportunity to work with them on the complicating factors in their lives which cause them to engage in excessive behaviors in the first place. The use of my

Roberts FLAGS Model is the best way to help them literally see how and why they choose to act out rather than deal with their problems.

If you are looking for a rationale as to why they should not drink and use, focus on health issues; not as scare tactics, but as realities they will have to deal with someday. It also a good idea to have them look at others around them and honestly examine the state of their lives. Help them to see that people who are addicted have very limited options in life. Get them to see how all-consuming the practices associated with addiction really are. Try to help them see what it is like to be around people who are addicted, and yet be clean and sober themselves. Focus on the realities that people who are addicted generally are not motivated to do anything positive with their lives. Point out the reality of addiction taking away the pleasure of getting high and simply becoming a need to maintain a certain physiological state in order to avoid withdrawal. Also point out the reality of everyone eventually having to make a choice to stop using and/or drinking in order to stay healthy and alive as well. Be careful to deal with the reality of everyone having the right to do whatever they want as along as it is not harmful to others. Point out how foolish it is to do things harmful to themselves even though they can choose to do so. Tell them regular use of alcohol and drugs will eventually even hurt those who care about the user. These approaches give kids the option to see that it truly is in their best interest to control all forms of substance use. Kids will rationalize alcohol, tobacco, and marijuana as not being so-called "hard drugs". Methamphetamines and cocaine-related drugs are even considered by kids to be moderate drugs. Heroin and LSD are the ones which scare them the most, especially when coupled with the idea of shooting up. As a professional you may have to settle for controlled use of marijuana and alcohol as a success, with the hope they possess some degree of control over their use. Like it or not, many people drink and smoke weed. It may take them getting in trouble on a job, at school, or with law enforcement before they realize the true consequences of regular use. If you have laid the groundwork they can build on it in the future as needed.

Always keep in mind successes with troubled kids are often few and far between. Also remember success for this population comes in less obvious forms than with higher functioning individuals who can more easily secure jobs, make plans for the future, achieve moderate to high academic standards, stay out of trouble, and stay clean and sober without much effort. Even one week of avoiding trouble at school or with law enforcement is a huge accomplishment for many of these kids. A month of perfect attendance, fewer problems at home, and an improvement in their overall outlook are tremendous successes. Each success should be acknowledged and reinforced by giving the kids a sense of their ability to control their lives, choices and destinies. It is also important to help them see how each success is in their own best interest and not for the benefit of others. While other people in their lives may benefit from their accomplishments this cannot be, nor should it ever be, the reason presented to them as to why they should want to do better. Never try guilt tripping them into doing something solely for mom or dad. The only person and perception which matters is the kid sitting in front of you along with what she/he thinks and learns about themselves in the process. If you can learn to be proud of relatively minor successes imagine how you will feel when you see a previously troubled kid graduate from high school knowing you were part of the process which helped graduation become a reality.

One particular intervention which is especially helpful for kids is to help them understand how much of the illegal activity in which they engage actually reflects various useful skills. Many kids who use drugs regularly often deal drugs in order to support their habit. Unfortunately a significant degree of criminal activity arises from their need to support and fund their drug use. Kids are generally shocked and amused to realize how many of their illegal actions build and develop useful skills relative to possible future legitimate career choices. Think about how much time and energy goes into establishing a drug dealing business. Kids learn a lot about planning, purchasing, market supply and demand, warehousing, pricing, competition, marketing, and establishing and maintaining a repeat customer base. While this may sound a little absurd, it is all true, and is helpful in getting kids to see the need to redirect their efforts and talents toward more positive and less risky legal ventures. It is not about kids changing with the goal of becoming someone different, it is about helping them use their energy in the right ways and changing their mindsets and frames of reference. The same energy which goes into illegal and risky behaviors is the exact same energy they would use for more beneficial and legal choices. It's about helping them to work differently with who they already are! These insights can actually encourage kids to finish school and even consider going to college to study different areas of business. Give them credit for their ingenuity and at the same time help them see and understand all of the reasons why engaging in any form of illegal business activities is completely wrong and immoral. Help them look at the devastating effects on the lives of those to whom they sell. Also get them to imagine the impact drug use has on the families of those to whom they sell. At the same time it is important to clearly point out the risks of continuing a career based in crime. However, it is really hard to get kids to let go of these pursuits given the fact these activities are very lucrative. However, it is necessary to try and get them to stop before it is too late. Give them an awareness of what even a juvenile criminal record can do to jeopardize their futures.

I cannot stress enough the need to look beyond what a kid does and see them for who they are deep inside and to see them for who they can become. No effective work can be accomplished with a kid unless they have total trust in your word and work. Kids must know you are there for their benefit only and not to serve some conscious or unconscious hidden agenda you may have on the table or in your head. Kids today are too sophisticated for adults to be able to pull something over on them. Troubled kids have usually had so many negative and damaging interactions with other adults before they got to you that you will have to work very hard to establish and maintain trust all along the way. Kids are very perceptive to and sensitive to efforts to manipulate or control them and will react by shutting you out or walking away. Always admit when you are wrong and apologize, and at the same time seek to repair any inadvertent damage which may have been done to the relationship you have worked to establish with your client, student or child. The use of positive psychology approaches allows everyone to emphasize the goodness in each kid and to then identify the obstacles blocking the emergence, growth and development of the goodness present in each child you meet.

Do not ever be hesitant to "join" with a kid in your efforts to assist them. The concept of joining is a family therapy term whereby the caregiver literally forms a bond of interest in and positive regard for their clients. This, of course, must be accomplished through appropriate professional limits and boundaries, and only within the context where assistance is being offered. Never make promises you cannot or may not want to fulfill outside the therapeutic or professional association. Kids will only get hurt and you will become like every other adult in their lives who has let them down. Never cross the line and bring a troubled kid into your personal life on any level. You must seek only to help them find and create what they have with you as a professional outside the professional context and within their own world and contexts. Many caregivers try too hard and cross lines which must never be crossed both for the sake of the kids and for the sake of the service provider. You cannot be everything to everyone, and to try this is both futile and foolish. The goal is to teach and empower rather than foster dependence and the appearance of a relationship which could never exist in reality. You can really be their "friend", but only within that professional context.

The need to look beyond what kids do and see them for who they are and can become is critical when working with high risk, troubled kids. Do not be afraid of foul language or curse words. Let them speak in any manner which will allow them to express themselves comfortably. Never let them cuss you out, but do not react if words like fuck, shit, piss, bitch, pussy or other such words if this is the way they need to tell you a story or details about their lives. After all, these are the kinds of words many kids use when speaking to their friends. The single most important thing in therapeutic interactions is to have the client talk with you. You can help them at some point to understand when such language is and is not appropriate, but ***LET THEM TALK!*** Do not be such a prude. Doing so will set up barriers between you and every troubled kid which can be easily avoided by simply focusing only on what is really important - the need to connect with them and get to know everything about them you need to know and understand in order to help them.

Furthermore, if you are not comfortable working with this population of kids, ***DON'T!*** However, if your heart goes out to them and you want to reach them, learn how to do so effectively. Be like a friend to them without crossing professional lines and boundaries. One of the biggest compliments a kid can give you is for them to refer to you as their "homie" or "dog". This level of comfort is a sign they see you as someone who they can trust to care about, help and protect them. At the same time remind them, if and when necessary, you are their therapist, teacher, mentor, etc. You will know when it is time to do this when they invite you to a party or to hang out with them and their friends. Never cross these kinds of lines, but be appreciative of their high regard for you. Have them imagine what it would actually be like for you and for them relative to everyone's ability to have fun at such an event or gathering. They will readily see it wouldn't work. After all, what kid would be comfortable drinking, using, or committing criminal acts in front of a professional whose opinion of them really matters? And what professional would be willing to risk everything just to be their buddy on this level?

A successful professional relationship with any kid can only be established if the kid feels and sees you are real and genuinely care about them. You must be interested in getting to know them on all levels before issues of addiction, criminality, and other critical matters can be dealt with and resolved to their benefit and satisfaction. All interactions must be appropriately informal to the deepest level possible with each individual kid. The limits on confidentiality must be clearly and thoroughly revealed at the onset of the initial contact, even when it comes to information which will or will not be shared with their parents or guardians. Unless an issue or behavior is life threatening, I never reveal such information to other adults under any circumstances. I have told many parents and other adults that I am not there to be their detective. Furthermore, I believe very firmly if a parent doesn't see or even suspect negative behavior, then it is not my obligation to reveal my insights to them except under very specific circumstances. I would never reveal anything, except as mandated by law, unless I have cleared it with the kid and have given them the chance to deal with others on their own first. I make all of this very clear to parents and other adults at the outset of my interactions with kids. At the same time I assure them I will not withhold any information I believe poses a danger to the kid or to adults involved in their lives. I cover all of this in front of the kid and during the initial contact. Most adults readily agree, and appreciate and understand the fact kids generally will not talk to adults close to them, including parents, about every aspect of their lives. Parents and other adults are usually appreciative of the fact their child has someone to talk to who they can trust. Without this arrangement upfront there is little chance of success with the kid. Kids will talk about virtually everything in their lives if they know they can trust the adult with whom they are speaking.

The only time I ever violated this position was with Jose. He was 13 at the time and would come into my office stoned every week. His mother was a very stern and strict woman and was blaming me for the lack of progress with her son. I warned him two weeks in a row that if he came back to my office stoned I would take him out to his mom and show her why nothing was working. He didn't believe me and left me no choice on the third week after my warning. After my intake interview his mom never came into the office with him except for that first session. This is often the case for parents of troubled kids who are simply looking for someone else to "fix" their kid. I never penalize a kid for the lack of parental involvement and never discourage parental participation. Jose's mom would drop him off at the clinic and would wait for him in the car. He would go behind the building and hit is marijuana pipe before he came into the office. By the time I saw him he was as high as a kite and thought this was really funny.

At this third session I told Jose I was taking him out to his mom in the parking lot. At first he didn't believe me until I stood up and told him to come with me. At that point he got really angry, cussing me along the way to the parking lot. All I could do was remind him that I had warned him, but assuring him I was not going to take the blame from his mom for his lack of progress. His mom saw us coming and got out of her car. She wanted to know what was wrong and I told her to look at her son. She didn't see how stoned he was, so I told her what was happening. To his surprise I made him empty out his pockets in front of his mom, exposing his bag of weed, his pipe, and a lighter. He was enraged with me and his mom was enraged with him. I told mom Jose's use of marijuana before our sessions was the reason no progress was being made. She made him get into the car and assured me she would handle this when they got home. I told him I would be here for him if and when he wanted to come back. He yelled some obscenities at me assuring me he would never be back to see me again. While I felt bad about all of this, I clearly knew he left me know choice. Out of my work with hundreds of kids over the years this was the only time I had to resort to such measures and was the only time a kid was angry with me as he or she left my office.

After a year or so had passed I was on one of the units at juvenile hall. As I entered the unit I heard a voice announce to the other kids and staff, "that guy's a rat!" This is the very worst thing a kid could ever saw about me or anyone and I had to address him in front of the other kids. When I identified the kid I was surprised to see it was Jose. I walked over to the table where he was sitting and said, "Hello Jose. Long time no see." He seemed surprised and embarrassed that I would approach him. Virtually every kid on this unit knew me and I couldn't let this go with his accusation of me being a rat. I said to him, "so you think I'm a rat, huh? Why don't you tell these kids and staff I ratted you out to your mommy about coming into my office stoned every week." He was horrified and knew he had really screwed up, then refusing to speak to me. I told him, "I'm still here if you need me." He finally looked up and said, "no way. Fuck you man!" The other kids laughed and I called the kid I needed to see into the office on the unit. The kid who knew me was really pissed off that Jose had disrespected me like he did. He wanted to jump him for me, but I insisted that would not be necessary since I had handled it in a way which didn't allow Jose to get away with what he said. I had to spend a little time with my other client assuring him I am not a rat and had to describe the reasons why I took the actions I did both a year earlier, and on this particular day. He fully understood and agreed to let it go with regards to retaliation towards Jose.

Another year passed and I saw Jose again in juvenile hall. I approached him and simply reminded him "I am still here for you if you ever need to talk." This time he simply said "no", and I gave him one of my business cards in case he changed his mind. One year later Jose was back in juvenile hall. Before I could even run into him he sent word to me through the staff he needed to see me. With this incarceration Jose was facing serious charges and was likely on his way to the California Youth Authority for a number of years. When I met with him the first thing he did was apologize to me for his disrespect. I assured him it really was okay and nothing he had ever done or said had changed the way I feel about working with him. He started crying and gave me the details of everything that had happened in his life since our first meetings some three years earlier. There was nothing I could do but listen to him and try to help him find some hope for the future beyond his impending sentence to CYA.

Jose told me he wanted to explain why he wouldn't talk to me when he had the chance initially. He told me about having been molested by a neighbor in his neighborhood when he was 12. The incident had been reported and the man was arrested and convicted of the molestation, but the incident had been very embarrassing to Jose and he didn't want to talk with anyone about it. Jose had no idea of the impact it had on him psychologically and didn't realize until this moment with me that talking about it with someone he could trust was exactly what he had needed all along. He was amazed at how easy it was to talk with me about this. I simply asked him a couple of yes or no kinds of questions so I would have a general idea of the extent of the abuse. He didn't have to give me details I could easily figure out from his yes or no responses. I felt so bad for him during these moments, but he readily understood his unwillingness and inability to talk with me previously was all his choice and had nothing to do with me or my efforts to connect with him previously. He also was able to see for himself he lacked the maturity three years earlier needed to see and handle things differently before now.

We spent three hours together that afternoon in an office within juvenile hall. This session was one of the saddest and most difficult sessions I have experienced before or since, and yet it was one of the most rewarding experiences of my career. Jose readily agreed if he could have talked with me previously he probably would not be facing several years at CYA. I helped him understand himself in ways he had never seen before with anyone else. We addressed the wounds left by the abuse and gave him ways to understand the incident and the impact on him to give him the relief he needed about his involvement and his future. As we stood up at the end of the session I went around the desk to hug Jose. He took my hand before he moved toward the door and said, "Doc, you'll see I'm going to be somebody someday. Don't be surprised in a few years when I show up at your office and prove that to you." We both had tears in our eyes as he spoke and I assured him I had the utmost respect for him regardless of anything he had done that got him into trouble. I also assured him I would be looking forward to his visit and to his future success.

These are the moments and memories which make it all worthwhile. I never heard from Jose again since that last encounter. There is no way for me to know how his life has turned out, or to know if he is even still alive for that matter. But, I know in my heart Jose connected with me that day like he had probably never connected with anyone else in his life. Because of that opportunity to talk with him and offer him some insight and guidance into some very complicated and difficult issues I know we both benefited tremendously from the experience. Never assume you haven't gotten through to any kid. Who knows, if I had stayed in California Jose may have come to my office looking for me. The one thing I know for sure is neither Jose nor I will ever forget the time we shared just before he left for CYA. Above all else Jose knew I genuinely cared for and about him. This is all it takes for one person to make a difference in the life of a kid.

This is one example of how kids try to cope with complicating factors by using and drinking. The real tragedy in this whole story is that Jose's mom didn't care enough to get more deeply involved in her son's treatment. She should have told me about Jose's history of sexual abuse, even if he had told her not to do so. It is tragic when people are unable or unwilling to see how all of us tend to act out emotion-based anxiety and depression. The lack of opportunities to gain assistance from adults who can be trusted to care and to offer assistance is tragic. When experiences and perceptions get buried rather than dealt with the severity of the experiences and circumstances determines the levels of helplessness and hopelessness which result and lead to acting out behaviors such as substance use and criminal activity. Anyone might develop pro-criminal thinking after experiencing any extreme violation or injustice, especially as a child who cannot defend her/himself adequately anyway. If Jose's mother had recognized and understood the need for Jose to face and deal with his emotions then Jose would likely have been able to make better choices as he grew older. Believe me, it is never too late to offer assistance. But, also believe me when I say it is extremely important not to become another complicating factor in a kid's life by mishandling your interactions with any kid. It will be far better for every kid for us to do nothing than to do anything which makes their lives worse than they already are! Please don't ever let that happen.

6

Sexual Issues and Concerns

The adolescent years are often a time of confusion and stress especially relative to sexual issues and concerns. It can be made more complicated with kids trying to figure out whether or not to become sexually active and even worse for kids who are dealing with sexual orientation issues. Kids nowadays are much more open to sexual activity and I think it is absolutely absurd that kids cannot be taught everything there is to know about sex in so-called sexual education classes. So many adults, especially people who are conservative and religious, are overly afraid of dealing with the sexuality of kids both as parents and professionals in various settings. Too many people have their heads buried in the sand when it comes to the realities of sexual temptations kids face even beginning in elementary school. Kids talk to each other and will make up the details if they are not given the full amount of information required for them to make informed decisions relative to remaining abstinent or deciding to become sexually active. Conservatives have way too much power in deciding what is appropriate relative to sexuality and it is time for law makers to put a stop to the fantasy of abstinence being the most likely choice by today's teenagers.

It is always interesting to me to learn how little parents and other adults actually know about what is going on in the private lives of kids.

As I described earlier, kids are sneaky and have many ways through the technology of today to engage in all kinds of activities without any awareness on the part of parents and other adults. Kids often have secret codes and language when it comes to discussing private matters, and especially relative to sex. Recently kids were wearing gel bracelets out in public in front of every adult in their lives both at home and out in the communities and schools. It was eventually revealed that the colors of the bracelets represented various sexual acts in which kids either would participate or had already been willing to participate. I learned about this from one of my female clients I was meeting with at a school site. She was very open about the bracelet system and how it worked. The most shocking aspect of it for me was the reality that in some areas a gang-like mentality was forming within some groups of girls which would actually result in open confrontation and violence. I never got the whole picture, but I got enough information to realize how alarming it was. Even very young girls in elementary school and middle school were wearing bracelets indicating they had allowed boys to engage in various levels of touching. Other bracelets indicated participation in oral sex, all the way to vaginal and anal sex as well usually by older girls. Girls who were willing to engage in sexual behaviors were referred to by boys as "girls with benefits". This system spread around the country and went on for months before adults became aware of what was actually going on in the lives of their kids.

With the Internet, cell phones, and other portable devices kids are in almost constant contact with each other both locally and even around the world if they so choose. Chat rooms for kids are quite common, offering a rather rapid means of spreading information to every other kid with access to the same communication possibilities. Web sites and chat rooms can even be used to ruin the reputations of kids or to threaten them with violence if they are unpopular, or are being brutalized by bullies. In my experiences, girls are much more brutal and ruthless than boys could ever hope to be in many different contexts. Because people fail to see the realities of what is happening there is a very strong double standard when it comes to punishing boys much more severely than girls for the same kids of offenses. This is true when it comes to sexual activity as well. Males are always given more serious consequences and penalties for inappropriate or illegal sexual contact than females receive. This was recently very evident in the case of a female school teacher who was sexually involved with a middle school boy. She received no jail time. If it had been a male involved with a female student the outcome likely would have been drastically different. Sexual misconduct is sexual misconduct no matter who commits the acts.

One of the most unfair situations relative to sexual activity between adolescents involves kids who are romantically involved and one (usually the boy) turns 18 and continues to have sex with his now underage girlfriend. I have known of cases where boys were charged with statutory rape for a sexual relationship that had been going on for quite some time before the change in age. There are girls who take advantage of boys sexually as well, and are equally as harassing in some of their interactions as any boy could ever hope to be. However, again the consequences for girls are generally less severe or even non-existent in some cases even when adults in various contexts witness the behaviors. Boys are still viewed as being the villain if they are the offender, and as the "bitch" or wimp if they are the victim. Sexual standards must become equally applicable to both genders given the realities of sexual interactions in general in today's culture.

Safe sex has two different meanings for today's kids. Some practice safe sex with regards to preventing both sexually transmitted diseases and pregnancy. However there are other kids who forget about sexually transmitted diseases and focus only on preventing pregnancy without any consideration of the spreading or contracting of diseases. This is likely the main cause for the increase of sexual experiences which do not involve vaginal intercourse. It is important to teach kids that anyone who is infected with some form of STD is contagious through virtually any form of sexual intimacy. Kissing is still safe unless there is the presence of some form of oral infection. Mutual masturbation is relatively safe unless one or both partners are infected with diseases which can be spread by touch. If one partner has any infectious secretions, sores, or warts then the infections can be spread if partners touch themselves after touching their infected partner, or by being touched by an infected partner if that partner had touched themself first. These kinds of contacts transfer bodily fluids and are potentially risky with the presence of any sort of infection – bacterial, fungal, or viral. The same logic applies with both oral and anal sex as well. While non-vaginal intercourse will eliminate the possibility of pregnancy, there is still the possibility of the transmission of STD's.

This kid of logic on the part of kids requires all aspects of sexual activity be addressed in sexual education classes. Girls are still technically virgins as defined by the act of vaginal intercourse being the means of taking a girl's virginity. This relates to the concept of limited sexual encounters supposedly practiced during the Victorian era as though the only sexual experiences strictly involve vaginal intercourse, in the so-called missionary position, between a man and a woman who have never had any other sexual partners. Very few adults limit their sexual practices to this range of intimacy. If the truth from the past could be known, it is unlikely that very many people throughout time limited their sexual experiences to such a quaint and acceptable act as vaginal sex in the missionary position. With all of the media exposure to and promotion of sex today people are much more likely than ever to experiment sexually than at any other point in the history of the United States. And kids are likely to be even more open to and about sexual experiences than many of their adult counterparts. Based on my awareness of sexual activity from the perspective of the kids I have worked with over the years, even many of the girls who pride themselves in being virginal by abstaining from vaginal intercourse are the very ones who come with other "benefits" as reported by the boys they are often dating. Sexual activity is sexual activity no matter how you look at it. This reality and the realities of the level of sexual activity in which kids of today are engaging require a very thorough education in all aspects of sexuality rather than the watered down and unrealistically limited sex ed programs being taught in most settings.

Kids appreciate this kind of openness and honesty when I have shared these considerations with them over the years. I talk to both boys and girls about these factors, admittedly using less vulgar or graphic language with the girls than I might use with the boys. However, the messages are the same. I also try to get girls to understand that in reality a lot of adolescent boys are only after sex. This is especially true with troubled youth who have very little awareness of how appropriate romantic/dating interactions look given the lack of appropriate role models in the contexts where they live and learn. Some of the most significant complicating factors in the lives and histories of troubled kids are directly related to the sexual indiscretions and obvious mishandling of dating and marriage on the part of their parents and parental figures. It is not uncommon for kids to have parents who have kids with multiple sexual partners, even with mothers and fathers acting out sexually at about the same rates. A lot of kids know very little about love and the realities that sex without love can easily confuse even the brightest and most experienced adults. Adults and kids are equally as likely to look for love in all the wrongs places without realizing or identifying their sense of desperately needing and wanting to be loved by someone - anyone. I have told girls in front of boys that some guys are dogs. The girls laugh and the boys ultimately agree given their admission of frequent score keeping of the number of virgins they "bag". I have actually worked with boys who put marks on belt buckles as a public display of their sexual conquests.

It is extremely alarming to me that many kids, and especially girls, believe having a baby will solve many of their problems. It is quite common for girls to want a baby as a way of having someone to love unconditionally who will love them unconditionally in return. Unfortunately many girls believe the only way to keep a boy is by having sex with him, or even worse believing they can get a boy to stay with them if they get pregnant. Some girls have openly lied to boys about being on birth control and have even resorted to poking holes in a condom with a pin in the hopes of getting pregnant as well. None of this ever works out as planned, again emphasizing the need of teaching kids about every aspect of sexuality, including the realties and responsibilities associated with parenting. In my book At the Mercy of Externals: Righting Wrongs and Protecting Kids, 2nd Edition, I have proposed teaching the concepts presented within that text to kids as early as middle school, but certainly by their first year of high school. The focus of my theories emphasizes adult roles and responsibilities and the resulting negative impact on kids when those roles and responsibilities are not met to the fullest extent possible. With the right combination of information, insight, and facts kids will be better prepared to make fully informed decisions about many of the choices they face during their adolescent years.

Sexual orientation and its related diversity are much more openly discussed among kids now than at any other point in our history. It is not uncommon to find boys and girls who openly and comfortably identify themselves as either bisexual or homosexual. Kids are much more accepting of these realties than are many adults, and people in general are much more accepting of sexual diversity among girls than they are with boys or males in general. I clearly believe this represents a double standard perpetuated primarily by heterosexual males in this country. Heterosexual males of all ages are commonly turned on by sexual activity between females, and are absolutely repulsed by even the notion of sexual intimacy between two males. Females together are hot and sexy in the eyes of straight males, and the males who engage in sexual activity with other males are somehow less than masculine if they engage in any form of homosexual activity. Homosexual acts are homosexual acts regardless of whether they occur between male couples or female couples. I think many heterosexual males are afraid of male-to-male sex, possibly having thought about or even experienced it themselves at some point in their lives. The teachings of religious radicals do not help any of this either. I have never met anyone who will tell me that any aspect of their true sexual nature is based in choice. Heterosexuals never even have to think about being straight. However, homosexual individuals have to choose how they are going to deal with their sexual orientation throughout their whole lives, with 'how to deal with it' being the only choice involved. This is a very significant issue for adolescents as many adolescent suicides successfully carried out are thought to be related to issues of homosexuality and the pressures to conform to heterosexual standards and expectations.

I always ask where an adolescent kid falls in the spectrum of sexual orientation which I believe exists as a continuum from completely heterosexual, to varying degrees of bisexuality, to the other end of being completely homosexual. Straight kids readily identify as straight and seem surprised I would even ask. Rarely does any kid admit upfront they are anything other than heterosexual. Even so I still explain the full range of sexual diversity and assure them we can talk about this at any point in the future if they have questions or need information. Steven, one of my previous clients waited for nearly three months to come back to this as an issue for him. It is unlikely he would have ever brought it up at all if I had not laid the groundwork at the outset. Steven was seventeen and was able to reveal his homosexual identity to me and we were able to help him come to terms with it during therapy. There was nothing about Steven that met any of the stereotypes, so he was able to hide his identity if he chose to do so. By exploring the issues with him he was able to see this was simply another part, and only a part, of his over all personality. I urge all kids and adults not to let any aspect of their sexuality to be the most obvious and overriding factor expressed outwardly regardless of their orientation. Unfortunately for many people the idea someone is homosexual still cancels out every other aspect of who they are in addition to this one aspect.

I believe the most reliable indicator of true sexual orientation can be found in the content of private masturbation fantasies. During the act of masturbation there is no reason to lie to yourself, or to even be overly afraid to explore experiences perceived to be wrong or forbidden by most. It is not uncommon for many adults to have some rather intense masturbation fantasies which can include rape scenes all the way to bondage and domination, as well as much more deviant scenarios. This is no less true for issues related to sexual orientation. When Steven first brought up his belief he might be homosexual I immediately asked him if he masturbated. He embarrassingly admitted he did. In response to my question about the gender of fantasy sexual partners he readily admitted they were always male and were often times guys he went to school with and who were on his football team. This is a good technique to use for kids who may be simply questioning their sexual orientation. In real life sexual situations it may be necessary to try and fake arousal or create a fantasy stimulus in order to get aroused, but during a masturbation fantasy there is no reason to hide from your real attractions and turnons. No one can physically fake an attraction to anyone they do not find to be attractive or arousing.

So in a very few instances when sexual orientation was an issue I have encouraged a kid to try and fantasize in private about sexual activity with a same gender partner. This will not be possible without some predisposition to do so, and is a very good indicator of where any individual falls in the range of possible sexual identities.

Over the years I have only worked with one kid who was HIV positive. Anthony had been infected at birth by his mother and had full blown AIDS by the time we met when he was 13 years old. He had been arrested for burglary and I was asked by probation to see Anthony while he was in juvenile hall. Even though he had an AIDS diagnosis he was being successfully treated with a variety of HIV medications and was in good health. However, the juvenile hall staff members were afraid of him and the idea they and other kids might be infected by him. I had to spend a great deal of time trying to educate the staff, with the help of one of the nurses on staff at the facility, about the spread of HIV and the limited precautions which needed to be taken in order to protect kids and staff with which Anthony had contact. In addition to infection issues I had to make sure everyone was aware of issues of confidentiality and the reality of Anthony being protected under the Americans with Disabilities Act. Unfortunately, by the time I got to Anthony, all adult staff members in the facility were talking about the fact he was infected.

Anthony was isolated from the other kids when we first met and I had to spend time with him addressing his fears of people finding out. I also had to warn him about his need to avoid fighting with other minors in order to avoid any form of blood-to-blood transmission. I was amazed at how uninformed Anthony was about his disease and spent time, again with the nursing staff trying to answer his questions and help him find some hope for the future. Anthony came from a very complicated family background, having been placed with extended family members after his mom and stepdad were arrested and imprisoned for serious drug related charges. Following the arrest and imprisonment of his mom and stepdad Anthony and all of his siblings had been permanently placed in the custody of different family members. Anthony's mom never took care of herself and had been very sick from time to time with AIDS related infections. His stepdad actually died in prison from AIDS related complications while I was working with Anthony.

Ultimately Anthony was released from juvenile hall and returned to an alternative school where I continued to work with him. However, it wasn't long before he got arrested for charges serious enough to get him sentenced to the California Youth Authority. I lost track of him after that and have no idea of his current condition or whereabouts. As far as I know none of the other kids who knew Anthony ever found out about his HIV status, at least not while I was working with him.

The only other case I had involving family members who had HIV/AIDS was that of two brothers whose parents had both died from AIDS related illnesses. The focus of treatment for these two boys centered around significant grief issues complicated by the reality of their parents having died from AIDS. The younger of these two brothers went on to be very successful in life relative to finishing high school and making plans for college as revealed to me the last time I saw him. The older of the two had become a serious drug addict and was involved in a number of serious criminal activities, with the younger brother significantly worried about whether or not his older brother might be either murdered or die from a drug overdose. Both of these boys were adopted by a loving family as prearranged by their father prior to his death. But, the impact on them was so tremendous as to alter their lives forever. Any death of a parent or parents when kids are still growing up is tragic, but because of the stigma associated with AIDS, these kinds of deaths seem to be more complicated. This is especially true given the reluctance of kids to talk with anyone about the realities of how their parents died. These brothers were especially upset with their father who apparently infected the mother as a result of his extramarital affairs. Many females get infected by their male partners without any awareness of their health status and often without any awareness of their infidelity.

When dealing with kids and sexual issues I try to get kids to understand the various ways in which HIV can be spread. They are usually shocked to learn it can spread as a result of physical violence. Any physical altercation involving exposure to open wounds will easily lead to infection if one of those involved in the fight is HIV positive. While this may be rare relative to the likelihood of occurrence it still needs to be explained to any kid who has a tendency to engage in any form of physical violence, and in addition to the practice of unsafe sex.

Another rather interesting form of sexual diversity has to do with fetishes. Jimmy was a 14 year old brought into our clinic by his father and step-mom after they caught him cross dressing. He was mortified and no one on our staff readily volunteered to take the case before I found out about it. I saw it as an opportunity to learn about another interesting aspect of human nature. Of course Jimmy denied having cross dressed to our front office staff, and our therapists expected he would continue to deny it even with them. I knew he was embarrassed about the whole thing, so I saved the cross dressing issue for last during our initial intake interview. However, when the time came in the interview to address his reason for being in my office, I asked Jimmy if he had any kind of sexual fetishes. He didn't know what a fetish was and I had the opportunity to open up the entire discussion by defining the term "fetish" for him.

I told Jimmy a fetish can be understood as any object or objects which lead to or are associated with sexual arousal and pleasure. He denied he had any feelings associated with gender confusion, and even denied he had any homosexual tendencies. His denial of homosexual tendencies continued over the entire time span I worked with Jimmy off and on for nearly two years. Personally and professionally I believe this is another aspect of his personality he will have to, or has already had to face since our termination of therapy some years ago. His father was actually okay with the idea his son might be gay and even agreed with me it was a possibility, but just couldn't understand or accept his cross dressing activities. Jimmy was using underwear and other items of clothing belonging to both his step-mom and step-sister. They were not amused to say the least.

Jimmy and I focused on several other aspects of his life including the divorce of his parents, specific feelings he had toward his biological mom, and the fact he had Attention Deficit Hyperactivity Disorder. He was a good kid and was rather intelligent, but in special education classes because of his hyperactivity and problems paying attention and staying on task.

Ultimately, the ADHD related symptoms were addressed and controlled through medication and he was eventually mainstreamed into regular classes. By helping Jimmy understand how much his cross dressing fetish deviated from the norm he was able to see his need to try and redirect his sexual interests toward more acceptable ideas and interests. My biggest concern for him was the fact he probably would have a great deal of trouble finding sexual partners in the future who would share or even be able to tolerate his cross dressing. I was also concerned about the additional embarrassment he would likely face someday if people outside his family found out. At the same time I was willing to go along with his fetish if he had insisted it was really important to him. Fortunately he was able to see how detrimental this could be to him in the long run and was able to compromise with me. Jimmy's most favored objects of women's apparel were high heeled shoes. I was able to help him imagine how attractive they were on women and he seemingly learned to settle for this image without needing to wear the shoes himself. This may all sound a little strange, but it was a very real issue for this kid. It seemed that as we resolved the problems associated with his ADHD symptoms, and helped him gain some much needed insight and resolve relative to his biological mom and his parents' divorce, his need to cross dress appeared to diminish.

When we successfully terminated Jimmy's therapy which extended over a two year period he was doing well according to self-report and reports from his family and school staff. We worked together on average once every two to four weeks. His father was fully involved in the process, and respected Jimmy's need to work with me privately on most occasions. Jimmy was fully involved in school activities and was a member of the cadet corps at school, participating in regular marching and other drill activities. This was a very interesting case and I made sure Jimmy knew I was available to him if he ever needed to return to therapy. Of course that option changed when I moved out of the area, but two years passed since our last session which was enough time for Jimmy to have graduated from high school. You never know what issues you will be asked to address with clients, so it is extremely important to keep an open mind and learn to be creative with your interventions. Never shame them or cause them to feel any more embarrassment than they may already feel. Also be prepared to support them in any direction they choose as long as they are not making choices specifically harmful to themselves or to others. Be sure to never take on a case you are not qualified to address, or in some cases not comfortable with addressing. An example for me would be trying to work with fully autistic kids, a population I know very little about, a population with very specific and special needs.

Another case involved a kid by the name of Gabriel who had been arrested for voyeurism toward one of his female cousins. He was caught several times at the age of 14 outside her bedroom window watching her undress while he masturbated. Finally his family felt they had no choice but to report him and Gabriel was arrested and charged with voyeurism and indecent exposure. He was convicted and labeled as a sex offender and sentenced to 12 months at a state program within the California Youth Authority for convicted sex offenders. Once he returned from CYA he was assigned to me by probation for therapy and monitoring through the mental health system. Gabriel was kind of quiet and obviously embarrassed about his actions and conviction. He told me he never felt like he fit into the program of sex offenders, but had to comply with their requirements and play the game in order to get out of the system.

During my initial intake Gabriel was able to give me the details which led up to his arrest and conviction. He told me his family had been very supportive even though they were angry, hurt, and embarrassed by the whole experience. He told me he never understood the origins of the compulsion which drove him to spy on his female cousin and invade her privacy. As we went through my normal intake interview he admitted to a history of heavy use of methamphetamines. He had been clean since his confinement and had not gone back to using meth since his release. One of the significant side effects of meth use is increased sexual arousal which is virtually uncontrollable for many users. This is one of the main reasons adults will use meth as an enhancement to their sexual activities. Gabriel readily admitted that every time he spied on his cousin he had been using meth heavily, and only felt this compulsion when he was really strung out. I have worked with several boys and girls who have described their meth related sexual compulsions as being insatiable, generally lasting for hours with a strong need for climax, but often without the ability to reach orgasm. Part of the compulsion is to satisfy themselves by achieving an orgasm which rarely if ever occurs. I worked with one kid years ago in juvenile hall who reported he masturbated frequently until his penis was raw and infected while under the influence of meth.

All of this registered with me as I interviewed Gabriel. When I asked him if anyone in the juvenile system ever asked him about his history of substance dependency he told me they had not. Given all he told me about not feeling like he met the profile of a sex offender, and only engaging in this kind of behavior while under the influence of heavy meth use, it was clear to me meth was the problem and not Gabriel. As soon as I revealed this to him he was shocked at how much it made sense, and readily agreed and started to cry. This was such a relief to him and he clearly knew I was not looking for an opportunity to make excuses for his past behaviors, nor was he looking for anything more than an opportunity to understand how he could have done these kinds of things to his cousin and to the rest of his family.

Ultimately I met with Gabriel's family and with his probation officer. Each one of them agreed with my assessment of the source of Gabriel's compulsion, especially in light of the fact he had no history of problems within any setting prior to his use of meth. Many other family problems were relieved, even in light of the fact both of Gabriel's parents were meth users. Gabriel and his siblings were removed from the home and placed with other relatives while their parents went through mandatory drug treatment. Eventually the family was reunited and efforts were made to improve their deplorable living conditions by giving them adequate housing and constant monitoring by social services. Gabriel was able to keep himself clean and sober and out of trouble, with a primary focus on his need to be there for his siblings in addition to wanting a better future for himself. The tragedy of all of this is the reality of Gabriel having a juvenile record as a sex offender for the rest of his life. Hopefully he had his juvenile records sealed as I urged him to do once he reached the age of 18. Maybe this offense will never come back to haunt him at any point in his future. There is no doubt in my mind that Gabriel was not a sex offender, only a meth addict who experienced this unfortunate side effect which manifested itself as inappropriate sexual behavior.

The last topic I want to address in this chapter is the issue of sexual abuse and its long range impact on kids. If you have read my first book, then you know about my RFLAGS model and the connections between abuse and victimization and lasting emotional damage which lasts into adulthood if not dealt with and resolved to whatever degree possible. The first of two cases I want to share with you is that of a kid by the name of Billy. He was 14 the first time I met him and was living with his dad who was an active alcoholic. Billy was referred to me by probation as were most of my cases at the time. He was living with his dad while his mom spent time in prison for charges of child endangerment resulting from her involvement in and the cover up of Billy's molestation at the hands of mom's most recent live-in boyfriend. By the time I met Billy he had already been in a lot of trouble with law enforcement and was one of the angriest kids I had ever met and worked with by that point in my career.

Billy's history of abuse was known to his father, but as time passed in my work with Billy the full extent of his molestation was revealed. It was very difficult for Billy to even talk about what he had been through, so we spent a great deal of time trying to focus on his criminal activity and on his need to deal with anger and face its sources. I had to work very carefully with Billy to establish and maintain a strong rapport of trust and compassion for him as a person and relative to his history of abuse. It took nearly a year before the full extent of his abuse was revealed to me by him, and after hearing the details I clearly understood why it took so long. His story was the most horrific and upsetting case I had ever heard and it broke my heart to learn how much Billy and his younger sister had suffered through their repeated sexual attacks by this pedophile.

According to accounts from Billy the sexual abuse started with Billy's sister. Once he found out what was happening to her the abuser turned on Billy primarily to gain control over him in the same way he was able to control his sister using threats and other forms of intimidation, clearly intended to instill the utmost level of fear possible in these two kids. The abuse occurred over a period of about four years for both Billy and his sister, and seemed more brutal and violent toward Billy. About one year into my work with Billy I pushed him one additional time to talk about the abuse. At first he was angry, but seemed to trust me enough by this point to believe me when I told him we needed to face his past. In spite of his anger and tears he was able to relate unimaginable details of the worst encounter he had with this man.

Apparently the man had a piece of land with a small house on it somewhere out in the middle of nowhere. Billy was told he and his 'molester' were going away for the weekend. Billy was helpless in his efforts to refuse and had absolutely no support from his mom. The weekend turned into the worst experience of Billy's childhood with the man drugging him repeatedly, tying him face down to a bed, and raping him repeatedly over the course of three days, even at times using various objects with which to sodomize him. Billy was about 11 years old when this happened, and even though he physically survived the brutal attacks, he was almost irreparably damaged emotionally by the experiences. Billy sobbed as he told me the details and I was unable to hold back my tears as I observed his intense emotional pain. He told me when they returned from the trip his mother completely ignored the fact he was physically hurt. At some point soon after this most recent event the abuse was exposed outside the home by Billy's sister. Authorities were called in, but before anything could be done Billy's mom took the kids and helped her boyfriend flee across state lines. They were on the run for months, with mom having full awareness of what had been occurring, and yet still helping this man escape the legal consequences he deserved.

According to Billy the abuse continued for both him and his sister until the man was finally apprehended and arrested. The offender and Billy's mom were taken back to the state where all of this occurred and Billy ultimately ended up in the custody of his dad, with his half-sister going to live with another relative. In a letter Billy received from his mom after she and the pedophile were convicted and imprisoned, mom talked about how much she still loved the man who had repeatedly raped her own children, telling Billy of her intentions to get back together with the guy after both had served their time. Needless to say Billy was devastated by his mother's lack of regard for what he and his sister had endured, and he openly hoped she and the boyfriend would not survive their time in prison.

Billy was an emotional wreck after relating all of this information to me. He agreed to let me go and get his dad from the lobby. I wasn't in very good emotional shape either. Billy made me promise I wouldn't tell his dad the details of what he had just shared with me. I agreed and assured Billy I would leave that up to him as to whether or not he ever told anyone about this again. When I approached Billy's dad in the lobby he seemed alarmed I guess by the look on my face. I assured him Billy had just revealed to me the details of his molestation and had asked that I not tell his dad what Billy had said. The dad readily agreed to this telling me he didn't know if could endure knowing what had actually happened without wanting to go after Billy's mom and her boyfriend. Even though dad was an alcoholic he worked and took care of his son. The scene in my office when I returned to Billy with his dad was one of the most touching sites I have ever witnessed. Billy and dad hugged each other tightly and both sobbed uncontrollably. I lost it as I listened to dad tell Billy how sorry he was not to have been there for him and his sister. Dad also told Billy how deeply he loved him, expressing a wish that he could have taken Billy's place in all of this.

I worked with Billy for a total of about two years until he got into more legal trouble. He was gang involved and was facing some very serious charges and was on his way to the California Youth Authority the last time we met. I never heard from Billy or his dad after that and can only imagine that Billy was probably never able to get his life on a different track than the one he had already chosen before I met him. In my heart I believe Billy's anger likely fueled every decision he had made and will likely fuel all future decisions as well. I don't see how this horribly damaged young man could ever recover from the extreme nature and extent of his abuse. He could never resolve his feelings of being less of a man because he had been the "bitch" of a pedophile. At times Billy even questioned his own sexual orientation, confused as to whether his abuse meant that he was now gay. No matter how hard I tried he never seemed to understand that the only thing left over from the abuse for him was the emotional damage he would have to face likely for the rest of his life. This was the only case I ever had where I truly believed there was little or no chance for this kid to ever be stable and productive in life. I think of Billy often and can only offer a prayer for his safety and for his soul.

The second case is that of a 16 year old girl by the name of Laura. This has a much more positive and hopeful outcome compared to the story of Billy. Laura had been arrested for assault resulting from a fight at school with another girl. She ended up on the informal probation program I described in chapter three and I was asked by probation to work with Laura at the alternative school site where she was attending school. Even more significant than her altercation at school was her habit of self-mutilation and her rather frequent suicide attempts, none of which her family had ever taken seriously. Laura had been hospitalized three times prior to our initial contact and the family had never followed up with services from the department of mental health as recommended as part of her discharge plans. The day we met she had several obvious cuts on her left forearm which I just happened to see when she moved her arm and her sleeve went up far enough to expose the wounds. I was conducting the interview without any family members present and at the school site where I saw a number of kids referred to me by probation.

While conducting the interview Laura revealed her history of suicide attempts and hospitalizations, which included three attempted overdoses and a number of incidents where she would jump out of a moving car. She looked like she was probably anorexic, but adamantly denied having problems related to an eating disorder. Laura described an extremely chaotic and dysfunctional family environment with parents who argued often, a dad who was emotionally unavailable, and a mom who seemed to be as emotionally unstable as Laura. Based on my experiences with other female clients who exhibit extreme emotional instability I was thinking during the entire interview Laura had likely been sexually molested as well. This is often true for girls who get into the juvenile justice system, with a very significant number of them having experienced varying degrees of sexual abuse and rape. When I asked Laura about this she started crying, and with much assurance from me, told me she had been molested for about four years by a next door neighbor.

Anytime a child or even an adult reveals they have been sexually abused in any way it is important to find out only the extent of the abuse. It is not necessary or important for any therapist to know all of the graphic details which occurred. In most cases it can be especially difficult for the victim to even discuss what happened especially if it is a female client talking with a male therapist. Professionally I believe it is even more difficult for boys in general to talk about any kind of male-to-male sexual abuse given the additional perceived stigma associated with male-to-male sexual contact. This is especially true if a boy was penetrated anally in any manner. The information needed by a therapist can be obtained through a series of simple "yes" or "no" questions, unless the client feels comfortable enough to disclose on their own. As a male therapist who also works with female clients I try to always be in control of any discussion of sexual matters. There is no effort on my part to unnecessarily limit the discussion. However, because of the fear on the part of every male therapist when dealing with female clients, I never want to be accused of any form of sexually inappropriate behavior. I know of male therapists who will not see any female clients behind close doors. I am not quite that paranoid, but realistically I have to be cautious.

The kinds of questions to be asked in order to understand the extent, nature, and frequency of any kind of sexual abuse or assault are as follows:

- Did you know the person who abused you?
- Were they male or female?
- Were they related to you?
- What was the nature of you association with them?
- How many times did the abuse occur?
- How old were you when it first started and when it finally ended?
- Is the abuse still happening?
- Was there ever more than one person involved?
- Have you been threatened in anyway if you tell someone about the abuse?

- Did the abuse involve inappropriate touching?
- Were you expected to reciprocate the acts?
- Did it involve kissing?
- Did it involve any form of masturbation – self, other, or mutual?
- Did it involve performing a sexual act while being observed or recorded?
- Did it involve oral sex?
- Did it involve vaginal penetration?
- Did it involve anal penetration?
- Did it involve penetration with any kinds of objects?
- Did it involve any type of bondage, torture, or shame/humiliation?
- Were you given alcohol or drugged?

It is important before asking any of these questions to remind the client of the limits on confidentiality. If there is any resistance after that to talk about what has happened it is of extreme importance to help the individual understand the importance of revealing the information. This is necessary in order to protect your client and to make sure the abuse doesn't happen to others as well. It is advisable to explain the reporting process and to make sure not to make any guarantees as to how it will be handled by the agency with which you have to file the report. Furthermore, it is good to make the client aware of what will likely happen once the report is filed. In the event the child is in, or may face imminent danger as a result of the report, or there is any possibility the abuse will continue, immediate action must be taken to protect the child. This can generally be handled when talking with the agency accepting the report. Many times I have written the report in front of an adolescent victim and have even called in the information while they were sitting in the room with me. This gives them the assurance I have been totally honest and accurate with them during the session and relative to what I report.

With Laura's case the abuse had occurred over a four year period with a man who lived next door to Laura and her family. Laura was age seven when it began and age eleven when it ended. The wife of this man and Laura's mom were close friends. In spite of Laura's efforts to resist being sent over to this house, her mother regularly sent Laura over to stay with this couple. The abuse only stopped because the old man died. Two years into the abuse Laura told her mom, but her mom not only refused to believe her, she also refused to investigate it further. As a result the abuse continued for two more years. This, coupled with all of the dysfunction within Laura's home/family context, left Laura with little recourse other than to turn her anger inward and toward herself.

Soon after I finished my initial intake Laura's mom showed up at the school that day to take Laura home. She agreed to meet with me and Laura as I requested and I began to question her about much of what Laura had told me. I told her that while there was no need to file a suspected abuse report given the fact the man had died, I did tell mom of my intentions to let Laura's probation officer know what had occurred. In front of me Laura's mom called her a liar. Before this went any further I confronted mom with her lack of concern and regard for her daughter's well-being relative to both the abuse and Laura's history of suicide and other self-injurious behaviors. I didn't even give mom a chance to respond before I openly told her she should be ashamed of herself for not taking better care of her daughter. My plans to report all of this to probation would at least help me monitor Laura's safety and would insure mom's compliance with my treatment requirements and recommendations. Mom felt threatened and outraged, but I told her I didn't care, assuring her I would do whatever I could do legally to insure Laura's safety. Laura was relieved and I was able to form a strong professional bond with Laura that day which lasted through nearly three years of treatment.

Out of all the kids I have worked with over the years Laura scared me more than any of the others relative to her suicidal tendencies and emotional instability. For the entire first 18 months of her treatment I worried she would end up dead. Fortunately with the right combination of medications and treatment approaches Laura finished high school and was attending a trade school to learn massage therapy as is used within medical settings. She was one of the most intelligent kids I have ever met, and this was likely the strongest factor in her favor and ability to resolve the issues of her past. Mom never fully accepted the fact Laura was molested, but Laura learned to resolve this as best she could even without her mother's support. Laura was hospitalized only two more times after I started seeing her and was able to stop self-mutilating altogether once she was able to approach this behavior from the viewpoint of an addiction. During all of this Laura's eating disorder also ended and her self-esteem went up 100%. She held her head up high and felt a great deal of pride in all she had accomplished and relative to all of the things she was able to face and overcome. My RFLAGS Model was paramount in helping her understand why she did the things she did given her extensive history of abuse and victimization, and her extremely dysfunctional home/family context. Just before I left California Laura was doing well and had fallen in love. Hopefully she will be able to put the past where it belongs – in the past.

As you can see sexual issues and concerns with high risk, troubled kids are quite complicated and numerous. It is very important to always seek out additional training and consultation when faced with a new therapeutic situation you are not qualified to handle. Many adults are given the opportunities to monitor and assist kids in need of support and guidance. However, as I have said many times, many adults with the very best of intentions often do the most harm, especially when they venture into areas where they have little or no training which would allow them to be effective. Arrogance is not a virtue, and each of us should realize the important need of working collaboratively with other professionals within various fields when working with troubled kids. No single person or institution can meet all of the needs of kids within this population.

7

Intelligence, Talent and Potential

Complicating factors disrupt and impede virtually every aspect of the lives of high-risk, troubled kids, including their academic needs, and academic successes and achievements. I cannot stress enough the need for everyone involved professionally and personally in the lives of high-risk kids to look beyond what they do - and in some cases beyond their lack of accomplishments – in order to see them for who they are meant to be and can truly become. Take some time to once again thoroughly review the list of complicating factors I included as an appendix in my book At the Mercy of Externals: Righting Wrongs and Protecting Kids, 2nd Edition. There is no point in moving forward in this book without a clear and very conscious awareness of the number of significant external factors which often interfere in the lives of this population of kids. At the same time we need to hold kids accountable for their mistakes and misdeeds, we must also look at those factors which likely motivated their behaviors and lack of progress. This is not a way of excusing their shortcomings; but a way of understanding their existence relative to what now needs to be done in order to help kids correct their mistakes and play catch-up in other areas of their lives.

Probably the biggest single factor relative to how kids view their potential for future success is based in their perception of how "smart" they are and how much academic progress they have achieved. My experience over the years has revealed to me how complicating factors impede success and achievement in a number of areas with these impediments then becoming additional complicating factors. The older a child gets the less likely they are to try and make the gains they need if they are to be successful in life or to develop a positive self-image and a sense of hope for their future. It is quite common for kids to equate their lack of academic skills to incompetence and the perception they are not very "smart". Once these beliefs become ingrained in their self-image these beliefs become self-fulfilling prophecies. Therefore, the longer we wait to intervene the less likely we will be able to do so successfully.

In my experiences of working with kids within various academic settings I have found there to be a combination of factors impeding academic success. It is not at all uncommon for troubled kids to engage in disruptive behaviors within the school context. Boys tend to act out, while girls tend to internalize. However, as previously stated, I believe in recent years this has begun to even out as girls tend to now become more aggressive and oppositional as they enter adolescence when coupled with a similar set of complicating factors as those experienced by their male counterparts. Because of the differences in how boys and girls still seem to respond to complicating factors early on, girls often get little or no attention, and boys tend to get excessive amounts of negative and punitive attention. Neither scenario works, and I hold teachers and other school personnel accountable for their unwillingness and inability to recognize acting out behaviors and withdrawal behaviors as indications of a deeper level of underlying issues and needs, which in many cases they are not trained to address.

One of the most significant factors hindering the education process for kids today is the reality that schools have become more of an environment for kids to socialize and/or "hook up", than for them to learn. For many kids the importance of socializing now takes precedence over getting an education. Kids are always about ten steps ahead of most adults when it comes to technology and various forms of communication devices. Many people, including parents, are becoming more and more addicted to these devices which facilitate a number of distractions for kids and school personnel. As a result priorities have shifted away from important issues such as education and accountability, to simply engaging in what are generally very trivial dialogues. Nowadays I have to frequently tell parents to turn off their cell phones even during therapy sessions. They are usually offended that I would have this expectation. Clearly parents are frequently modeling a set of priorities that are not in step with reality. Low performing schools tend to also be battle grounds for gangs and other forms of criminal activity and recruiting as parts of social networking.

The suggestion that low performing schools should be shut down is probably unrealistic given the fact that schools are generally set up to serve certain geographical areas of any given city or region. However, it is extremely necessary to hold teachers and school officials responsible for being both ineffective and incompetent relative to the right approaches needed to simply engage kids in the education process. Those school personnel who do not meet even minimal standards relative to the academic outcomes of their students need to be fired. If they then want to return to the educational setting, teachers and other professional staff will need to be retrained, and in many cases re-educated and re-credentialed, before being allowed to take any position within any school district. Teachers' unions and corrupt school systems need to be completely reevaluated and totally revamped relative to the programs being offered and the professionals providing both administrative and classroom services. No educational group should be able to sustain itself based solely on its abuses of power and authority sanctioned by people only interested in protecting their jobs regardless of appropriateness or effectiveness. Too much money is being wasted on poorly trained and uncaring staff.

Most professionals, as previously addressed, who choose to work with kids often enter their fields with an idealistic impression of the unhindered good they will be able to do. Unfortunately this unrealistic view ignores the full range of complicating factors professionals are likely to encounter within the settings of their chosen careers. Many quickly become disillusioned and disheartened, while others label kids as some form of undesirable element and seek to have them removed from the setting. All professionals need to be better prepared before they enter their professions to deal with the full range of human nature which exists, even among children of all ages. I believe a careful screening process and continuous monitoring relative to the effectiveness of every adult professionally involved in the lives of kids is critical. The concept of "No Child Left Behind", or any other school program, will be a joke unless the needs of every child are identified and met within all contexts, and by whatever means are required.

One of the biggest errors made within many academic settings is often the unwillingness on the part of school officials to spend the money needed to evaluate and then offer programs to meet the needs of kids who somehow fall outside the range of the so-called "mainstream" students. Too many kids within the juvenile justice system have serious learning disabilities which were never caught, and if caught were never appropriately addressed. I never use the term "learning disabilities" with kids. Instead, I refer to "learning difficulties" which make it more difficult for some kids to learn compared to other kids who seem to have less trouble moving ahead. In my mind the word "disability" suggests to a child that they have a defect which makes them unable to learn. By simply substituting the word "*disability*" with "*difficulty*", kids will be much more likely to put in the extra effort as long as they know they eventually will be able to accomplish the task at hand. Like it or not, some kids really need additional assistance in order to move forward academically. Educational professionals should always be held accountable for any failure to assist a child who has any form of special needs. Much can be accomplished in many cases with one-on-one tutoring which many schools are reluctant to provide. A reduction in much of the bureaucracy of many school districts would free up a great deal of money needed to help the kids succeed. Also a simple enforcement of national, state, and local regulations and mandates would resolve much of the neglect and failure to comply.

One of the most alarming factors relative to a child's academic success is the lack of awareness on the part of parents relative to both student and parental rights within educational settings which are guaranteed and protected by law. Unfortunately, many school districts take advantage of this lack of information and in fact do not want parents to know the full extent of services schools are required to provide. Parents are always amazed and enraged when I inform them of their rights to have their child evaluated when academic progress is not occurring. Many times I have confronted school staff during meetings held to determine student needs. These types of meetings are often referred to as "individualized education plans" (IEP) and are often conducted with the hope of parents not asking too many questions and not being fully aware of state and other mandated guidelines. This is one of the reasons schools look at professionals, such as me, who do not work within academic settings as "outsiders". Many districts will go out of their way to keep people from outside the academic setting from attending IEP meetings. One of the biggest threats school districts face today are the actions of advocacy groups who will intervene on behalf of the child and their parents. In many cases school districts are reluctant to work collaboratively with other agencies such as mental health groups in order to avoid taking responsibility for a child's needs and the risk of exposure for not doing their jobs as required by law. However, school officials will readily demand that parents take to child to a mental health center for medication if the child is considered to be a behavioral problem within the school setting. In Mobile, Alabama some school officials tell parents not to bring their kids back until they are medicated. This is absolutely against the law.

A perfect example of this involved one of my middle school kids who was facing an "opportunity transfer" to another school for disciplinary reasons. I knew enough about this case to know Jimmy was not receiving any of the services he needed. Furthermore, I knew none of the teachers or staff at his school liked him. Jimmy's mother asked that I attend the meeting as Jimmy's psychologist and the school granted permission for me to do so. My hope for being present at the meeting was to help school staff work differently with Jimmy while I continued to work with him and his family on a number of rather serious issues present outside the school setting. However, it became apparent early in the meeting the school staff had made up their minds to simply get rid of this kid.

I listened quietly for a while, trying occasionally to offer some suggestions and to let them know some details of the work I was trying to do with Jimmy and his mom in my office. They were not interested in any of my input and it became apparent they no longer wanted Jimmy around. The man leading the meeting started trying to convince Jimmy and his mom why it would be to "Jimmy's advantage" to change schools and start over in a new setting. Within another school district where I had worked previously I knew this was referred to as an "opportunity transfer" and I called the school staff on their deception, pointing out the reality of the only people benefiting from this transfer were the school staff at Jimmy's current school. In front of the staff I began to inform Jimmy's mom of her rights and of the school's obligation to try several other options which had never even been mentioned. Needless to say, the man directing this meeting was outraged, but had to contain his anger as he agreed with my observations of the situation. The school staff finally agreed to help Jimmy change teachers, and agreed to give Jimmy a behavior contract which would put all of this on Jimmy if he failed to meet their requirements.

This was a very fair agreement and settlement. Jimmy and his mom were elated. During the meeting I stressed the importance of Jimmy not blowing this opportunity to remain at his current school, pointing out I had put my neck on the chopping block for him. In spite of Jimmy's assurance to me, his mom and the school staff, Jimmy only lasted two weeks before he blatantly violated the contract and ended up being transferred as originally planned. My actions during the meeting were actually very professional and reserved, but I still got my point across. I was extremely disappointed in Jimmy's unwillingness to comply with their expectations and was able to make him take responsibility for his own outcome of getting, in effect, kicked out of school. The school staff never confronted me on my methods, but readily rubbed it in my face when Jimmy failed to live up to the agreement. I had the satisfaction of holding them responsible for their obvious deception, and word spread quickly around the district I was an advocate for my clients. A great deal of care was taken over the years to keep me from finding out about other meetings even with other clients. However, I made sure every parent and client who was involved in any form of individualized education plan agreement let me know when meetings were scheduled. While I was not liked by school staff, I was respected and appreciated by my clients and their families. Think of the countless number of times this and other school districts are able to deceive kids and families all around this country. This reinforces my belief in the need for independent monitoring and accountability at all levels within institutions and agencies, especially when it comes to service provision to kids.

Positive Psychology is a recent trend growing in popularity and applicability within the general field of psychology. This approach to dealing with clients of all ages was introduced in 1998 by M. P. Seligman, past president of the American Psychological Association. References to this theory can be found online in an extended abstract entitled "Positive Psychology: An Alternative Vision", by Derrick Klaassen, from Trinity Western University. It is available and can be viewed and/or printed out online at www.meaning.ca/articles/print/positive_psychology.htm. Mr. Klaassen gives a wonderful summary of the concept and suggests ways for it to be applied within the entire field of psychology. The main premise of Positive Psychology is to move away from focusing only on what is wrong with someone (pathology) to focusing on and identifying what is right with them. This approach offers therapists and other professionals an opportunity to look for the good in their clients as I have been doing throughout my career. The theory offers a tremendous opportunity for all people within the so-called "helping professions" to help individuals focus on the issues of optimism and choice, and has the potential to have a profound impact on the re-shaping of society and social standards. It fits into the Existential and Humanistic philosophies of emphasizing the value of the person and the importance of freedom to make choices and the need to accept responsibility for the choices we make.

A very useful and compatible theory within the field of education is that of Multiple Intelligences developed in 1983 by Dr. Howard Gardner, professor of education at Harvard University. A summary of the theory and a short, but useful bibliography are presented by Dr. Thomas Armstrong online at www.thomasarmstrong.com, and is entitled simply "Multiple Intelligences". Dr. Armstrong lists the "eight different potential pathways to learning" which are:

- Words (linguistic intelligence)
- Numbers or Logic (logical-mathematical intelligence)
- Pictures (spatial intelligence)
- Music (musical intelligence)
- Self-reflection (intrapersonal intelligence)
- A physical experience (bodily-kinesthetic intelligence)
- A social experience (interpersonal intelligence), and/or
- An experience in the natural world (naturalistic intelligence)

In another online offering available at www.multi-intell.com/MI_ chart.html, you can find a chart-like format describing in detail each of the realms of intelligence mentioned above. This approach to education and the relatively new approach of Positive Psychology go hand-in-hand when dealing with high risk, troubled kids. Our perception of how smart we are is a very important factor in determining our overall perception of self-esteem and self-image. This is no less true for kids of all ages. I would encourage readers to look into both of these theories in order to get a deeper and broader understanding of their relevance to this discussion and to their applicability as compatible approaches to understanding troubled kids. One of the most outstanding premises of the theory of Multiple Intelligences is the concept referred to as "islands of competence". This suggests that each of us is competent within at least one of the areas listed above. It is safe to say many people, including kids, possess some degree of competence in many, if not all of the areas, with everyone having those areas of competence which are dominant. These areas of emphasis represent more the innate potential within everyone, and only serve as a place to start relative to identifying and developing skills within all areas to whatever extent possible respective to each individual. Keep in mind the word "ignorance" means nothing more than to be lacking in knowledge or awareness. It does not indicate an inability to learn – although it often suggests an unwillingness to learn or the lack of opportunities to learn.

As professionals working with troubled kids it is extremely important to figure out all of the good qualities and characteristics which all kids possess.

In many cases it is necessary to help kids see how many of their ill-chosen negative behaviors and activities represent these islands of competence. One example of this is represented by my previous explanation of the qualities and skills exhibited by criminal activities such as drug dealing and weapons sales. So many kids who are troubled possess almost unimaginable and underdeveloped skills, which fall under the headings of several, if not all of the above categories. It is our job in working with troubled kids to help them see how these skills can be utilized more positively and productively in their lives. This can only be done by educating them about the existence of these skills and the opportunity to understand them and implement them appropriately. This falls under the realm of our roles as teacher and mentor with this population of kids. While it is important to identify and address therapeutic issues, it is equally important to identify areas within a kid which are simply unrecognized and underdeveloped. To fail to do so is to further support the shortcomings kids experience within the academic settings where these kids are often labeled as unreachable and incorrigible. It is our job to foster hope within these kids by helping them see they are not the screw-ups they have been told they are.

In order to educate kids about their levels of intelligence, talent and potential we must help them understand they are indeed capable of much more than they realize. There is no greater joy for me than to watch as a kid discovers who they really are and can become as opposed to their negative self-image created internally and based on misinformation from outside – my concept of being at the mercy of externals as addressed in my first book. Depression is thought to be based in negative and pervasive thoughts and patterns of thinking which perpetuate the depression and related helplessness and hopelessness associated with depression. A simple change in perspective can bring about remarkable results in the lives of troubled kids as they change what they believe and know about themselves. It is so important to understand that this change in perspective must be established on a conscious level within the psyche of each kid. In some cases this takes a great deal of time given the limited amount of time we are able to spend interacting face-to-face with our clients. Therefore, it is important to use designated time wisely by first joining with the kid to gain a keen awareness of their potential and their goodness, and then working diligently to help them see this for themselves.

The importance of changing their thought patterns relative to beliefs and what they think they know to be the truth lies in the need to address unconscious, habitual ways of thinking and seeing life and the world around them. Most of these kids lack the presence of positive role models who can model and encourage these ways of thinking, so we have to become in effect surrogate parents in assisting them to understand things differently. This process of thinking begins by identifying and spelling out their erroneous thoughts and beliefs which are automatic. From there it is important to help them understand and create a process of making this new way of thinking an intentional, conscious process which must be established to replace their negativistic thought processes and belief systems about themselves and the world. One of the most exciting parts of working with this population is learning as a professional to think creatively and actively in order to tailor-make a scheme which will work for each individual under your care and supervision. This is likely the greatest challenge to professionals as it requires a great deal of intelligence, talent, inspiration, and potential on our part. However, this is what makes the journey of working with these kids so rewarding and such a wonderfully creative experience for those of us who serve as teachers and mentors in their lives. Rather than simply seeing ourselves as fulfilling some specified professional role in their lives, we need to understand we are joining with them in a joint effort to create something new for them – foundations and tools upon which, and with which they will be able to build their own road to success for the rest of their lives.

The term "success" needs to be addressed as well. It is important to remember that successes with this population will not always be bold, huge steps forward. Therefore, every step forward relative to insight which leads to positive changes internally and then to progress in life externally must be acknowledged and reinforced. Never let these kids down or disappoint them! While it is not possible to be perfect, it is important to work toward perfection relative to our abilities and skill levels when working with this population. When you make an error in evaluation, assessment, or observation immediately acknowledge it and apologize for it. Then give the kid the opportunity to explain why you were wrong from the perspective of the kid. Be adult and strong enough internally to allow this to happen so you will learn from your mistake and then be better able to help this kid and the kids who will follow.

No professional is ever just in the teacher role, especially with this population of kids. Troubled kids have much to share and to teach us as professionals about the realities they face and the issues they are trying to understand and resolve. Understand that most actions and thought processes of troubled kids represent their best efforts to cope with and make sense of their lives and the world. It is very important to understand these perspectives as their truth or reality, even if they are factually incorrect. Before you ever challenge what a kid believes or thinks, it is of the utmost importance to understand their perspective on everything around them. When you know that their perceptions are right, even if they are harsh in content or presentation, you must acknowledge the accuracy and legitimacy of their interpretations of people, events and other realities in their lives. This is true even if kids are saying negative and angry things about adults in their lives whether these adults are their parents, relatives, teachers, probation officers, law enforcement officials, or any other adult within their range of experiences. To do anything less is to insult them and will drastically jeopardize your ability to continue working effectively with them. Do not make the mistake of defending adults whose behaviors and words are indefensible and inexcusable, a huge mistake often made by adults in positions of power and authority. Never expect or accept anything less from a kid than you would from an adult. Also, never talk to a kid in any manner you would not use with an adult. If you do you will be "just like every other adult" in their lives.

When kids reveal to you the presence of negative role models in their lives it is critical to help them learn how to deal effectively and appropriately with these obstacles. At the same time you acknowledge the accuracy of their impressions you must guide them toward accepting the existence of these realities. At this point in the process it is necessary to help kids understand that accepting something as real is not the same concept as liking whatever the negative reality is or represents. If you can get them to accept the existence of any reality it is then possible to help them develop coping skills which will help keep them out of trouble and on track toward making progress in their lives. This is where the concept of 'what is in their own best interest' comes into play. As you can see, even the realities of their lack of academic progress can be addressed from this perspective by helping them understand how it is in their own best interest to try and make up for lost time. Unfortunately the realities in the lives of many of these kids are unchangeable. This is especially true relative to people and circumstances present in their lives which are unlikely to change. However, there are a number of ways they can learn to work around obstacles as long as they know they have support from whatever positive resources are available.

Ignorance on the part of professionals involved in the lives of troubled kids is inexcusable. When this ignorance is coupled with the arrogant belief that we know without question what is best for them, this is truly abhorrent. Therefore it is extremely important to learn all we can before we ever attempt to interact with them. Furthermore, it is extremely important to understand our roles with these kids as both teacher and student. It is only by working consciously and deliberately to continue expanding our knowledge and awareness of the realities and issues these kids face on a daily basis that we can ever hope to even reach them, much less help them. Case conferences and consultation with well trained and knowledgeable professionals should be sought out on an ongoing basis throughout our careers. Always read about new theories and approaches in order to increase your base of knowledge and awareness of changing factors and trends. Attend regular continuing education seminars. More importantly let the kids share with you their knowledge of and awareness of life in the streets so to speak. This kind of information from them is invaluable and will serve you well in joining with them in an effort to see the world and life as they see it. Most of all be sure to follow the inspired and compassionate whisperings of your soul. If this makes no sense to you then you should never work with this population of kids.

As you evaluate the intelligence, talents and potential of each individual client, look for their islands of competence. Much of this insight into their capabilities will be gained through an understanding of their efforts to cope with and interpret those external factors present in their lives. This means looking at the criminal acts they commit as a way of identifying their creativity, ingenuity, resourcefulness, resilience, and the ability to transcend the obstacles and challenges life has presented to them. For example - and in addition to drug dealing and the selling of weapons - look at the artistic skills kids exhibit through graffiti created in the streets. While these acts are illegal they will reveal the level of artistic ability a kid possesses. After assuring them you won't "rat" them out or "snitch" on them, if possible look at their art pieces either in person or by asking them to bring in photos or sketches of their work. Pay attention to the tone and content of the piece and ask them to explain what it means to them. One of the most well thought out forms of graffiti are the murals painted in honor of friends and family members who have died. Through this form of artistic expression it is possible to see the depth of their emotions and their ability to feel pain. Their pieces often represent their own sense of the RFLAGS of **F**ear, **L**oneliness, **A**nger, **G**uilt, and **S**hame. It also reveals their sense of pride and bravado, and gives us an opportunity to understand what motivates and excites them.

Never underestimate any aspect of who and what these kids are in the present as all of this information also reveals what and who they are capable of becoming in the future. What an incredible and awesome opportunity to be part of the process which brings their positive potential into reality. Potential is potential either way; and energy is energy either way as well. The main role of professionals is to simply help them use the same energy which they use negatively in a more positive manner. Our work with them is never about making them "change", because you will find this suggests to these kids that in order to become successful they have to "change" into someone else. This could not be any further from the truth with the reality that you only want them to change how they use their potential and the energy which makes that potential a reality. This kind of challenge they can achieve and likely will be willing to accept it, because they will understand they simply need to change how they work with who they already are, and nothing more. It represents a change in perspective and motivation, and not in a change of person.

JJ was one of the most intelligent, perceptive and insightful kids I have ever met. As with many other kids he was searching for an opportunity to engage in a very deep and intellectual discussion with someone who understood him as he really was. On the surface he was very entrenched in the gang culture and was very committed to its causes. At the level of his soul he was eager to learn and share what he knew with someone who could appreciate his good qualities. We spent many sessions talking about many philosophical issues such as spirituality, human nature, political and social issues, and purpose in life. His eagerness to participate was evident and he enjoyed the opportunity to appropriately show off his ability to think. JJ was wise beyond his years and he was one of those kids I tend to see as an "old soul". By taking the time to get to know JJ on a very deep level he was willing to let me see parts of his nature he had never revealed to anyone else. People knew he was smart, but had no real idea of his depth of wisdom and potential for tremendous personal and spiritual growth and development.

I worked with JJ over a period of three years. He finished high school and was gainfully employed. JJ had dreams of going to college and wanted to eventually become a psychologist "like you Doc". What an honor to have a kid like and respect you enough as a professional that he or she wants to emulate many of the characteristics they see in you both personally and professionally. He was especially interested in the spiritual concepts and perspectives I shared with him. These included the concepts of individuality, uniqueness, karma (which all kids understand as "what goes around comes around"), altruism, God as the energy that is us, an afterlife, unconditional love and expectance, the possible connections between us and others who have died, and the importance of making observations rather than judgments. At the age of 19 JJ became a father, and while the relationship with his girlfriend didn't work out, he fought for and was granted custody of his son because his girlfriend was proven to be an unfit mother.

Things were going well for JJ until two of his closest friends were killed in gang related shootings. Daniel, the second one of these kids who died, was someone I had worked with a few years earlier who had already been shot twice in a previous gang related incident. The last time I saw Daniel before I went to his funeral was in juvenile hall and just after the first time he was shot. He swore that he had learned his lesson and was done with the whole gang scene. Daniel went to the California Youth Authority for two years. When he was released he was working in a construction related career and was doing quite well. I learned at his funeral that after the shooting of the first kid who was a mutual friend of both JJ and Daniel, that Daniel again resumed his gang involvement to retaliate for the death of his friend. Within a matter of weeks Daniel was ambushed by the rival gang as he drove through an intersection apparently on his way to carry out his own act of retaliation. Another kid in the vehicle with Daniel was critically injured, but survived.

All of this was too much for JJ to face and he apparently decided to carry out the acts of retaliation Daniel and the other kid had planned to commit. Ironically, JJ's level of intelligence, coupled with his pro-criminal thinking would be the unfortunate combination of factors which led to his downfall. JJ always believed he was smarter than the law enforcement officials who tried to bring him down over the years. He believed he would never get caught for any crime he committed and had apparently been able to pull this off since early in his adolescence. The deaths of his two friends rekindled his allegiance to the gang culture and JJ was arrested and charged with one count of murder and one count of attempted murder. By this time JJ was 20 years old and entered the adult criminal system for the first time, and unfortunately in a big way. I found all of this out when his picture flashed up on the TV screen of a local news broadcast as the reporter announced his capture and arrest. The announcement was also made that JJ would be facing two consecutive life sentences if convicted.

I was devastated and angry with him all at the same time. Our interactions had decreased over time as JJ started working, but he would occasionally call me or drop by my office fairly often just to check in. Because he was in the adult jail I was not able to have any private contact with him as I could have done if he had been in juvenile hall. About three weeks after his arrest JJ's brother told me JJ wanted me to visit him at the jail. At first I was reluctant to do so, primarily because I didn't know what to say to him. I knew him well enough to know he already knew how I felt about what he reportedly had done, also knowing it was now too late for me to help him.

After a few days of thinking about this I decided to go to the jail with JJ's brother. Because we had to talk on a monitored phone line through a glass panel there was really very little we could discuss. The opportunity to talk openly and freely was gone. The look on JJ's face when he walked through the door into the visiting area was one of being glad to see me. However, his expression changed drastically as he realized the circumstances under which we were meeting. We talked to each other via this monitored phone system, often times with tears in our eyes, for about 15 minutes. He told me of his plans to fight his case as an act of self-defense, but I knew the DA was going to really go after JJ as they did with other gang members in an effort to send a message to the streets that no gang violence would be tolerated. JJ talked about his son and the fear he would never be there as the child grew up. Toward the end of the visit JJ apologized for letting me down. I accepted the apology because I knew he was perceptive enough to know the depth of my disappointment. I assured him I would always care about him, and would always regret the choice he had made, even though I understood why he felt he had to make it. I told him I felt really bad for everyone who had died in the process of retaliation between the rival gangs. We focused on their families and on JJ's family who would experience a devastating blow if he was convicted as charged.

The last thing JJ said to me before I left the jail was, "Doc, I found out I can become a psychologist in prison." We put our hands together on our respective sides of the glass and I told him, "There is no doubt in my mind you will find a way someday to do what's right." I have no idea how all of this turned out since I left California soon after this visit. He knew I was leaving and returning to Alabama. Someday I will track him through the system and find out where he is and how he is doing. I knew within myself I had done all I could do to try and save this kid from himself and the streets. In spite of this awareness I grieved the loss of what he could have done if he had made the right choices. Believe it or not, I still have hope for him and still believe in the goodness I know to be present in his soul. I do hold him accountable for screwing up his life as well as the lives of many others involved on either side of the incidents which led up to JJ's actions and arrest.

This example of JJ represents very clearly the reality that no matter how hard we try with this population it is completely impossible to control everything going on internally or externally in their lives. Therefore, it is necessary to never base any interaction on controlling a kid as the approach used by the professional. With law enforcement officials and in certain other contexts control of the situation and circumstances is necessary, but efforts to *only* control the kid set up a very destructive atmosphere of competition. This is represented by what I call the "yes-you-will; you-can't-make-me" kind of interaction which must be avoided at all costs in order to keep the interaction from becoming a pointless power struggle. Sometimes within specific settings "no" is simply no, and "you can't do that and get away with it" must be enforced. But, remember with kids it is important to give them the opportunity to learn from their mistakes and understand why it is critical for them to make the right decisions. In other words help them see what is in their own best interest and why this is so. If you as the authority figure cannot accomplish this goal then collaborate with others who can.

Even though JJ was unable and, to some degree, unwilling to withstand the pressures of certain realities in his life, there have been hundreds of other kids I have worked with over the years who were able to resist. Most of my kids finished high school and very few of them ever entered the adult criminal systems. If they did get into the adult system it was generally limited to the local or county level, and not to the extent of the state or federal levels. In fact many of the kids I served over the years simply disappeared from my points of reference and environments where I would have encountered and interacted with them again. This is what you want; to have kids reach a level where they are able and willing to move forward on their own. After all the goal of every "parent" should be to teach their kids the right ways to live so they will someday successfully leave the nest.

8

Psychological Issues and Concerns

One of the most alarming realities of incarcerating juvenile offenders is that incarceration alone is not a sufficient deterrent to pro-criminal thinking and activity. In fact incarceration often increases pro-criminal thinking and related activities. This reality becomes even more obvious as kids continue to re-offend and are re-incarcerated. The deeper a kids gets into the system the less likely they are to be rehabilitated, with the odds of them becoming adult offenders only increasing. However, when incarceration is coupled with appropriate and effective mental health services and other forms of redirection and support the chances for rehabilitation are greatly increased. The key words in the previous sentence are "appropriate" and "effective" relative to treatment approaches with this population of troubled kids. Not all troubled kids will become juvenile offenders, but it is very accurate to say the vast majority of juvenile offenders are troubled kids. Of course, many law enforcement officials now see this population of kids as job security, especially at the juvenile offender level. These officials now work to maintain the status quo rather than seek out more effective ways of working with this group, such as the theories and approaches I am offering and have used successfully for many years now. Remember, if juveniles stop offending there would be no juvenile justice system in any part of this country. This is one of my goals – shut down juvenile justice nationwide! This kind of thinking makes me a real threat to law enforcement officials, rather than an inspiration for them to assist versus incarcerate.

Generally speaking staff within the various settings of juvenile detention, including juvenile hall facilities, various residential placement programs, and state level juvenile detention centers, are not trained to work effectively with these kids relative to mental health needs. More money is spent on punishing these kids than is spent on trying to intervene in a manner which will increase the likelihood of their success and prevent future offenses. I believe this is true as well within the adult systems. The difference is that kids are much easier to reach than are the adult offenders given the reality of the personalities of kids being much more fluid than those of adults in their mid-twenties and older. Therefore, it makes sense that early intervention in the form of appropriate and effective redirection and support efforts would decrease the number of adult offenders.

There are many factors associated with this issue, the biggest of which I believe to be the ignorant arrogance of law enforcement agencies in general who make crime a game between them and the kids they seek to arrest. Unfortunately kids who re-offend begin to see their interactions with law enforcement as a competition, just like the cops and robbers game I played with my friends as a kid. Even more unfortunate is the reality of law enforcement officials being the very ones who set this scenario into motion. A rather alarming number of law enforcement officials see themselves as the only people who can control and stop crime. We need law enforcement officials to be part of a collaborative solution, rather than contributing negatively to the problems which already exist. As I stated previously, no single individual, institution, organization, or agency can be all things to these kids.

Most of the efforts of so-called peace officers are concentrated within the communities which have a high prevalence of low income families. It is common knowledge these areas are prime breeding grounds for crime, not because of the people living there, but because of countless complicating factors which in reality are often beyond their ability to control and influence. The hurricane season of 2005 hit everyone in this country with the horrors associated with the ever expanding divide between the rich and the poor. We were shamefully exposed worldwide relative to the realities of the different classes existing within our own society. The entire world witnessed what should have been experienced by every American as a disgraceful crime against humanity right here in the United States of America. This fact was laid bare by the existence of lower class citizens created and perpetuated by our own society and culture. Like it or not we are a society divided into upper, middle and lower classes and it is time to put an end to this!

Psychological disorders are much more prevalent within low income communities and populations compared to higher income groups and communities. This in no way suggests low income people are somehow innately more impaired than others. Rather this fact represents the significant impact of complicating factors which are much more numerous and prevalent among low income people than among their higher income counterparts. Poverty easily leads to despair as low income people fight simply to survive while facing ever increasing hardships with very few opportunities to pull themselves up and out of their environment. Poverty tends to be multigenerational in many cases as the need to survive outweighs the need to seek out opportunities to get ahead. Realistically low income families often depend on every family member to contribute financially to their existence. All too often low income individuals see government handouts as a quick fix, failing to realize their income will be forever limited and determined by government agencies, institutions and politicians. There is no security in this kind of solution and low income adults need to be aided in ways which will give their children the opportunity to complete their education and move on to bigger and better jobs. This approach utilizes both prevention and intervention as approaches to break the cycles of poverty and despair.

Poverty can easily become a mindset if individuals buy into the notion there is nothing I can do about this. If the right amount of money was spent to intervene with kids and their families, then the money saved over time by reducing the numbers of adult offenders could be used to provide the kinds of ongoing support services needed to fight against poverty. Low income

European American families tend to live in less densely populated rural areas of the country, while low income non-European American families tend to live within more densely populated urban and suburban areas. This is likely representative of the disproportionately higher percentage of low income non-European American groups as compared to their European American counterparts. The higher the level of concentration of low income families within any area increases the likelihood of increased crime levels and decreased levels of opportunities to fight against their socioeconomic positions. This fact alone demands attention and demands remedy through intensive efforts to intervene and prevent the complicating factors which perpetuate poverty. As a nation it is imperative that we reprioritize and maximize our efforts to assist people in need. This is the only way to decrease the gap between the haves and the have-nots and to stop the ever increasing divide between these two groups.

One of the most shameful aspects of our political system is the reality of so-called conservatives being much less concerned about the plight of those who are "left behind". The current administration has guaranteed that the lives of low income people everywhere will only get worse as cuts are being made in the very programs needed by low income individuals in order to survive. The irony of all of this is conservatives supposedly represent those who are devoutly religious. However, their need to promote their own biased agendas is more important than following the Biblical teachings they use to promote their own self-serving causes. Because many conservatives have a natural tendency toward punishment and war they fail to recognize everyone's interconnectedness and the need to find non-violent solutions to various situations whenever that is a realistic option. Under the most recent conservative control and reign we have had more money being spent on war and law enforcement than at any other time in our existence. This is true because of legislation such as the Homeland Security Act and the US Patriot Act both of which bring war efforts and law enforcement into some kind of holy, infallible union. There is no doubt in my mind that deception and corruption are more widespread throughout this country than at any other time as well. My beliefs are based in the ever increasing number of scandals and violations of our rights which are being exposed at the political level, coupled with my own experiences of witnessing the unfair and unjust treatment of kids and their families through my work as a psychologist. There is no God in any of this and I find it hard to believe that the misuse of money appropriated for homeland security is not being monitored more closely throughout the country. We are being lied to and the low income people within our nation are paying a particularly high price for governmental arrogance, secrecy and elitism. So far none of this has changed very much even under the Obama administration.

Because of the above mentioned factors and misuses of power the psychosocial issues and concerns, especially as they apply to low income groups, will only become more serious and pervasive. Also, because of the current political climate it is unlikely that any law enforcement group is going to be willing to give up funding for their jobs and so called missions. Of course some of these missions are aimed at our troubled kids with law enforcement officials able to treat them as domestic terrorists at even the slightest hint of criminal involvement. Too much of what drives law enforcement agencies and institutions is self-preservation in the form of the old money and numbers game. As long as they can give some proof, even if it is exaggerated and inaccurate at times, that there is a vital need to maintain the status quo they will be able to push the fight to preserve their existence. More and more around this country various professional groups become increasingly territorial. These groups will defend their ways in spite of evidence indicating money could be better spent if reapportioned more appropriately and effectively. Unfortunately, many of our current political leaders support the "strong arm", "iron fisted" approaches to fighting unrest rather than preventing its emergence and existence. Investigations after hurricane Katrina, coupled with other incidents are finally beginning to expose some of the corruption and abuses of power and authority which has existed and increased since 9/11. A lot more still needs to be done to change the current mindset in Washington DC.

A search of the literature relative to psychological disorders among juvenile offenders supports my strongly held belief of many of our juvenile offenders needing opportunities for redirection and support from various agencies and institutions. There is no other way for them to break their cycles of engaging in crime-based acting out behaviors as long as they are driven by emotional and mental instability. While there are numerous articles available one of the articles I found online brings everything into focus. The article is entitled "Psychiatric Disorders in Youth in Juvenile Detention", (L. Teplin, K. Abram, G. McClelland, M. Dulcan, and A. Mericle; *Archives of General Psychiatry*. 2002; 59: 1133-1143.) Their findings were in line with all of the articles I read and this article was published much more recently than some of the others. Their findings also back up my own stated professional observations based on my work with this population since September 1992. Their diagnostic determinations were based on diagnostic criteria printed in the Diagnostic and Statistical Manual of Mental Disorders, Third Edition, Revised (DSM-III-R).

The research conducted by this team utilized a total sample of 1829 male and female youth, ages 10 to 18 years, and screened within the Cook County Juvenile Temporary Detention Center. Statistical data are broken down into the categories of male, female, African American, Non-Hispanic white, Hispanic, and Other. Included in the sample were 1172 males and 657 females. The numbers broken down by ethnic diversity were 1005 African Americans, 296 Non-Hispanic whites, 524 Hispanics, and 4 "Other". The average age of all participants was 14.9 years. A summary of their findings is as follows and presented as percentages of the total sample:

- 66.3% males and 73.8% females met criteria for at least one diagnosis.
- 60.9% males and 59.7% females met criteria for diagnoses excluding Conduct Disorder which is a common diagnosis for most juvenile offenders.
- 13.0% males and 21.6% females met criteria for Major Depression.
- 12.2% males and 15.8% females met criteria for Dysthymia, a milder form of depression.
- 2.2% males and 1.8% females met criteria for Bipolar I, most recent episode manic.
- 1.0% for both males and females met criteria for Psychotic disorders.

- 21.3% males and 30.8% met criteria for at least one of the Anxiety Disorders.

- 16.6% males and 21.4% females met criteria for ADHD - Attention Deficit/Hyperactivity Disorder.

- 14.5% males and 17.5% females met criteria for Oppositional Defiant Disorder.

- 37.8% males and 40.6% females met criteria for Conduct Disorder.

- 50.7% males and 46.8% females met criteria for one or more substance use disorders, with marijuana and alcohol use being the most prevalent.

A summary of their findings relative to ethnic diversity and gender specific to each of the three categories is as follows and presented as percentages of the total sample. Abbreviations for each category are African American Male/Female (AAM/F), Non-Hispanic White Male/Female (NHWM/F), and Hispanic Male/Female (HM/F).

- 64.6% AAM, 82.0% NHWM, and 70.4% HM met criteria for at least one of the DSM-III-R diagnoses.

- 70.9% AAF, 86.1% NHWF, and 75.9% HF met criteria for at least one of the DSM-III-R diagnoses.

- 18.6% AAM, 13.8% NHWM, and 21.5% HM met criteria for one of the DSM-III-R affective disorder diagnoses – Major Depression, Dysthymia, or Bipolar I.

- 26.2% AAF, 23.4% NHWF, and 28.7% HF met criteria for one of the DSM-III-R affective disorder diagnoses – Major Depression, Dysthymia, of Bipolar I.

- 1.0% AAM, 2.6% NHWM, and 0.7% HM met criteria for a Psychotic disorder.

- 0.9% AAF, 0.0% NHWF, and 2.1% HF met criteria for a Psychotic disorder.

- 20.9% AAM, 14.4% NHWM, and 25.5%HM met criteria for one of the Anxiety disorders.

- 31.2% AAF, 30.0% NHWF, and 32.6% HF met criteria for one of the Anxiety disorders.
- 17.0% AAM, 20.9% NHWM, and 13.7%HM met criteria for Attention Deficit/Hyperactivity Disorder.
- 20.0% AAF, 22.2% NHWF, and 29.3% HF met criteria for Attention Deficit/Hyperactivity Disorder.
- 14.4% AAM, 19.4% NHWM, and 13.6% HM met criteria for Oppositional Defiant Disorder.
- 15.8% AAF, 17.8% NHWF, and 26.2% HF met criteria for Oppositional Defiant Disorder.
- 35.6% AAM, 59.9% NHWM, and 41.7% HM met criteria for Conduct Disorder.
- 34.3% AAF, 58.9% NHWF, and 50.2%HF met criteria for Conduct Disorder.
- 49.1% AAM, 62.6% NHWM, and 55.4% HM met criteria for one or more of the Substance Use Disorders.
- 42.3% AAF, 61.9% NHWF, and 51.7% HF met criteria for one or more of the Substance Use Disorders.

As you can see from this data there is an alarming presence of mental and emotional disorders, coupled with substance use disorders found within this population of troubled kids who become juvenile offenders. The percentages are likely very similar for adult populations, with a general consensus of many adult offenders also having serious unmet mental health needs. Keep in mind the more serious psychiatric disorders do not completely develop until late adolescence and early adulthood. Therefore as kids get older the percentages of late adolescent kids would likely rise if they were followed into the adult systems. Of further importance is the fact of kids not being diagnosed with adult personality disorders. This is due to the accepted reality that the personalities of kids are still fluid and can more easily be redirected with the right combination of interventions and approaches.

Another interesting component of the data revealed by these statistics is that while Non-Hispanic White males and females were the smallest ethnic group within this sample, they had the highest percentages of impairment. First of all, I believe the relatively small number of Non-Hispanic White juveniles simply reflects the disparity relative to ethnic and other cultural differences. In my experiences most European American kids who got arrested rarely were ever locked up to the same extent as their non-white counterparts. In many cases European American families are more likely to be able to afford effective legal representation than are families in the other groups. The other big factor is the greater likelihood of kids from ethnic minority groups being pursued with greater fervor and intensity by law enforcement groups in this country.

My experiences with adolescent populations have taught me it is much more difficult to reach kids under the age of fifteen. This is due to their lack of maturity, coupled with their lack of ability to reason and think abstractly. From the age of fifteen and up it is much easier to reason with kids to help them see what is in their own best interest given the reality they are approaching adulthood. At this point it is easier to help them understand, in spite of the presence of numerous complicating external factors in their lives, that to some extent their own choices and reactions have shaped their lives so far. During this critical period of transition from adolescence to adulthood it is possible to help kids see that their choices will continue to shape their lives into the future. This is accomplished by helping them learn to consciously make the right decisions at this point in life when, consciously or unconsciously, they will be making future decisions anyway. It is important to move these kids away from reactionary motivations toward carefully thought out plans and strategies which will give them hope for the future. Set your expectations high for these kids, but not so high as to make them unrealistic and unattainable.

The chronological years of seventeen and eighteen are especially significant given the reality of eighteen year old kids being recognized as adults under the law – younger than eighteen for certain types of violent crimes. This is a time to help them see the importance of putting any criminal past behind them, making sure not to create an adult criminal record which in most cases will follow them for the rest of their lives. This is also the time to help them face any unaddressed or otherwise unresolved needs in their lives, such as mental/emotional health issues, and unmet academic needs. Believe me, this will be the last chance for many kids in this population.

My work with high risk, troubled kids was often done without parental participation or involvement other than establishing eligibility for services and signing consent forms for me to treat their child. When kids were locked up or in residential placement permission for me to see them was granted by the courts. When kids were living within their communities I usually met with them in school settings during school hours, with only a few afternoon appointments at my office. The kids I saw in my office were generally the kids with more serious mental and emotional problems who were also being seen by our psychiatrists for medications. Even when families were present in my office I always met alone with a kid for the greatest part of the time scheduled. Parents were more than welcome to participate, especially if they had information I needed to know about changes in their child's behavior, academic problems, parenting issues, etc. Because parents could see I was getting through to their kids they valued my time alone with their child. They also respected my insistence on confidentiality when it came to the privacy kids need in order to feel comfortable when disclosing. There were very few times I have had to share a kid's personal information revealed to me in sessions with parents or guardians, other than as required by law.

I made it really clear to all parents and guardians I am not here to be their detective. I have always felt if parents are so uninvolved in the lives of their kids as to not know what they are up to, then why should I give them such information. This is especially true with kids who are in the 15 and up age bracket. My ability to join with kids on an appropriate level is always critical to the success of my treatment approaches. Kids always enjoy the opportunity to talk openly with an adult who understands them and the way they see things. This is why it is so important to ignore such things as bad language, clothing style, and other factors which have nothing to do with the work at hand. The last thing troubled kids need is another authority figure telling them how to talk, dress, sit, walk, and act. Working with this population of kids in a very relaxed yet professional manner is one of the most enjoyable parts of my job as a psychologist. Even though the atmosphere is "kick back" as the kids call it, we are constantly working during every aspect of our interactions. My role as an active listener is critical in the process of understanding the kid and their related issues. One of the best ways to accomplish this task is to simply engage them from time to time in a conversation about their friends and routine activities. The more kids talk, and the more they trust me, the more completely I will be able to help them redirect their energies and efforts toward worthwhile goals and activities.

Involvement by family members is especially helpful when trying to get an accurate history on every client. However, it is important to understand the only realities and perceptions which matter are those believed and held by the kid sitting in front of you. While their realities and perceptions may not be accurate, the way they see and interpret everything in their lives is what motivates them either positively or negatively. It is helpful to be able to correct their misinformation when possible, but it is not a necessary factor. You will often find that parents and guardians will only give you their perceptions of the child, and are rarely ever honest about themselves and the part they have played in complicating their kid's life. I never let them get away with this as I always ask the question "What mistakes have you made in life which have complicated your child's life?" I do this in front of their kid and expect them to be honest. If the information is too sensitive, or something I think the kid doesn't need to know, I meet with the parent or guardians alone. Anytime I meet alone with a parent I always assure my client I will not violate their trust, and I NEVER do! After all, the case is under the kid's name and not the name of the parents of guardians. With younger kids involvement by parents or guardians is critical, but with older kids their presence and regular involvement will actually impede the kid's progress in many instances.

Fortunately only a relatively small percentage of kids have serious mental disorders such as Bipolar Disorder or some form of Psychotic Disorder. The more common problems will be different forms of depression, anxiety, behavioral problems, learning difficulties and abuse issues. The most common diagnoses for troubled kids are: Major Depression,

Dysthymia, Conduct Disorder, Oppositional Defiant Disorder, specific Learning Disorders, and Polysubstance Dependence (or at least abuse). Diagnoses like Attention Deficit/Hyperactivity Disorder and various Learning Disorders only make all of the aforementioned conditions more complicated to address. I personally believe kids born into any kind of stressful environment with repeated exposure to stressful stimuli will very likely meet criteria for one or more of the possible childhood diagnoses. In many cases children have a genetic predisposition to certain temperaments and coping styles. A stressful environment will only make the manifestation of these genetic predispositions more pronounced. I refer to it as being "pre-wired for sound". The continuing level of stress, along with the numbers of complicating factors, will determine the level of impairment as the child grows older. This relates directly to my Roberts FLAGS Model explained in detail in my first book, At the Mercy of Externals: Righting Wrongs and Protecting Kids, 2nd Edition. It is critical for each of to you read and understand the concepts in that book in order to gain the utmost benefit from the contents of this current book. This is the reason for combining the two books into one publication as of 2010.

I am not a promoter of medication for anyone unless it is clear they are too impaired by their disorder to function adequately and safely in life. Severe forms of Major Depression, Bipolar Disorder, Psychosis, ADD, and ADHD require medication, as in many cases it is impossible to even work effectively with someone who is extremely impaired by their mental and/or emotional state of mind. Keep in mind mental and emotional disorders are in some cases organic in nature and are very frequently the result of hereditary factors. This can easily be determined by obtaining a thorough family history of other family members who have exhibited the same symptoms. Rather than think of people as having a mental illness I help them understand extreme forms of mental and emotional states are nothing more than brain-based disorders. This helps kids and adults deal with their mental health issues without the stigma of being "mentally ill". It is possible to help people deal more effectively with the concept of a brain disorder which is chronic and needs to be treated as much as any other chronic physical disorder would require. This approach goes along with the current push to reclassify every mental disorder to a medical condition if it is chronic, hereditary, and needs to be treated medically.

The biggest obstacle with disorders needing to be treated with medications is the issue of compliance due to the adverse side effects of many drugs. Therefore it is important to work closely with psychiatrists to find the right balance of medications needed to control symptoms and limit the adverse reactions so often experienced. Recent research indicates medications not only help control symptoms, but help regenerate brain cells and stop further degeneration of brain tissue. Because we still have a lot to learn about the brain it is difficult to help people diagnosed with serious disorders find hope for the future. However, with the current levels of research and advancements increasing frequently, it is possible to help clients understand that all of these conditions will someday be controlled and/or eliminated without having to deal with negative side effects. In spite of the hope for advancements in treatment and in the understanding of brain functioning, compliance remains a major obstacle in working with people who have serious symptomatology. This is equally difficult for both children and adult populations.

(As an aside, I believe the most significant contributing factor to what appears to be an increase in various physical, mental, and emotional disorders is the willful disregard relative to ever increasing sexual promiscuity and indiscriminately risking pregnancy with virtually every sexual encounter. I firmly believe that the more people are acting out due to their own total lack of impulse control, the more likely they are to be carriers of what I call "bad gene soup". This mixed with the "bad gene soup" from their equally as out of control and impulsive sexual partner increases the likelihood of more severe childhood psychological and medical diagnoses of all kinds. I bring this up to every single parent I now see who has several children from different sexual partners - who, along with the kids, are impaired genetically - and they readily agree with my perception. At times I even go as far as to suggest that they not continue having additional children who will likely develop the same or worse kinds of conditions, and they readily agree with me on this point as well.)

For kids who are deeply involved in the juvenile justice system medication compliance is a little easier to maintain when they are incarcerated. Once they are released follow up with mental health services for medication is rare. Even when they are locked up kids have the right to refuse medications and must be informed of this right. All too often I have watched as juvenile justice staff try to force medication compliance with threats of legal consequences if the kid refuses. These individuals get very upset when I refuse to back them on this issue. The most I can do is to try and help kids see how it is in their own best interest to comply, but this does not always work.

For about 18 months I worked with kids in Desert Youth Academy, a lock-in residential placement program housed within the Indio Juvenile Hall Facility in Indio, CA. This is the program run by the Riverside County Department of Probation I mentioned in chapter three. These kids were generally ages 16 to 18 and this was their last opportunity before being sentenced to the California Youth Authority system which was overcrowded, and which is basically state prison for kids. Every kid housed in this program had failed at least two other placement programs and had almost unimaginable criminal records, often times coupled with heavy involvement in gang activity. This was a 20 bed, all male unit and at least 25% to 30% of these kids required medication if there was any hope of successfully completing the program. Because I saw them regularly on the unit, spending extended amounts of time with each of them as needed, I was able to keep them compliant with medications I believed to be necessary as part of their treatment and successful release from DYA. While on medications these kids performed extremely well and I was able to reach them on a level which would have been impossible without medications.

The stability provided by the right combinations and amounts of medication gave me the opportunity to provide insight-based therapy with kids who would have otherwise been unreachable. It was obvious to everyone when they stopped taking their meds as their symptoms would return very quickly, and frequently with a major rebound effect of even more exaggerated symptoms. The changes in their levels of self-control were astonishing when their medications wore off. Therefore, it was impossible for the kids not to see the differences for themselves relative to how much they needed medications. A great deal of progress was made by all kids on this unit. Those who needed medication at least left the program with the awareness of their conditions and the stability they gained when they were med compliant. Most of these kids lived in other parts of Riverside County and outside the area where my office was located in the desert. Every effort was made to hook them up with mental health and other support services once they were released, but unfortunately many of those needing medications never followed up with treatment.

One of the most remarkable aspects for me in working with kids in this placement program was the reality that I had never known most of them outside of the facility. Therefore, I knew them only under the kinds of conditions which encouraged right actions and behaviors. They were motivated to be successful since failure in this program meant very serious consequences. So many of these guys were extremely intelligent and possessed amazing skills, talents, and potential. For many of them this was their first time to shine and get a glimpse of the positive things they were capable of doing. The stories of these kids were heartbreaking, with many of them coming to this program after years of being in foster care. These kids had faced more complicating factors collectively as a group than any other kids I had every served. My work with them was the most rewarding part of my career to date and was a tremendous learning experience for me relative to what can be accomplished even with the most trouble kids when the right approaches are used with them. All of the staff associated with this program knew my presence and work with these kids was one of the largest factors contributing to the success of the kids and of the program itself. As you can imagine being banned from this program because of a child abuse report I was required by law to file against senior staff, was devastating to me. Then on top of that to be told this population of kids was no longer a priority with the California Department of Mental Health was infuriating. But, for 18 months I dedicated my life to the kids on this unit and gained insight and wisdom which will be invaluable to me throughout the rest of my career. I have the satisfaction of knowing every kid I worked with was given a glimpse of themselves they had never seen, and I know for a fact they will never forget the amazing experiences we shared.

Because most of the kids in the lock-in placement program were from other parts of the county once they were released I had no further contact with them. However, I always gave them my contact information at the Indio clinic so they could at least reach me by phone if they needed to or wanted to talk with me following their release. In addition to many complicating factors common to all troubled kids, a very high percentage of these kids were also dealing with issues of extreme grief and loss. In many cases these kids had lost one or both of their parents either by death or abandonment, or they had experienced the deaths of a number of their friends and extended family members as a result of gang violence. Many of these kids were chronically sad and angry relative to many external factors which were beyond their abilities to control or influence.

Evan was one of the most remarkable kids from this program. When he was sentenced to this placement program he was already being successfully treated with Lithium for extreme Bipolar I Disorder. Evan was prone more to the manic end of this disorder rather than to the depressive end – with mania and depression being the two opposite poles of this "bipolar" disorder. Evan was extremely intelligent and talented, and at 15 years of age, was one of the younger residents. He was very mature for his age and he had unlimited potential – in either direction. Having never known Evan when he was off his medication it was readily apparent when he stopped taking his meds. His mania was marked by racing thoughts and being hyper verbal, with little ability to keep himself on track during a conversation.

The only time during his stay when he refused his meds the change in his ability to interact with me on a rational and calm level was drastic and uncontrollable. At first I couldn't figure out what was happening until I finally asked Evan if he had stopped taking his meds. Initially he denied this, but finally admitted he had started "cheeking" his meds two days earlier. None of the nursing staff or unit staff was aware of this, but everyone could see a tremendous change in his personality. It didn't take long for Evan to realize how critical his medication was and he was enraged by this reality. With a great deal of encouragement on my part he finally agreed it was in his best interest to go back on his medication rather than face removal from the program and re-sentencing to the California Youth Authority. After this incident I had at least four months to work with Evan before he was successfully released from the program. Once released, Evan returned to the eastern part of the county where he was to be monitored by that division of probation for a six month after care monitoring program.

Once out on his own Evan stopped taking the medications he was given at his release. His mom, who according to Evan's account was apparently bipolar herself, convinced Evan he didn't need the medication. Evan never followed up at the mental health center in his area and rather quickly returned to his previous history of self-medicating with heavy alcohol use. Within a relatively short period of time Evan resumed his previous use of crystal meth and re-involved himself in his gang culture. He had an almost unimaginable history of extreme physical abuse at the hands of his mother and was again faced with the all of the demons from his past when he returned to his home/family context. I talked with Evan twice by phone and it was obvious he was out of control with his Bipolar I symptoms. There was nothing I could do to make him realize his need to go back on his meds and it was clear he was spiraling out of control in every area of his life. I have no idea what became of Evan since I left California, but my fear is that he is either in more trouble legally and with his substance use, or even worse he could be dead by now. All I can do is hope he remembers how good it felt to be stable mentally and emotionally while he was locked up. If he is still alive I hope someday he will be able to deal realistically with his brain disorder and will learn to take care of himself. He is one of those kids I will never forget.

Evan's story is not at all uncommon. The fact he had very few after care resources available to him once he was released was one of the reasons for his downfall. Evan's case represents many of the overwhelming complicating factors faced by troubled kids on a regular basis, all of which are greatly intensified when there are serious overriding mental and emotional disorders involved. When you add to that the devastating realities many troubled kids face within their communities and family contexts it is no wonder many high risk kids are unable and unwilling to see their own potential for success. None of this will change until the political and social climates in this country change in the direction of a strong desire to reach out collaboratively to those in need, especially those labeled as society's underdogs. I plan to be a very active participant in making these changes in attitude and perspective a reality.

9

Be Part of the Solution and Not 'Just Another Problem'

In this day and time I believe our society has become rather adept at renaming realities in ways which are either more politically correct or in some cases in ways which disguise the truth. This is especially true when talking about our different socioeconomic strata. Rather than talk or think about lower, middle and upper classes, we talk about groups described as low income, middle income, upper middle income, and upper income. However, we tend to distinguish the "haves" and the "have-nots" as either high class/high society or low class. These terms conjure up stereotypical images of the characteristics often associated with and attributed to those who are rich and to those who are poor. The rich are generally characterized as being arrogant, greedy, and privileged, while the poor are represented as ignorant, dirty, and worthless. Depending on the context of a conversation the terms high class and low class are often times used as insults against those who seem to think they are better than others, or against those who do not measure up to a certain level of standards arbitrarily set as the norm. Race or ethnicity is not always a part of these kinds of taunts as these labels tend to separate the haves and the have-nots within any cultural or ethnic group. Anyone within any of the socioeconomic levels can be referred to as having negative characteristics associated with either the high or low class stereotypes.

Imagine being born into poverty where poverty has been a multigenerational legacy. Most of the daily efforts are focused on struggling to survive and not much on getting ahead since this seems to be the illusive dream. The chances are you are living in substandard housing located in a "very bad neighborhood". You were probably born to a single mom or into a very conflicted marriage or live-in relationship environment, in which diapers and formula are bought using money needed to provide food and other necessities for all family members. The chances are you will be sustained by programs offering handouts rather than real opportunities to improve quality of life. There are few if any positive role models in your immediate contexts of home/family and community, and you are likely surrounded by substance use, abuse, violence and criminal activity both inside and outside the home/family context. Your days will likely be spent indoors for safety reasons, or you will be allowed to roam freely without supervision depending on the ability of the adults in your life to parent and protect you.

Over time you will likely have several father or mother figures to deal with, most of whom will not like you because *you're not really their child*. If you are the oldest sibling you will likely be given unreasonable responsibilities relative to caring for the adults in your life who cannot take care of themselves or the younger siblings you are likely to have. On the other hand, if you are an only child or the youngest child you will likely be either neglected, or babied to the extent there are no distinctions or boundaries between you and the person or people who baby you to satisfy their own unmet emotional needs. School performance will be dismal and minimal since you will probably have very little self-control or ability to focus on schoolwork because of the lack of emotional stability in your life. Much needed quality medical care will likely be unreachable, nutritional needs may be lacking, and the likelihood of developing significant emotional, behavioral, and psychological disorders will be almost inevitable due to the numerous complicating factors present in your life and surroundings. The number of complicating factors within your home/family context correlates directly to the level of Fear, Loneliness, Anger, Guilt and Shame (FLAGS), along with helplessness and hopelessness, you will experience. Any form of abuse and victimization will only make all of these factors worse, and your chances of developing appropriate coping skills and behaviors will be very low. Unless someone within some context teaches you to dream of better things for the future, and provides you with the opportunities and support to make those dreams become realities, your future won't be much better than the life you had as a child.

This chapter is about adult roles and responsibilities covered in depth in my first book, At the Mercy of Externals: Righting Wrongs and Protecting Kids, 2nd Edition. Again, it is very important to understand the material presented in my previous book to fully understand the important perspective of this chapter. Righting wrongs refers to the need to intervene with older adolescents and adults of all ages, hopefully before they become parents and continue the multigenerational process of abuse and victimization they experienced as children. Protecting kids is the prevention part whereby we work with parents and kids to help them understand how to make better choices by understanding how their past has shaped their lives and often times continues to live in their present. All too often the adults in the lives of kids are a big part of the problem and they need to be taught how to create solutions for themselves and their children or other kids in their charge. Adult roles and responsibilities go way beyond the home/family context and extend out into the other five contexts of community, school, society, politics and religion. This means any adult who has any level of influence and authority over a child as a parent, extended family member, professional, law enforcement, educator, minister/clergy, politician, or any other chosen role must be prepared to right wrongs *and* protect kids.

As a means of identifying the numerous adult roles and responsibilities take each letter of the alphabet and think of every word beginning with each letter which represents one adult role and responsibility. For instance with the letter "A" you get a list that includes: accept, acknowledge, appreciate, assist, accentuate, acclaim, applaud, accommodate, accompany, accord, activism, admire, admonish, affection, affirm, aid, advocate, ally, alleviate, amend, adjust, adapt, analyze, assess, apologize, appease, articulate, aspire, assert, assure, attend, and avert. If you do this with every letter, using a dictionary as I did, you will be astounded at the number of existing adult roles and responsibilities, even if we ignore them.

Because of the extremely high number of adult roles and responsibilities, I believe very strongly it is necessary to teach these realities to kids before they become sexually active. The content of this book and my first book should be part of a Parenting 101 class which every adult should take before they try to move on to more complicated issues of active parenting. This applies to adults in other roles outside the home/family context as well who need to fully understand what works and what does not work when trying to guide, teach, assist, or otherwise interact with kids of all ages. A thorough understanding of the adult roles and responsibilities, along with a full awareness of the numerous complicating factors all troubled kids face are essential in knowing how to effectively and appropriately interact with kids in our charge.

Another important area of concern relative to teaching these realities is the importance of an explicit, realistic and thorough approach to teaching sexual education classes. I firmly believe if kids understood all that is required in order to be effective in their parenting roles they would be less likely to get pregnant before they have made important accomplishments in their lives. Such accomplishments include: getting an education; preparing for a worthwhile and rewarding career which will allow them to support themselves and a family; and working on undoing any emotional and psychological damage they may have experienced while growing up within the different contexts.

I also believe kids and adults need to understand having a baby should be based in the desire and readiness to become a parent. The most common mistaken assumption of many kids and adults is that a child will solve many of their problems. Very little consideration is given to the welfare and wellbeing of the child relative to complicating factors the child will face if the parent(s) are not ready to assume their parental roles and responsibilities. The decision to engage in sexual activity which puts someone at risk of becoming a parent should be based on fully informed awareness of what causes pregnancy and of everything which will occur once the baby is born. This is especially true if the pregnancy is accidental and the child ends up being unwanted. The best way to prevent excessive use of abortions is to make kids and adults fully aware of the ways to prevent pregnancy beyond the unrealistic notion of an abstinence only approach. An abstinence only model ignores the lack of maturity, awareness and self-control of even many adults. All too often lives are complicated and even to some extent ruined with an unplanned pregnancy, especially if the child is unwanted and born into a less than favorable environment which will not benefit the child.

Not every disadvantaged, low income home/family context is dysfunctional. However, the complicating factors kids will face by just being in the low income category will demand that the home/family context be as functional and stable as possible. Let me help you get accustomed to the kind of language associated with kids you need to accept and deal with rather than challenge every time a curse word or vulgar term is spoken. One of the most profound statements ever made to me by a parent was this: "fucked up parents raise fucked up kids." I was so taken aback by this, but all I could do was agree and even laugh at the frankness and conviction with which this statement was uttered. This single mom had a 17 year old son, Vince, referred to me by probation for drug-related charges and gang affiliation. As time progressed it also became apparent that Vince was developing strong symptomatology related to Schizoaffective Disorder which is a combination of psychotic symptoms and extreme emotional/mood instability. His serious addiction to alcohol, marijuana, and crystal meth only made the symptoms of his brain disorders worse.

Vince's mom had in recent years obtained a nursing degree and was working in a hospital. She readily admitted that the early years for Vince and his younger sister had been fraught with extreme substance use and domestic violence within the home/family context. When Vince was about 12 years old his father had been arrested and sentenced to many years in prison. Mom filed for divorce and sought out counseling for herself and was able to get her life on track, just not in time to save her children from the emotional damage done during their early years. There was a significant history of emotional and psychotic disorders from both of the biological parents even though Vince's mom had never developed any of the symptoms herself. Mom's poor choices as an adolescent were the result of the extremely dysfunctional and complicated environment she experienced as a child and recreated for her children. Her mom had the same Schizoaffective Disorder as Vince was beginning to develop in late adolescence.

Vince's situation represents one of the worst sets of complicating factors any family could face. Not only were there many complicating factors which truly put them at the mercy of externals, there was also a multigenerational history of poverty and extreme brain disorders manifested as serious emotional instability and psychotic symptoms. Vince's mom was lucky enough to have the innate qualities of resilience and the ability to transcend the complicating factors from her past. She also never developed any of the symptoms of the disorders for which she carried a genetic predisposition. As her children got older she was also determined to pull herself out of poverty by using her intelligence and insight to get a good education and enter a career where she could help others in need. Vince's mom readily admitted that, while she deeply regretted all of the chaos she helped create in the lives of her kids, there was nothing she could do to change the mistakes of the past. She also had to face the reality Vince had serious mental and emotional disorders which would plague him for the rest of his life, especially if he continued to drink and use, and refuse the medical treatment he so desperately needed. Vince's younger sister had a baby at 15 and never finished high school. Vince's mom was trying earnestly to help her daughter change the direction of her life, both for her daughter's sake and for the sake of her grandchild.

I hope you can see from this example the importance of allowing people to be who they really are when they are sitting in front of you and seeking help for themselves and their family members. If I had been offended by this mom's bold statement of perception and fact, I would have spoiled the entire opportunity for her to express herself and share her insight with me in her own way. Vince's case was not one of my successes given the fact by the time I had the opportunity to work with him he was so entrenched in the gang culture, and his substance addiction was so serious. The complicating factor of extreme emotional and mental disturbance also impeded his ability to face his future with the hope he would someday be stable enough to function effectively in life. I referred Vince to our adult services at age 19 and he was generally non-compliant with the services he needed to stabilize the symptoms related to his brain disorders. There were several times Vince came back to see me for help and guidance. I was able to at least establish a professional relationship with Vince from the beginning which allowed Vince to trust me fully and to know I truly cared about him and the issues he was facing.

The last time I saw Vince's mom she told me Vince had been arrested for drug related charges and now had an adult criminal record. The likelihood of him getting deeper into the adult system was high, with this system being the only way Vince would possibly accept the help he needed for his inability to control many aspects of his existence. I have no idea of Vince's current situation, but I can only imagine he is likely locked up. I can deal with this possibility better than thinking about the possibility he could also be dead. Sometimes all we can do is try. Even that can be enough to reach someone in a way which will help them in the future, assuming we have made a connection, starting from the point of our initial contact, which will facilitate their ability to remember their experiences with us favorably. I cannot stress enough the importance of dealing with kids and people in general by looking beyond the bad choices they may have made and seeing them for who they were meant to be and can become. When serious mental and emotional problems are present the odds of seeing extreme achievement is reduced, but never eliminated. People with serious mental and emotional disorders must be given hope for future medical advances which will make their symptoms more manageable. We must all hold out hope for eventual cures for these types of chronic brain disorders as we learn more about how the brain functions.

When I think about a family like Vince's I cannot help but wonder where were adults within other contexts who could have and should have tried to intervene and assist this family. Even if efforts were made to assist this family early on in their struggles, they were not successful. Vince's mom told me she wished on many occasions that someone along the way would have tried to help her and her children rather than judge them by the actions of their father and the family histories on both sides. All too often law enforcement officials and even educators will hold a family history against the children of parents with police records, mental disorders, or poor academic performance records. This kind of thinking only guarantees the likelihood of kids following in the footsteps of the parents and other family members that law enforcement officials and educators may have known under less than favorable circumstances. It is wrong to assume the next generation will be exactly like the previous generations. Such an assumption may even explain some of the thinking within this country which has helped to create the classist society we now have. Because Vince's mom was able to get her life on track after her husband's incarceration and their subsequent divorce, this potential had to have been there all along. This example is one where I firmly believe the right interventions early on may have helped stabilize this family before it got to the point of becoming so much more complicated than it already was.

One of the most interesting and challenging cases I ever had involved Gracie and her six children. There were three different fathers involved, none of whom took any responsibility for their roles as fathers in the lives of their kids. This family was known to every social service agency in the area and they were referred to me for family counseling. My work with them covered eight of the last nine years I spent in California. All I can say about Gracie was that she was quite a character. She had a heart of gold, was as immature as any one of her children, and yet very intelligent at the same time. Gracie's criminal history and criminal involvement were rather extensive, and I learned very quickly not to ask too many questions about things which didn't pertain to issues directly related to family dynamics. She was known as a gang mom and a protector of the kids in the streets. The most amazing thing about this woman was the level of trust and respect she gave me in working with her for the benefit of her children.

During the years I was involved professionally with Gracie and her children I was not aware of any active criminal involvement on her part. However, because of my desire not to know more than I needed to know, primarily for my own safety, this was not information I sought. If I had learned or witnessed something I would have had to act on it and I tried very carefully not to put myself in that position. As a psychologist or any other category of therapist working with extremely high risk kids, it is important not to get overly inquisitive in some aspects of people's lives which have included an extensive history of criminal involvement. If you are really good at your job as a therapist with high risk families you will gain a level of trust from people with extreme needs. This will require from time to time that you remind them you are their therapist and not a close personal friend of the family. I had to do this regularly with Gracie.

Gracie's biggest obstacles were her serious health issues which often times made caring for her children very difficult. However, she always managed to get by and never neglected them. I spent a great deal of time occasionally referring her to agencies which would provide her with temporary financial assistance, along with food and clothing. Anytime there was a campaign within my agency to adopt a needy family, I always nominated them, which meant on two occasions Gracie and her kids had the best Christmas holidays they ever had. Gracie was estranged from her immediate family, so there was no assistance available to her from relatives. This was likely her fault given the kind of life I suspect she had lived in the past.

Because Gracie was so respected and protected within the gang culture, she often had assistance from them. By knowing Gracie and her family she helped me gain a tremendous amount of respect from all of the gangs in the area, with her assuring them I was only there to help their children make it in life. Many of my referrals came indirectly from her and I always appreciated her support without feeling obligated to her for it, and she clearly knew this. Her two oldest sons eventually joined a local gang in spite of my efforts to prevent this. Law enforcement officials had their eye on this family constantly to the point of harassing them from time to time. On numerous occasions I defended Gracie's two older boys to law enforcement, especially on occasions when I overheard their derogatory comments made in my presence without any awareness of my professional association with this family. Both of these boys ended up deep in the juvenile justice system, but I never gave up on trying to get through to them at any opportunity I had. This family knew I cared and they were the only people I have ever served when on a very limited number of occasions I spent money on food for them myself when they were truly desperate and couldn't find other assistance in the community.

One of my rather frequent interactions with Gracie and her kids took the form of home visits. I would go into their home and take on somewhat of a father role with the kids by admonishing them for not helping their mother out with simple things like keeping the house and themselves clean. I never felt uncomfortable in their home and always made sure my office staff knew I was going to visit them, always giving an estimated time of return. Sometimes I would admonish Gracie for not doing more than she was doing to take care of herself. The really tragic reality about all of this was that, in spite of my efforts to assist this family, things always seemed to get worse again after a period of relative stabilization. The complicating factors in their lives, along with numerous negative influences immediately available to the kids in their community worked against everything I ever tried to do.

Just before I left California Gracie's health had declined to the point where she was no longer able to care for her four younger children and they were placed in foster care. Because they were placed in foster care due to Gracie's inability to provide the care they needed, Gracie was given the opportunity to visit them when she could and to talk with them by phone. She was devastated and I felt helpless in trying to help at this point, especially since I was basically meeting with her during this time to end our professional association in light of my relocation efforts back to Mobile, Alabama. I believe the younger children may have a better chance in foster care than they would have had with their mom given the realities of her struggles just to take care of herself. I am not sure what she did to push away her extended family members, but no one would even take in her children rather than see them go into foster care. The boys were adjusting well to their new environment and were old enough by this time to understand what was happening to them and why. The oldest of the six boys was there with Gracie and the next oldest was soon to be released from detention. I can only hope her oldest sons were able to pull things together to give their mom the help she so desperately needed at this point in her life.

With this case I had to fight the feeling of having somehow failed this family. I worked very hard to keep the professional limits and boundaries from getting blurred. This is something I learned very quickly when working with this population. There is only so much I can and am willing to do for my clients and to go beyond those realistic limits would be wrong for them and for myself, and in addition to being unethical. My heart breaks at times because of the work I do which results in exposure to almost unimaginable realities many people face on a daily basis. I have never been afraid to try or afraid to learn by admitting I don't always have the answers. Unfortunately, not everyone can be helped to the extent I would like to accomplish. But I have learned over the years to never assume I haven't made a difference by at least trying. There is no way Gracie or any of her six sons will ever forget my interactions with them. Because of this I trust my efforts will someday pay off for these boys and the kids they will likely have someday. At least this is my hope. I turned their case over to another therapist and have not followed up on Gracie since. It was best for me to just live things as they were and wish all of them the best. Sometimes that is all you can do. What a tremendous learning experience this was for me. I value every experience I have ever had both personally and professional, as each has made me a more capable and stronger person and psychologist.

Let me say a little bit more about the risks involved when working with especially high-risk, troubled kids. Professionals within all fields have the legal obligation to report child abuse/neglect, and any threats from someone to hurt or kill themselves or others. While in most situations this is not that difficult or complicated, with kids involved in rather serious criminal activity such reporting can pose a real threat to you personally. Over the years I have learned to clearly and rather frequently repeat the limits on confidentiality. On numerous occasions I have actually stopped a kid from telling me about something harmful they intended to do to others within a criminal context. It is important to learn to watch for this especially if you have been able to establish a very trusting association with your clients. Joining with a kid requires a frequent review of the limits and boundaries of your professional relationship with them. It would actually be unfair for us to unintentionally set them up to disclose information which could get them or us injured or even killed. When this comes up I quickly stop a kid from telling me anything I would have to report. From that point I then tell them I am going to address what I think they may have been alluding to in a way of trying to talk them out of any sort of illegal activity. While this may be a bit controversial I am not willing to put my life on the line to report a possible street crime which will likely occur anyway. Not only would the planned act be carried out, retaliation against the professional and the kid would most definitely be carried out as well. You will need to learn very early in your career to avoid exposure to this kind of risk.

Another interesting factor each of us should be aware of is related to the safety of others outside of the professional relationship you have established with your client or student. If you are really good at joining with troubled kids they are likely to reveal some details of criminal incidents they encounter. On two occasions I was listening to two different clients talk about retaliation from one gang to another. While the details were vague, they gave me enough information to figure out who the intended target(s) were in both cases along with which gang was going to carry out the retaliation. Because I had gained such a high level of respect and trust within all of the gangs in the area of Riverside County known as the Coachella Valley, I decided to take a risk and go to kids in the retaliatory gang I knew could stop this from happening. In both cases the kids giving me the very limited details were the intended victims. Understand this was my own personal choice and I am not suggesting you follow my exact example, but I had to do something to try and save the lives of my clients. Believe me my supervisor nearly had a heart attack after I told him what I had done in both of these cases. He was surprised to find he actually agreed with this being the only way to likely resolve this situation without putting my own life in very real danger and still save the lives of the intended targets.

After giving all of this a great deal of thought over no more than a 48 hour period I went to the kids in the rival gangs who I knew I could talk with openly. These kids were also my clients and knew me well and respected the work I did to try and help them. I approached the rival gang kids with the same vagueness relative to details I had been given. I assured them no one had ratted them out, reminding my clients in the rival gang of how I work with them and of the level of trust they also had with me. I stressed how important the life of each of my kids is to me and essentially pleaded with them not to kill one of my kids. Remember, I stopped the conversation with the intended victims before they put me in a position of having to report anything to authorities. Even though I pieced things together, I had no specific names of shooters and no specific dates or timeframes. In both cases the kids I approached and pleaded with to spare the lives of my kids honored my request and no one on either side got hurt or killed. Because of the way I handled these situations on both sides no one ever knew specifically who I thought the intended victims were, but readily admitted they knew what I was referring to. Furthermore, I never told the intended victims what I had done because I didn't want any of this discussed on the streets, even for the sake of the kids I approached and made my appeals to save the lives of my other kids.

Let me assure you this was the only way to handle this situation without jeopardizing my own life and the lives of the intended victims. If I had obtained enough information to put me in a position of being obligated to report these incidents to the authorities, the number of deaths likely would have included my own. If I had allowed this to continue to the point of having no choice but to report, then the deaths of the intended victims would have been assured. My own conscience would not have allowed me to do nothing, even though I would have been in no danger if I had simply left things alone. However, there is no doubt in my mind my actions saved the lives of the intended victims and gave me more credibility within the gang culture than I had prior to my interventions. Two of the kids I approached in one rival gang told me "Doc, you've got balls, and we've got your back."

Even though all of this goes against everything which is considered to be usual and customary, the decisions I made in both of these situations were the most realistic and ethical actions to take under the circumstances.

I could not have lived with myself if I had allowed the concerns about my own safety to lead to the deaths of two kids I could have saved. My decisions in both instances were very well thought out and were calculated risks I was willing to take. In my early years of training I could never have foreseen these kinds of double bind situations down the road. My boss never asked me to promise him I would not do this again. I was very happy he understood why I did what I did in these situations, and I didn't tell my supervisor any of this until after the second intervention. As far as I know my supervisor never told anyone else in the organization I had made these choices and had taken these actions. The only reason I told him then was to request that he look for me if I ever failed to show up for work without reporting in to indicate I would be absent. He agreed. Several times during Law and Ethics workshops I shared enough of the details of my stories to let others know in many cases things are not as black and white as we want them to be. Each time the instructors of these workshops agreed that, while my actions were unconventional, they were the best choices to have made given the realities of the situations.

When working with troubled kids in general I believe it is necessary to be somewhat unconventional in our approaches toward them. I would never advocate or support anything illegal or unethical, but I am willing to meet them at their level of understanding and reality if that is what it takes to reach them. Like I said I am not offended by language as long as it is not being used toward me. The manner of dress and appearance of kids in general is not a big deal when my main goal is to get to know them for who they are in order to more clearly figure out how that relates to who they are meant to become. At the same time, I try to help kids understand what is necessary and appropriate dress and language within specific contexts and environments, especially relative to the workplace and appearances in courts before judges.

I hope to establish the same levels of trust and respect with the kids and the communities in the area where I now live and work in Mobile, Alabama. However, the black gangs in Mobile are much more dangerous and ruthless that the Hispanic gangs I served in California. I never felt really nervous about my work with gang kids until I moved back to Mobile.

Now I am much more cautious and to some extent less directly involved. This reality may be the result of the fact gangs have become much more violent on a national level in recent years then they were when I still live in California. I attribute much of the rise in youth violence to the extreme abuses of power and authority sanctioned under the US Patriot since 9/11. However, my goals still include the desire to teach others in this area and even around this country to understand kids the way I do. Kids where I live now do not generally refer to themselves as gang members. Rather they refer to their territories as "hoods", and to themselves as thugs. Regardless of the terminology used this is still the mentality associated with gang involvement visible in virtually every large city in this country. No matter what terms are used to describe or designate their perspectives, these are still kids who deserve the opportunity to look at things differently and realistically. Therefore, it is still of the utmost importance for adults in all professions associated with working to assist troubled kids to always see these kids first and foremost as kids!

It is extremely important not to use labels which define their existences as though their existences accurately reveal identities of the kids involved. Existences for troubled kids only reflect the realities the kids within these existences must deal with and face. These are kids who do bad things, but are not bad kids. These are kids who face hopeless odds, but are not hopeless kids or lost causes. These are kids who have problems, but are not problem kids. The labels we use to describe and categorize kids always reflect our own biases and ignorance. The only way to become knowledgeable is to admit we do not understand, and then seek to understand rather than judge and label. And the only way to understand is to look beyond what kids do and see them for who they are really meant to be. To do anything less is to be just another problem rather than part of the solution.

10

Interview Techniques and
First impressions

This chapter is about your very first contact with a new client or student. While most of the content within this chapter will focus on an initial interview within a clinical setting, professionals within other settings and contexts could adapt this model to their specific purposes. In reality therapists and social workers within clinical settings are not viewed, and should not be viewed by anyone as authority figures. Therefore, we likely have more freedom to be relaxed with kids than other professionals can risk. First of all the depth of information needed during a clinical interview is much more intensive than would even be appropriate in a less formal and less focused context such as a school. However, the need for the interviewer to be real and genuine is essential if any progress is to be made relative to getting to really know who the individual is beyond such external factors as their behaviors and appearance. The content of this chapter is focused on working with troubled, high-risk kids *only*, and will attempt to help you understand what I mean by the level of comfort and rapport needed to work effectively with this population. In other words allow them to be themselves with cuss words, slang and graphic details of their real life situations, as long as they are simply trying to open up and communicate with you as needed. You will know the difference between kids trying to comfortably communicate as compared to deliberately trying to shock and/or offend you. Their desire to shock or offend will likely occur if we mishandle of our initial approach and our attempts to connect and begin to join with these kids in a professional manner. The outcome of our initial contact with any high-risk kid depends solely on our level of training, compassion, knowledge, and caring; and based solely in our abilities to convey all of this immediately.

In most settings the single most important factor to know relative to what a new client is thinking about you or expecting from you as the adult is that this experience will not be favorable. The chances are you will be viewed as just another "asshole" in a long line of previous "assholes" who have tried through stereotypical fear tactics and deception to impose unwanted controls on the kid simply for the sake of control. In a clinical setting there will likely be the additional stigma that you as the therapist will think the kid is "mental". The kid will likely be resistant to interacting and will even be suspicious and apprehensive about what may be about to happen. The most critical step at this point is to handle this with the knowledge and desire that this interaction is going to benefit this kid in ways he or she could never even imagine. This can only be accomplished if you as the adult in this situation are very passionate and sincere about your work with this population, and if you have the ability to put the kid at ease rather quickly. Any missteps at this point will jeopardize all future interactions.

As I have stated before kids today are too sophisticated to be fooled by any adults who are nothing more than arrogant, ignorant, insincere, control freaks. Kids may comply with demands, but only out of a sense that a power struggle would be pointless, representing a form of surrender rather than a willingness to learn and grow from the interaction. Let's face it, most adults can 'win' in any professional situation if winning is the only goal. Competition between adults and kids is a lose/lose exchange. Even if the adult wins what have they really won – nothing more than the defeat of the kid they were supposedly trying to reach. The old "I'll show you who's boss" routine doesn't work with today's adolescents. Keep in mind that many kids are not mature enough to resist the stubborn stance of "you can't make me." Kids will often times deliberately fail to succeed if they feel like succeeding is equivalent to kissing the ass of some adult. This is the reason that helping a kid understand what is in their own best interest is the best and only approach which works, especially with troubled kids. The only way an adult can know what is in a kid's best interest is to first of all succeed in joining with the kid and being able and willing to try and see the world through the eyes of each individual kid. Nothing short of this attempt at building a strong positive rapport and a high level of trust will facilitate an alliance with the kids who often need the most assistance and guidance. Each kid must see that you are real and can deal with them and the very real complicating factors they face on a daily basis. It is imperative that they see your compassion and earnest desire to understand before you can assist. None of this can be faked without the adult looking like a insincere fool in the eyes of any kid.

As you enter the waiting area where your client will likely be sitting with family members, always approach the kid first by extending your hand to him or her and introducing yourself by name. A simple, "You must be (kid's name). I'm Dr. Roberts and it is a pleasure to meet you." The parent(s) will be a little taken aback in some instances that you did not acknowledge them first, but ignore this. After all the case you are about to open will be in the name of the kid and not in the name of his parent(s) or guardian(s). In reality most of the experiences involving kids and adults, adults generally acknowledge each other before they acknowledge the kid who actually will be their main focus. After the initial introduction I always tell the adults present that I will be working alone with their daughter or son for the first session, assuring them I will give them a little time if possible or at least bring them in initially at their next appointment. I handle the first contact with virtually every kid this way unless they are under the age of six. Adolescents will be able to hang in with you for the entire first session, whereas younger kids will only be able to take so much before you will need to get the adults to join the session. This is the only way to put kids at ease and give them the freedom to openly express themselves and tell you why they think they are in your office. If you inform the adults that this is your standard and consistent approach with every client they will usually understand. I handle this quickly enough that they don't have the opportunity to object before the kid is already in my office and they are left sitting in the waiting area.

For the kid to trust you fully they must be present at every meeting with adults unless it is clearly in their best interest not to be there. Even then it is important to make them fully aware of the nature of such a meeting both before and after the meeting occurs. There has *never* been a time that I didn't end my initial intake interview with the kid having a completely different and more positive demeanor. This is so obvious to the family members or guardians that in some cases they are actually speechless. I bring the adults in with the kid after I have completed my extensive interview and explain to them how I work with my clients. If necessary I also ask for clarification on some historical details relative to family and medical issues. Of utmost importance is for adults to understand and accept that I am not there to be their detective and that I expect them to respect the privacy of what I discuss with their daughter or son. I remind them that kids in most cases are not generally completely honest with those who are responsible for their well-being. I explain that the only way for me to work successfully with their child is for them to trust me and my work so the kid will have at least one person in their life with which they can discuss anything. Furthermore, I tell the adults that I will make sure their kid knows about every contact I have with them between sessions so the kid will know I am not going to side with the adults against the kid at any time. The only information provided to me by adults which I withhold from my client is information which would be in some way damaging to the kid. The best examples would be: the child being the result of a rape, or of a parent's very personal history of abuse and victimization.

My primary caseload includes transitional age, troubled kids, ages 15 and up. Kids from other age groups are welcomed, but I find this group of troubled kids to be the most reachable. This really depends on how out of control their lives are relative to problematic behaviors and other types of bad choices. Kids under the age of 15 are less mature cognitively than older adolescents and are more prone to give into peer influence and follow their impulses to fit in and prove something to others. From the age of 15 and up kids are better able to see that they are growing up whether they want to or not. This gives me a greater chance of helping them understand their need to make better choices based in what is in their own best interest given the reality they are fast approaching adulthood. Most kids will understand that the kinds of accomplishments they need to make during their teenage years are much more difficult to achieve as they take on adult roles and responsibilities. Furthermore, this age group generally represents those adolescents every other program has failed to reach; so, for them this may be their last chance to redirect their lives through guidance from at least one caring adult. It is, therefore, critical that professionals at all levels not screw up this opportunity by approaching these kids inappropriately and ineffectively. Plus, kids in this age group talk about wanting to leave home by the time they are 18. This gives me the opportunity to help kids set goals which would make this option manageable if that actually becomes their choice at 18. Parents are able to see that using this as a goal will only help insure their kid's progress prior to reaching that age. Most kids do not actually choose to leave home at 18 once that day arrives. However, knowing the option will be a viable plan if they make the right preparations will help them see why certain changes are in their best interest.

In many cases after the first session parents are able to see significant changes in the way their daughter or son is behaving and thinking, and they welcome the opportunity for me to work alone with their child as much as possible. Family members are always welcomed in my office, but the majority of my time and focus must be on my client. Children under the age of 12 or 13 are more likely to be dealing primarily with family issues needing to be resolved. However, by the time a kid reaches the age of 15 or higher, the focus must be on them and their future. In reality if interventions are not started before they reach 15 then the chance of impacting the family dynamics are unlikely anyway. At this point, especially with troubled kids, the focus must be on helping them identify and cope with whatever realities they have experienced in the past so than can move forward in spite of these potential obstacles. Many of the adults in the lives of troubled kids are not interested in making changes for themselves, but expect someone to fix their child for them. Fixing a child is not the issue. Redirecting and supporting a child and the way they use their energy, abilities, and thought processes are the goals. Sometimes with troubled kids this is less likely to occur if the family members are directly involved in their treatment. So do not penalize a kid by refusing to work with them if the family does not want to be involved. In many cases this actually works out more favorably for your client. Always follow the laws of your state regarding parental consent. However, a signature is all you need and participation of adults should not be required as the only way you will agree to work with the kid!

Keep in mind that in many instances by the time a kid reaches your office for therapy they have attended any number of meetings regarding their behaviors and/or lack of progress academically. In these kinds of meetings the kid is usually in the room with several adults who sit around and talk about the kid as though he or she was not even present. In order to get my clients to understand and trust that I will never disregard their worth or input I purposefully exclude the adults in their lives from our initial session. This simple change in the process of getting to know a kid through their own eyes is much more valuable than having a room full of adults who often only express their biases against the kid. In reality you will find that adults have a tendency to play the victim role and exaggerate or outright lie about their issues and concerns of a kid. Parents and teachers are really bad about this and I always confront people regarding the parts they play in making things worse rather than finding effective solutions for the kid. Two powerful questions directed at adults are: "what have *you* done to further complicate the life of this kid?"; and "what have you done for this kid that has *helped* rather than made things worse?" I firmly believe in holding adults accountable for the damage they have done regardless of whether or not it was done intentionally.

Let me actually take you through one of the most interesting interviews I have ever conducted. This particular intake session truly represents everything I have shared with you so far in this chapter. I will explain the information I am trying to obtain on a section-by-section basis and will then actually set up a narrative of the interaction. Please bear with me as I think you will find this informative and interesting. Many of the details, including the kid's name, will be changed, but everything else I share will accurately represent the tone of the entire session which lasted about two hours. Generally at least 90 minutes is needed.

The Interview

I enter the waiting area, looking around for the kid I believe most likely to be my new client. It is rather easy since, at this point in my career, I am the only therapist in the building who works with the truly high risk, troubled kids. I spot my target and walk up to him with my hand out and say, "You must be David Ortiz." He remained seated and shook my hand as I told him, "I'm Dr. Roberts and I'm going to be your therapist." I looked to the woman sitting to David's left and asked her if she was with David. As I shook her hand and again said "I'm Dr. Roberts and I'm going to see your son alone for the first session as I do with all of my kids", she introduced herself as his mother. " When we are done I'll bring him out to you and then you can come into my office with him if we have enough time. If not I'll be glad to meet with you at the beginning of his next appointment with me." With that David got up and I walked with him back to my office.

As we approached the lobby door I explained that I would have to use my key. I told David, "Don't worry. You can get out. You just can't get in without someone opening the door for you." Once through the door I explained, "This is a children's service unit so you'll have to ignore all of the pictures (obviously for younger kids) on the wall. My office is just down this hallway and is the second door on your left." As we enter my office I tell David, "Please sit in the chair by my desk for this session only. I have to do a lot of writing and it's just easier if I can ask questions and write down information without having to turn around all the time. The next time you come you can sit wherever you like."

David sat in the chair I had indicated and immediately slouched down with his right leg crossed over his left at his knee, his right elbow and right knee resting on the edge of my desk, his ass nearly hanging off the front edge of the chair, and his head back against the wall. David was wearing a blue bandana on his head, and was dressed in hardcore California street-style gang attire, which at that time mimicked the way prisoners dress inside the penitentiaries – khaki pants and shirt, with the shirt buttoned only at the very top; very baggy pants, with a "wife beater" style undershirt exposed by his open top shirt. His boxers were visible through his undershirt and his pants were worn very low beneath his waist. Last, but not least, David was wearing the signature Nikes and black framed sunglasses with very dark lenses associated with the standard gang uniform of the time. His body language clearly expressed a "fuck you" kind of attitude, with his posture in the chair telling me he was bored and was not going to be part of this exchange. I ignored all of this and proceeded with my introduction as to the manner in which I work with all kids.

"David, the most important thing I want you to know is that everything in this room is confidential and I can assure you I will never betray that unless you tell me you are being abused, or have the intentions to hurt or kill yourself or someone else. When you are in this room I don't care how you talk – shit, fuck, damn, piss, or hell are all okay as long as you're not using those words against me. Believe me I will never give you a reason to do that. The only thing that matters to me in here is that you talk to me in any manner that makes you feel comfortable. I will never lie to you about anything and my only goal today is to treat you differently than you have ever been treated by any other adult so I can simply get to know you better. Do you have any questions so far?"

"Nope", he replied with a slight and curious smile on his face.

"Then let's get started. Today I need to ask you a lot of questions and I will be writing down a shortened version of what you tell me. I have no secrets and nothing to hide here, and I'm not here to trick or deceive you in anyway. If at any time you want to know what I'm writing down I will show it to you and let you read it, or I'll read it for you. If I ask you a question about something you have done in the past, let me know if this is or is not on any of your records at school or with the courts. If it is not known to anyone else then I will not write it down. Even though it has never happened to one of my clients, your records from this office could be subpoenaed, especially if you go out of here and blow up a McDonald's or shoot kids in a playground or school yard. Then people are going to want to see what I missed and will look in my records to try and find it. Because this could happen I will never write down anything that could cause you more problems that you have caused for yourself by that point. The *last* thing I want to do is to create more problems for you. Anything you tell me that is not known to others will be written down in a way which will only remind me that you appear to have an extensive history of criminal activity and refused to give me the details. I will never bullshit you about anything! Do you have any questions about any of this?"

"Nope", He says and then asks, "Fuck dog, are you for real?"

I laughed and said, "Yep!"

With this I knew I had gotten through to him. I had not acknowledged any of David's mannerisms or the way he was dressed. I had treated him with respect and like a human being, rather than like the thug he wanted me to see. The kid within him came out rather quickly by me being real with him and by assuring David that I was there to get to know him, to help him as much as possible, and to defend and protect him if that became necessary, and if it would be appropriate for me to do so. He also knew that I was not there to judge or misjudge him, or to mistreat or deceive him in any way. This kind of approach is the only approach that works and works consistently with troubled kids.

As I sit shuffling my papers, trying to get organized and ready to begin my intake interview, I told David, "I have only one request."

"What's that?", he asked.

I replied, "I need you to take off your sunglasses."

Obviously offended, David asked, "What for? Do you think I'm fucking stoned or something?"

"No", I responded, "I just want to be able to look into your eyes while we are talking."

With that David smiled, almost trying not to laugh, and sat up in his chair. He took off his sunglasses, folded them carefully, and placed them on my desk. In the process he had uncrossed his legs and his entire demeanor changed. I had never witnessed such an immediate and complete transformation in my entire life, and couldn't help but laugh and ask, "Who the fuck are you now?"

David asked, "What the fuck are you laughing at?"

"Not at you," I assured him. "You're just not the same kid now who walked into my office 15 minutes ago. You know, those glasses are going to get you killed someday."

With that clarification David started laughing. He could clearly see how the simple act of removing his sunglasses had allowed him to literally remove that hardcore exterior image he felt he needed to portray in order to protect himself from me and my attempts to invade his privacy. I asked him, "Are you ready to get this interview over with?"

David laughed and said, "It's okay, Doc."

"I know your name is David Ortiz and that you are fifteen years old. Are you still in school?"

"Yep", he replied, adding, "but I get into a lot of trouble at school and they don't want me there."

"What grade are you in and what school do you attend?" I asked.

"I'm in the ninth grade and attend (XYZ) High School."

"Did you fail a grade?"

"Yep, I got held back in the third grade because I was having a lot of trouble with reading."

"Are you in special ed?" I asked.

"Yep, and I hate school!", he added.

Do you feel like you're getting the help you need in school, or do you feel like they go out of their way to harass you?"

"They fuck with me all the time" David replied. "Every time I turn around they're searching me for drugs or weapons, or I'm being sent to the office for something I didn't even do!"

"Do you dress like this at school?" I asked while surveying his attire.

"Yep.", he answered.

"Then you understand you are just asking for trouble aren't you?"

"Yeah, but it isn't fair", he reasoned.

"Fair or not, it's a reality that isn't going to change. I'm not suggesting you do anything to change the way you dress for school.

I'm just asking you to be aware that you will always be treated with disrespect as long as they see you kind of flipping them off by the way you dress. When we meet I'll never tell you what you have to do. I'll just try to give you some things to think about so you can decide what behaviors and choices are in your best interest. Let's move on. Tell me what gang you're in."

"Why do you want to know that?" he asked.

"Well it's rather obvious that you're in a gang. Does probation have a record on your suspected gang involvement which includes the name of your gang?"

"Yeah."

"Then just tell me which gang so I'll know as well. Because they already have it on record I'll write it down in my notes so I won't need to ask you again in the future. Like I said earlier, if there is no record anywhere of any part of your life you want kept secret, just tell me and I *will not* write down what you say. Remember, too, I'll show you my records today or at any point in the future if you want to check to see if I have lied to you about anything."

"No, I believe you Doc. My gang is Eastside Desert Locos," he announced proudly while throwing up his gang sign. (This gang did not exist.)

From there I asked several questions about his history of gang involvement, including when he got jumped in. He gave me the details of how bad the initiation was, announcing with pride that, "Those fuckers didn't even knock me down once!"

"What do they call you in the gang?", I asked.

"What the fuck you wanna know that for?", he asked defensively.

"Just to see if you trust me. I promise I'll never write it down or tell it to anyone else. Plus it will give me a chance to see if I have ever heard of you from other kids."

With that explanation he proudly told me, "They call me Little Bro."

"I have heard of you from some of the other kids I work with. Do you know Little Peeps, and Cyclone?"

"They're in my gang. How do you know them?"

"They were referred to me from probation just like you were. Ask them about me and they'll tell you I'm for real", I explained.

I use this approach frequently with this population *only*. The longer I work within any certain area, the more kids I get to meet. This is happening in Mobile with the kids I am seeing here as well. Eventually all of the kids on the streets either will have met me or at least will know about me by word-of-mouth. I never give out personal information of the other kids and always assure the kid in front of me at the time that I won't do that to him either. I am not concerned about the confidentiality of this as much as I am concerned with trying to put these kids at ease relative to the work I do with them and their friends. In reality all of the kids will likely see me at some point with other kids either in a school setting or when they get locked up. I never do this with other populations of kids.

"Without going into any details just tell me if you have any history of criminal activity related to violence and weapons. Also let me know if there is a record of any of these actions." I continued.

"Yeah Doc, I have been charged with assault with a deadly weapon, and there are other things I have done that I don't want to tell you about now", he answered.

"Do you have any other charges such as burglary or anything related to drugs and alcohol?"

"Yeah, I got arrested for a beer run and once for possession of marijuana."

Rather than dwell on the gang issues and criminal activity I decided to move on for now. These are factors I will continuously monitor throughout the entire time I will work with this kid and other kids. It is important to at least get a glimpse of what their criminal history may include, without appearing to be too nosey at this point. Don't over go overboard during the first interview. The level of rapport and trust needed to explore these kinds of issues in more detail will develop more fully over time. It is always important not to write down details of activities which could cause problems for a kid later on if any kid's records are requested by his parents or, are ever subpoenaed for court.

"Tell me what kinds of drugs you have tried, and give me the list of drugs you use regularly. It will be okay to write this information down since you would have to get caught using any substances for you to be charged with a crime. But if you don't want me to write down anything other than what is known by your family or by probation I won't do that. Just tell me."

"Fuck Doc, I've tried a lot of things, but the only ones people know about are alcohol and marijuana. I drink a lot on weekends and smoke weed every day. I sometimes use meth and have tried cocaine, but you can't write those down. I am afraid of hard drugs because I see what they do to people around me."

"I don't mean to offend you by asking, but are you being honest with me? The only reason I'm asking is so I can understand how important drugs are as a part of your life. I'm not here to judge you or to even try to control you. You can clearly do whatever you want to do, but it is my job to at least warn you about the dangers and health risks of these kinds of choices."

"That's cool doc, but I am being honest."

"I appreciate that and I believe you David."

"Do you ever hear things or see things that other people don't see?"

"What do you think I'm fucking mental or something?"

"No David, I just have to ask. You'd be surprised to know that sometimes the answer to that question is 'yes'. It's just part of what I need to know about you. I don't think you're mental and I'm glad that doesn't happen to you. If it did we would need to deal with it though."

"Do you ever get really depressed about things in your life?"

"Sometimes I get down about my friends who have been killed, but when I drink and smoke weed it goes away. I never think about killing myself."

"Drinking and smoking weed are not going to make your feelings go away permanently. Hopefully you will let me work with you on the deaths of your friends so I can help you learn how to deal with their deaths in ways that will help you and maybe even protect you."

"We'll see Doc."

"Did you at any time in the past think about killing yourself?"

"I used to before my father got arrested."

"Tell me a little about that."

"He always drank a lot and would beat up my mom. I tried to stop him and then he would beat up on me. My mom always tried to protect me, but things only got worse."

"What was your dad charged with?"

"Selling drugs. He's going to be locked up for a long time. I haven't seen him since I was 10. I'm glad the son of a bitch is gone!"

"It sounds like you still have a lot of anger toward him. Do you use that anger on the streets?"

"Sometimes. I really hate it when guys beat up on bitches, so I always kick their asses when I see this happen! I would never hit a girl."

"But you call them bitches. We need to work on the way you see females in your life."

"Whatever, Doc."

By this point in the interview you can see that I have accomplished a number of things with David and have gained his trust and respect. These two components will always be very fragile with this population so you must work consistently to never let your clients down. As you can see I know a lot about David's home/family context and about his experiences within his community and school contexts as well. David has willingly shared a great deal of information with me about his criminal history and his use of various substances. The single most important accomplishment occurred when David removed his sunglasses and was able to clearly see the two very distinct sides of his personality. None of this would have been possible if I had approached David any differently than the way I did. In later years of running into him as he got older the two things he remembered most were the realization associated with the sunglasses, and the fact I treated him differently than any other adult previously involved in his life. David will carry these experiences with him for the rest of his life.

During this first part of the interview I now have an idea of David's emotional state and know that he doesn't appear to have any desire to commit suicide, and has no psychotic symptoms. I can tell from his ability to express himself that he is rather intelligent, a characteristic that I suspect very few people ever recognize in him. The only way other people would be able to see David as I was able to see him would be by using the exact same kind of approach I used. Because most adults would have focused exclusively on David's obvious outward appearance and behaviors David would not be able to let down his guard and allow people to see his soul. By using this approach with kids I am able to get a very clear picture of their intelligence, talents and potential. I am also able to see who they really are and who they are meant to become, even if these potentialities never fully take hold. By the time I finished working with David even at the end of our first session, David had a different perception of himself than he had likely ever had. With my awareness of his potential and his intellect I asked the next question intended to challenge his self-perception and at the same time introduce another perspective.

"Tell me David, how smart are you?"

"Not very. I can't do math and I still have trouble reading."

"David, I didn't ask you about your school performance, I asked you about how smart you are."

"What's the difference?", he asked.

"Your lack of progress in school clearly has nothing to do with your level of intelligence. You have been actively involved in every part of this interview so far and have clearly understood everything I asked. You also showed me that you put a lot of thought into figuring out things in your life, like the way your dad's drinking and violence affected your life."

"I never thought about it that way. I always thought that because I am in special ed that I must be kinda dumb.", he said, expressing both surprise and relief by the tone of his voice.

"David, I would imagine that you are probably lucky to be alive, Right?"

"Yeah."

"This tells me that you obviously have the ability to make plans and carry them out in ways that have allowed you to survive many things in your life, right?"

"Yeah!"

"I would also imagine that you have probably participated in activities that required you to do a lot of planning related to business deals you have made, right?"

"Yeah. How the fuck do you know that Doc?"

"I've been working with kids who have lives and problems similar to yours since 1992. I even worked and trained in East LA and upper South Central LA before I moved to the desert. In LA I worked with kids from 18th Street, White Fence, Sangra, Playboys, Avenues, Lomas, Hazard, Red Door, Red Dragon, and Asian Boys. The only difference between you and them is that you live outside of LA.", I explained.

"Whoa, Doc. I didn't know you have worked with all of those gangs.", he said sounding impressed.

I continued, "All kids involved in street crimes generally have good planning skills and a great deal of business experience. I'm sure you know about marketing and advertising, getting and keeping new customers, competing for sales, setting competitive prices, buying and selling, warehousing and storing, and profits, right?"

"Yeah, Doc, I do!" he said laughing in disbelief.

"Then you have valuable skills you could someday use in ways that won't get you killed or locked up, huh?"

"Yeah Doc, but you make a lot more money my way than by being legit."

"Yeah David, but making money illegally always comes with a price doesn't it?"

"Yeah Doc, it does."

"Then all I want you to do is to at least think about what I have said and to be aware that you are much smarter than you have ever been able to see before today."

Kids will always be amazed when you tell them how useful their skills are even though they were obtained from illegal activities in which they are involved in the streets. It is very important to not let them think you are validating their activities as valuable. Rather, that you are simply pointing out how they can turn the negative misuse of the skills and energy into positive endeavors if they would choose to do so in the future. This rather simple reality puts a different twist on their self-perspective relative to their levels of intelligence, talents, and potential. It gives them a chance to also understand that not all of their time has been wasted, even though they put everything on the line every time they engage in illegal activities. Revealing other possible results of their activities will also give them some sense of hope relative to their potential to become someone other than who they have become so far. This approach also gives them the opportunity to understand that you are not asking them to change into someone new. You are just asking them to work differently with who they already are, relative to the true nature of their soul and their potential for good in the future. Always work with kids in this population with the notion of "what goes around comes around". This is their slogan for the concept of Karma which is found within all spiritual teachings. By pointing this concept out as Karma you can also give them a glimpse at how they already use basic spiritual concepts in their lives. Of course with troubled kids this phrase is more related to the idea that "if you kick my ass I'm going to kick yours." They can be given the opportunity to understand that this concept has far greater application, including the fact that when you put good things out there good things will come back to you as well.

The rest of the interview revealed that David had an older half-brother and two younger sisters. It is important to ask kids to tell you who lives with them in their home. Always start by listing the adults living in the home/family context and find out their ages and the specific relationships they represent, such as parents, mom/boyfriend, dad/girlfriend, step parents. Always ask if adults are married, divorced or never married. Don't be shocked or even react if a kid tells you they have a homosexual mom or dad who has a same-sex partner living in the home. You will need to ask how the dynamics of all of these relationships impact the kid sitting in front of you. Also ask if the parental relationships work or if they are conflicted and involve a lot of arguing or even domestic violence which can go both ways between partners. Don't forget to ask if mom beats up her partner. This is more common than you might imagine. Be sure to discuss the details of any immediate family members who have died.

When asking for the list of siblings, always get the ages of each sibling and get their last names. Different last names will give you an indication of how many different fathers are involved and how many half siblings there are. Always ask about relationships between siblings and get a clear indication of who is responsible for the care of siblings – older siblings, or the parent(s) or guardian(s). Ask about siblings who live away from your client's home/family context. Find out if they have simply grown up and left home or if the parents have children with other parents besides the biological parents of your client. Always get names and ages. Believe me this is all important in getting a clear picture of your client's family constellation, which may at times involve distant galaxies as well. Getting this kind of detailed information will give you clues about other questions to ask. Write all of it down. If it is really complicated show the diagram to your client and point out how the family dynamics really complicate their life in ways that are beyond their control. Kids must be allowed to see the numbers of complicating factors present in their lives. This will give them the chance to see and understand that their problems are more about where they have come from and what they have been through, and much less about who they really are and are meant to become. At the Mercy of Externals; Righting Wrongs and Protecting Kids, 2nd Edition, was a title chosen very carefully for my first book relative to the realities of kids within this population of high risk, troubled kids.

After exploring all of the family members and respective relationships you only need to find out more about your client's medical history, including what they know about their mom's pregnancy and delivery. It is important to learn if mom drank or used during her pregnancy and if there were any complications. Obviously some of this will need to be clarified with the mom if that is possible. Included in this category is the family history of illnesses and hospitalizations to include mental and emotional disorders as well. You may have to be creative in obtaining this information by asking questions such as: "was any member of your family ever thought of as being strange or weird?" This will get some interesting responses.

The last topics to be explored will be specific educational needs and goals, including the kid's take on whether or not they think they will finish high school. This must be explored in detail, with attempts made to encourage educational pursuits in light of the realities associated with failure to make even minimal academic achievements. From there it is important to focus on future plans and goals. One of the biggest problems created by educators today is the lack of efforts they put into helping kids imagine what they want to be when they grow up. You will find that many of the troubled kids you will work with have never even thought about this. Their biggest concern is with simply growing up. They have very little awareness of trying to imagine anything beyond that accomplishment. It will be part of your work with your clients to teach them how to dream and to help them understand the importance of doing so. If a kid suggests something that is highly unlikely given what you know about them or about the odds of anyone achieving that goal, then help them explore some alternatives just in case.

I had the opportunity to work with David for about six months. During that time we made a lot of progress in helping David understand differently many aspects of his life. Unfortunately David didn't finish school. But the last I heard he was alive and I know he never got re-incarcerated within the juvenile justice system. I saw him at his house when he was 19 and it was obvious that he was still deeply involved in his gang activity. He told me he seldom ever used drugs anymore, but still drank on weekends and smoked weed occasionally. He looked really healthy and we laughed about the incident with his sunglasses. I have no way of knowing what has become of David, but I do have the satisfaction of knowing that I made a positive impression on him and on his way of thinking. At least that is something, and hopefully something he will pass down to his children someday.

* *

<u>List of Critical Interview/Assessment Items for Troubled Kids</u>

- Identifying information
- School attended and current grade or grade completed
- Diagnoses

- Referral source(s)
- Current medications and dosages
- Presenting problems
- Assessment for harm to self or other to include suicide, homicide, and all forms of self-injurious behaviors
- Assessment for any form of abuse
- Mental status exam
- List of all family members and people living in the home. Always include ages, first and last names, relationship to child, living or deceased, and marital status. This section should also include lists of parents living outside the home, stepparents/significant others, half and step siblings, and any other relatives or non-family residents living in the home.
- Assessment of family relationship dynamics between all involved
- Child/family history of physical, medical, mental, and/or emotional problems and hospitalizations
- Academic history and related issues
- Social interactions of child
- History of criminal activity of child and parents/others
- History of substance abuse by child and parents/others
- Most traumatic life experience
- Most traumatic event witnessed
- Most offensive act committed
- Sexual activity (if age appropriate)
- Sexual orientation (if age appropriate)
- Knowledge of STD's and pregnancy prevention (if age appropriate)
- Personal changes and improvements client would like to make
- Fears and nightmares
- Sources of anger
- First childhood memory
- Immediate and long-term goals

11

Focus and Funding Needs

For anyone to work effectively with troubled kids it is necessary to be both earnestly interested in working *with* them and genuinely interested *in* them. This must be the focus of every interaction. It is also important to put aside all professional pretense and superiority and truly enjoy the time you spend with each kid, every time you meet. Dress somewhat casually and learn to speak and understand their language. Be familiar with their music and their fads and trends. If a kid uses a phrase with which you are unfamiliar, ask them to explain what it means. There is a big difference between being "cool" and making the mistake of trying to be one of them. At all times you must be the cool, caring adult who is actively seeking to serve every kid to the fullest extent possible relative to your professional role with them. Be the authority figure only when the situation and circumstances demand this stance. Otherwise be professionally relaxed and casual in your efforts to reach out to kids who are starving for positive and supportive adult interactions.

The example of David in the previous chapter was a good example of what is required to reach even the most reluctant of participants. If I had approached David any differently than I did he would never have opened up to me, nor would he have continued working with me. This level of willingness to participate must be established during the first interview if you are to be able to proceed with therapy, counseling, teaching, or mentoring relative to troubled kids. Your effectiveness depends on your ability as an adult to carry the lead in conversation with kids in general. Kids who are not in the "troubled" or "high risk" categories are usually more polite and will tolerate your interactions even if they are perceived as disingenuous. Troubled kids feel absolutely no obligation to tolerate anything given the realities that their lives have been about nothing less than compromise after compromise within every context in order to survive. Never expect a troubled kid to settle for less than they deserve or need. After all, why should they? If, as a professional, you are motivated by any other drive than that of serving and meeting needs, then you should find another professional role involving populations other than troubled kids. It's that simple!

The focus of treatment and other forms of interaction is different when dealing with troubled kids as compared to kids who fall into other categories. Non-troubled kids who present for treatment or some form of assistance are more likely to be dealing exclusively with learning disorders and other types of disorders which are strictly physiologically based. These types of disorders would include Attention Deficit Hyperactivity Disorder, Attention Deficit Disorder, Post Traumatic Stress Disorder, situation specific depression and anxiety, developmental disorders, and symptoms suggesting early onset of more severe mood and/or psychotic disorders. While troubled kids may be dealing with some of these diagnostic categories, they will also have a collection of serious complicating factors coexisting in and dominating their lives as well. They will present with referrals from various agencies and institutions for more extreme behavioral problems which match symptomatology of Conduct Disorder and Oppositional Defiant Disorder as primary diagnoses. Secondary disorders will likely include emotional and mental disorders with the overriding emphasis on the behavioral problems represented by the primary diagnoses of Conduct Disorder and Oppositional Defiant Disorder. Accompanying secondary disorders which are most common for troubled kids include ADHD, Learning Disorders, Major Depression, and Polysubstance Abuse. Even though there may be indications of developing personality disorders, such diagnoses are never made for kids given the fluidity of their emerging personality traits as compared to those of adults.

After my initial interview with David we met on a regular basis and he willingly kept his appointments because he looked forward to our time together. If nothing else David was initially curious about me and the difference he perceived with me compared to other adults in his life. As I got to know him better, it became much easier for me to identify and define who he was meant to be and to nurture that potential in a way that my perceptions could become his perceptions. My insights were of no use to him until they became his insights tailored according to his own need and ability to understand and apply them. And only those insights which were appropriate and accurate were useful to him. Many of the good qualities I saw in David were difficult for him to believe until he began to try them out in different areas of his life. The fact alone that David didn't get any deeper into the juvenile justice system is proof that something clicked within him. He may not have finished high school, but I got his attention as evidenced by his own successful redirection of at least some of his energy. David was proud to know me and openly talked with his friends about me, many of whom I knew professionally as well. What an amazing and humbling impact to have on a kid considered by most to be worthless and unreachable. Failure to accomplish this level of trust and regard with any troubled kid is almost as abusive as anything else that has gone wrong in their lives. The ability to simply keep a kid engaged is a sign of success even if they are reluctant initially to open up. This is why it is critical that adults be able to take the lead in guiding the interactions toward the goal of getting to know the kid. It is the only way for any kid know how it feels for someone to truly take an interest in them and care about them and their realities.

Depending on how complicated a troubled kid's life is the therapy, outreach and support could cover a period of several years. It is not uncommon for troubled kids to get locked up, sent off to placement, or even be on the run for extended periods of time. However, they will eventually resurface and it is important to always look for them and reach out to them on an ongoing basis. They will never tell you to "fuck off" unless you do something which shatters their impression that you truly care about them. ***NEVER LET THIS HAPPEN!*** You may have to accept their desire to terminate their association with you, but make sure this happens on a positive note and with an open ended return and availability policy such as: "Unless something unforeseen happens in my life, I will always be here for you when you need me!" They will never forget this promise and will look for you when the time is right. If you have treated them with the respect they deserve and have successfully demonstrated your ability to care about them, they will eagerly come back to you knowing that you will never see them as a failure. Meet them wherever they are in life and start from there in helping get them back on track or to guide them in an entirely different direction. Your ability to care must never wane, no matter what they do or have done. A certain level of occasional disappointment is appropriate, at the same time knowing they understand your level of frustration with and unspoken disapproval of certain activities and choices. Their connection to you indicated by their return to you reflects their appreciation for the differences between you and them relative to life choices they have made or are making. They don't expect you to bless their misdeeds, but they do expect consistency in your ability to guide and assist them when they are sincerely seeking assistance.

As I mentioned earlier in this text, don't make every meeting a counseling or therapy session – at least not obviously so. Each encounter with a kid should always constitute some form of therapy or counseling since you should always be looking for insight into the kid's experiences and perceptions. However, this can easily be accomplished by simply engaging them in a conversation about the events since the last session or by showing an interest in the time they spend with their friends. Don't be judgmental of their accounts of how they party or pass time with their friends. Use these accounts as opportunities to warn them of danger and to give them some reality checks relative to any misperceptions they may exhibit. Do not be overbearing with these observations either, always remaining conscious of your inability to control the choices they make. Remember that the most you can hope for is an opportunity to offer them some insights into their actions and choices which will give them the desire to change relative to what is in their own best interest. Never deceive yourself about your ability to set limits for them. However, it is appropriate to let them know how much you worry about their safety and to tell them how much you would be impacted by their incarceration, death or serious injury. It is also appropriate to remind them that death can be both literal and figurative – physical death, and death by incarceration for life. By admitting your limitations relative to impacting their lives and choices you keep the responsibility squarely on them. By letting them know how much you care you give them something to think about that will at some point be useful in helping them make better choices. This is especially true when they get locked up and have a lot of time to think.

Keep in mind too that the kids you work with have the ability to help their friends make needed changes in their lives as well. All you need to do is to help them recognize these opportunities and see how helping their friends can be accomplished without making your kids look like "pussies" or "bitches". One of the hardest things kids have to face on the streets is the death of a friend or a family member. By getting them to understand that there will be moments when they can save lives by simply being the one who keeps a level head they will be able to step up and do what's right. When the time is right a simple statement made to their friends could help diffuse a situation which is potentially dangerous and/or life threatening. Such a statement made out in the streets by the kid you serve could be, "Wait a minute. Let's think about this before we do something stupid given the fact we are all fucked up." This is especially helpful in a situation where everyone involved is drinking and/or using, which is often the case. It is easy to get your kid to become aware of how alcohol and drugs cloud everyone's ability to think things through before acting impulsively. There is no doubt in my mind that by sharing these kinds of skills and insights with my kids over the years, countless lives have been saved as a result. In many instances your kid can and will become the catalyst for change on the streets and in other contexts with her or his friends.

If all of us handle things right with the kids in our charge we can have a tremendously far reaching impact on kids within an entire geographical area. This alone is one of the reasons for the importance of seeing every interaction with each kid as being extremely significant, and possibly your last relative to circumstances beyond your control. With this perspective it is possible to increase our efforts to be more appropriate and effective in our contacts with troubled kids. You will be astounded to learn how quickly the word will spread that Mr., Mrs., Miss, Officer, or Dr. so-and-so is really cool and can be trusted if you need someone to talk with about your problems. Think about how quickly the word spreads about anyone who is experienced by kids as being an asshole or a bitch. Either way these labels stick in the minds of kids. The same is true for each of us as adults who hear and think certain things about the adults or kids within our range of experiences. Remember that negative reputations are difficult to change.

If a kid tells you someone in their life is an asshole or a bitch and you know this to be an accurate observation, acknowledge it as appropriately as you can. Then take care to help the kid deal with this reality in a way that will serve their own best interest without giving the so-called asshole or bitch any further opportunities to complicate the kid's life. This has happened many times in my career since in many cases I have known most of the authority figures directly involved in a kid's life and experiences. Many times I have told a kid that "I agree with you. However I am going to trust that you will not tell others that I said so as this could create serious problems for me professionally. Now, what can you do to keep this person from causing you more problems given the reality that they will probably always be the asshole or bitch you think they are?"

Even when I do not know firsthand that their observation is accurate, I accept it as their reality and encourage them to prove the adult wrong by doing what is in the kid's own best interest. Clearly at times the behaviors of kids can make it difficult for others to like them, but adults within all contexts should make every effort to always separate what a kid does from who they really are. If adults could be more objective in their interactions with troubled kids, they would be able to see serious mistakes they make which only incite and escalate a kid to anger and obnoxious behaviors. By challenging kids not to give adults the opportunity to be right about kids being lost causes, kids can get a lot of satisfaction out of making changes which will prove the adults to be wrong. Sometimes this scenario involves kids' perspectives of and interactions with family members as well.

While this approach must be handled in a professional manner, failure to acknowledge the kid's perspective will only make you "just like every other fucking asshole/bitch in my life." This will defeat your purpose of working supportively with your kid and will also jeopardize your ongoing professional relationship with her or him. Sometimes kids are just trying to be manipulative, but in a majority of cases with troubled kids their perceptions are very accurate. Keep in mind that most of the authority figures involved in their lives do not like them anyway. Therefore it is easy to assume that a kid's interpretation of their experiences is likely accurate. Many adults are often guilty of siding with adults no matter what the truth is. Be sure to resist this temptation and do not allow yourself to be pulled into an agreement when you know the truth contradicts what any adult is saying about a kid. This is part of the arrogance I am referring to relative to adults who have authority over kids. Adults very frequently gang up on troubled kids because in many cases the adults have done things they know to be in direct violation of the kid's rights and needs. This is especially true within the contexts of law enforcement and educational settings. Like it or not everyone knows that it is quite common for adults to cover for other adults if the general consensus is that of not liking a kid and not wanting them around. Believe me, troubled kids are especially sensitive to and aware of this kind of reality in their range of experiences within many, if not all of their environments. Like I said in a previous chapter, be part of the solution and not just another problem.

* *

Matthew Stevens was seventeen when he was referred to me from probation for mandatory counseling. He was in the eleventh grade and was always getting into trouble at school. The principal at Matt's high school was 'finally' able to get him charged with assault and placed on permanent probation. Needless to say Matt was pissed about this. While Matt was viewed as a troublemaker he was well liked by many school personnel.

Matt is a prime example of the importance of making the kid your focus of treatment and or interaction, rather than siding with the adults in her or his life. This is especially true with kids who are older and more mature as was the case with Matt.

Matt initially came on to our clinic with his mother to be registered for services. As was the case with many of my new referrals, I was not there at that time of day to meet Matt or his mother. The front office staff scheduled Matt for my next available intake slot on the following Tuesday. Most of the time a kid is accompanied to the office by his parent or guardian. However, Matt was alone, having taken the bus in order to keep his first mandated appointment with me. Even though he was a little apprehensive about the experience of meeting with a psychologist, he told me he was glad that his mom was not present, explaining that she always embarrassed him and made him mad. He told me his mom was mad at him for getting into trouble and didn't have time to be part of his treatment at a "mental clinic". I went through my usual routine and put Matt at ease very quickly. He was so glad to have someone to talk with who respected him and he opened up to me very willingly.

Very early in the interview it became obvious that Matt was extremely intelligent and that he had no clue of the extent of his intellect. He was very articulate and insightful relative to numerous complicating factors dominating his past and his present. All Matt knew for certain was that he was really pissed off about the way his life had been and the way it seemed to be going relative to his family. When we got to the family profile part of the interview he told me that his mom was married to a man of a different ethnicity than hers. His biological father had died a few years before our meeting, but had not been part of Matt's life until just before his dad died. Matt found out from his father that Matt's mother had kept them apart because Matt's father knew things about her past she didn't want Matt to know. Matt's mom told Matt about his dad and his whereabouts only because Matt's dad had contacted her to tell her he was dying from cancer and wanted to see his son. She apparently agreed in spite of her reluctance for Matt to have contact with his dad and Matt got to spend a relatively short amount of time with his dad before his dad died. During all of this

Matt learned that the man he always thought was his dad was in fact only one of mom's many boyfriends from the past.

Matt learned that his dad's cancer was associated with his history of heavy drug and alcohol use. While Matt had some idea about his mother's own history of drug addiction, he never knew that he had been born addicted to heroin. His dad told Matt that he was eight weeks premature and was not expected to survive, at least not without serious brain damage. To everyone's amazement Matt not only survived, but he beat the odds and had only minimal deficits relative to his cognitive functioning. Matt knew he had some problems with memory and comprehension, but had learned over the years to compensate for these deficits rather than let them impede his progress. However, Matt had no idea that all of this was related to his mother's addiction to heroin, a secret she had wanted to keep from him.

Obviously Matt confronted his mother with all he had learned. She reacted with a sense of righteous indignation, expressing her regret that she had told him about his real dad. Her regret was for herself and the fact that the truth came out about her past and the impact it had on Matt's health and wellbeing early in his life. Apparently the physical complications Matt had when he was born had given mom reason to stop using heroine, even though she continued to drink and use other substances until Matt was fifteen. Matt's mom was extremely abusive to him over the years and he deeply resented her for this. Learning the truth about her past and about his dad only deepened his resentment toward her for all she had put him through. The only thing that made this bearable was the fact that as mom cleaned up when Matt was fifteen and she tried to make all of this right with him. However, the damage had been done. In spite of mom's efforts to set things right she continued to live a very complicated lifestyle which had a very negative impact on Matt even at the time when I met him.

It is important to keep in mind that troubled kids usually have parents who were or are more troubled than the kids. Furthermore, it is not uncommon to work with kids who are more intelligent and insightful than their adult counterparts. Sometimes this is related to the extensive history of substance addiction for the adult which has negatively affected their ability to reason and function. Because of this it would be wrong to refuse to work with any kid because their parent(s) do not want to be involved in their treatment or other attempts to intervene on behalf of the kid. In reality all you really need from a parent or guardian is their signature giving you permission to work with their kid. As I stated previously, even when troubled parent(s) are involved, their involvement often creates a toxic environment in which very little progress, if any, can be made as long as they are part of the therapeutic process. This would have been the case with Matt and his mom. This is why it is so important that the main focus of treatment or other forms of intervention always be on the kid. Others should be involved if and only if it is in the best interest of the kid, and then only if the kid agrees to their involvement when you are dealing with a kid who is 15 years of age and older. Make sure that you as the professional are always in control of the process being implemented on behalf of any kid, regardless of their age. Do not be afraid to stand up against other adults if it is in the best interest of the kid. Believe me, some of my most successful interventions have resulted from my willingness to set very clear limits with adults by confronting them on their self-serving overindulgence and deception. The mom of one of my clients told me she respected me because I was not afraid of her, telling me she would remove herself from the process since it was clearly in her son's best interest that she do so.

Keep in mind that adults are not usually motivated to make changes. The more impaired they are the more likely they are to have serious personality disorders. These disorders become permanent and ineffective ways of trying to cope with life. For older adolescents in these situations the only solution is to work with them separately from the negative adult influences in their lives. By this point in a kid's life, it is generally too late to help the family repair itself. The longer a family stays broken the more likely it will become irreparably damaged. In this case the only thing to do is to try and literally save kids from these circumstances. This is the only way to keep them from repeating the mistakes of the parents by helping them identify and understand what the mistakes were and will continue to be. Part of my hope with the kids I see is that even if they cannot make the changes for themselves, they will at least protect their own children from harm when they become parents.

As I continued my interview with Matt he reluctantly revealed that he and his family were living in one of the local motels (referred to as "roach motels") occupied by people who had no other place to live. Matt was really embarrassed by this and no one in his life knew about this reality. He managed to keep it away from all of his friends even though they had been living in the motel for several months. The real insult about their current living situation was that Matt's mom and stepdad lost their last two apartments because of their recently acquired gambling addictions. No matter how much Matt begged them to stop gambling and save up the money they needed to get a new place, they continued to waste their money at the local casinos. The marriage between Matt's mom and his stepdad was really conflicted primarily because both of them had so many complicating factors present in their separate lives and personalities. Apparently because of their financial problems Matt's mom had started drinking again. Things were really bad for Matt and it became apparent to me why he was getting into trouble outside the home/family context. The thing that really surprised me that was he was not getting into more serious trouble than he actually was.

During this first session I was able to give Matt a glimpse into his unrecognized and unrealized potential. I helped him understand the two most amazing characteristics he possessed – resiliency (the ability to bounce back), and the ability to transcend or rise above the complicating factors present in his life. In this first session he was able to realize the level of his intelligence in spite of the fact his mother had always told him how stupid he was. Matt was able to see that he had the ability to continue beating the odds as long as he nurtured and maintained the desire to do so. He was also able to see that the problems he had in life were about where he came from and what he had been through, and had nothing to do with anything inherently wrong with him. I was able to help him make observations about his family which gave him insight into many realities present in his life which were beyond his control to either influence or change. This included the reality that his mom would likely never change to the point of being stable and likable. He was able to see that all he needed to do was find and hold onto hope for the future as a way of surviving until he was old enough to leave his mom. Thank God he was 17 and not even just a few years younger. At least at this age I could help him see that every day is one day closer to him being able to become independent as long as he prepared for that to happen by at least finishing high school.

I worked with Matt for about 18 months. By that time he had turned 18 and had his high school diploma. He faithfully and willingly took the bus every two weeks in order to keep his appointments with me. Each visit was filled with new insights and awakenings, coupled with the continual reinforcement of Matt's belief in himself and in his ability to succeed. After a few sessions I scheduled his appointments so he was my last client for the day. With that I offered to take him back to the motel where he lived rather than have him walking or taking the bus after each session. At first he was reluctant for me to see where and how he was living. After assuring him that his living conditions were a reflection on his parents and not on him he agreed. It took a few times of taking him to the motel before he agreed to let me meet his mom.

Keep in mind that parents of troubled kids who are troubled themselves often want to play the victim role. Matt's mom was no exception to this rule. She came out of the motel room rather than have me see the real conditions under which they were living. Matt stood beside me as I listened to his mom tell me how complicated her life was and how much trouble Matt had caused her especially in recent years. I had warned him about this and he had agreed to let me handle it for him, assuring him that I would if it became necessary.

After listening to this bullshit for several minutes, I simply told Matt's mom that I knew the truth about her and her past, and also knew the reasons why they were living in a motel. I told her she should be ashamed of herself for not realizing what an amazing son she has, telling her how sad it was that a relative stranger saw more in Matt then she did. With Matt standing right beside me I told her she should be grateful that her son had recovered from his addiction to heroine, which he acquired during her pregnancy, without having any serious residual effects as a result. I told her that I was offended that she would treat Matt with the level of disrespect and disregard she obviously displayed for him, with the assumption I would not see through her efforts. Furthermore I assured mom I was not buying any of this, and gave her a very vivid description of who I believed her son to be.

After a while mom started crying, telling me that she was sorry for the way she had talked to me about Matt. She told me that I was right about him and that she owed him more credit and respect than she was giving him. I assured her that I knew Matt was not perfect, but that he was a lot better off than he should be given all she had put him through. I told her I was not there to judge her, but that I would never allow her or any other parent to get away with attempts at such deception. None of this was done in a threatening manner and mom knew that I was simply right about what I had told her. She knew that I had not bought into her lies like other adults had always done in the past at the expense of her son. She acknowledged that since I had been working with Matt everything in his life had improved drastically. I told her that Matt was doing that for himself first and foremost and not for her, even though there were benefits for her in the changes Matt was making. Before I left I told Matt's mom that she was welcome to come to my office anytime she wanted to do so, but only if she was there to support and offer something positive to the work I was doing with him. I gave her my direct office phone number and urged her to call anytime she felt there was something significant I needed to know about Matt and any negative choices he might be making. She agreed and thanked me before she went back into the motel room.

Matt was astounded that his mom had allowed me to address her like I did, telling me she usually went off on anyone who challenged or crossed her. I pointed out that I did not once approach her in a manner that would have given her cause to feel the need to defend herself. He agreed that by stating my awareness of the truth so boldly I let her know that I was not going to buy into her one-sided, self-serving tales of woe. Matt also told me that no one had ever defended him as I had done with his mom or with anyone else for that matter. He clearly appreciated the fact that I not only believed what he had told me, but that I cared enough about him to stand up for him. There is no way Matt will ever forget the experiences we had together professionally. As he neared the end of his senior year I was able to write a grant request to the local police department and was given enough money to buy a complete computer system for Matt. He was shocked and very grateful, assuring me that he would make good use of the computer when he started college in the Fall at the local community college. Matt's mom was grateful for the support and assistance I was able to offer her son. When I terminated my sessions with Matt he and his mom and stepdad were still living in the same ratty, rundown roach motel where they were living when Matt and I first met. The difference now was that Matt had a diploma, had reached the age of 18, had a job, and was making specific plans for the future which would take him out of that situation permanently.

Treatment goals for kid such as Matt are really quite simple. The three most common goals I make for each of my troubled kids are these:

1. (My client) will not engage in any activities or behaviors which could result in any form of disciplinary action within the school setting and will work to maintain a GPA equal to her or his intellectual capabilities.
2. (My client) will not engage in any activities or behaviors which could result in such negative consequences such as arrest, confinement, retaliation, addiction, injury to self or others, or death.
3. (My client) will make future plans and goals to include getting a diploma or GED, securing a job, seeking out advanced job training and/or educational opportunities, and focusing on career possibilities which can be easily and readily verbalize.
4. Do what's right even when I don't want to. (represents both self-control and self-discipline)

As you can see these are very simple and straightforward goals which address virtually everything that could go wrong in a kid's life between sessions. They also address the need for forward thinking relative to a future which will come even if they are not prepared to face it. Each of these goals is specific and measurable, and can be easily monitored during the course of treatment which must include assistance and support to facilitate the achievement of these goals. I have taken many kids to visit job training programs such as Job Corps. On a number of occasions I have taken kids to register for school at a local college or trade school, and have helped them fill out the necessary forms to apply for financial aid. Frequently I talk with my kids about the need for establishing and maintaining a high credit rating, explaining the outcomes and obstacles they will face if they fail to do so. I have explained why the rewards received through criminal activity are more risky than they are worth. With every kid I explain the importance of having a strong work ethic along with the awareness that no one owes anyone anything. Furthermore, I work with each kid to get them to understand the limitations and demeaning effects of hand outs and so-called easy money. As often as possible I have met collaboratively with kids and their teachers, social workers, and/or probation officers in an effort to garner additional support from others and to make sure everyone involved in my client's life is on the same page.

Collaboration is much harder to accomplish now that it was when I first started working with this population. Law enforcement agencies and educational institutions have become much more closed to outside collaboration in recent years. I believe much of this is based in their need to protect themselves from scrutiny relative to the realities of the lack of assistance and support kids are now receiving within these contexts. There is no doubt in my mind that there are many ethical and legal violations occurring within these institutions. As a result the civil rights of many kids are being violated on a regular basis. The survival tactics of isolationism and territoriality relative to job security and the money and numbers games played by many institutions and organizations have become more important than the greater good and welfare of those they are meant to serve. There is no survival of the fittest. Rather, there is the survival of those with the greatest political power and influence needed to maintain themselves and guarantee their existence without any regard to effectiveness and appropriate use of funding. Ignorance quite often feeds arrogance, and arrogance feeds contempt and complacency. There is no room in the lives of society's underdogs for such thinking, or for these kinds of pissing contests.

All of my experiences over the years since 1992 with this population have given me a great deal of insight into the needs of these kids regardless of their geographical locations. Furthermore, my observations relative to the decline in services for this population cannot be denied either. The current political and social climates focus on punishment and incarceration rather than on any form of effective rehabilitation efforts toward redirecting lives and destinies. I know all of this because of my opportunities to look behind the scenes and look into the minds and closed societies within the agencies and institutions which are the biggest perpetrators of these injustices. All too often I have heard law enforcement officers literally state that the only way to deal with troubled kids is to get them off the streets. Some of these officers do not care if the kids are locked up or dead since either stated reality accomplishes their goal of getting troublemakers off 'their' streets. This is especially true between officers and kids when law enforcement officials have set up the competitive atmosphere of "we'll show you who's boss". This perspective explains the many occasions when I have had full awareness of the exaggerated and intentionally erroneous police reports which get these kids deep into the systems. And this observation is backed up by my awareness of statements made directly to me by cops and probation officers stating they will never waste their time writing up charges they cannot "make stick". The problem is that I cannot prove any of this because it all involves juveniles and juvenile records which are protected from outside scrutiny. I know for a fact that the proof of many of these kinds of injustices has been destroyed or altered to protect officials from disciplinary action or prosecution. Everyone behind the "blue curtain" knows that what I am saying is true, including those involved in prosecuting the cases.

The other biggest culprit is the educational system in this country. Here again, as I have stated previously, kids are denied access to much needed services. In many cases efforts are made behind the scenes to block awareness of both student and parental rights, and the existence of such services and laws. As with law enforcement agencies I know all of this first hand as well. However I have no way to prove any of this given the fact student records are protected and officials have ways of covering for each other rather than have any of this exposed. Just this week in Mobile,

Alabama a local news station investigated and exposed the outrageous expenditures of school board members relative to travel expenses. The trips were reportedly for training seminars and conferences. However, the expenses included very expensive meals and hotel accommodations for these school officials. There is no doubt in my mind that a significant percentage of the administrative overhead in virtually any school district could be cut drastically. This would free up more funding for student services rather than wasting it on bureaucratic overkill. Talk about entitlement programs! While teachers deserve to be paid well for their services, they must earn their level of pay based on academic results and progress of their students. Teachers unions and contracts have greatly hurt the public school systems and give teachers undeserved protection from accountability.

All of this said, I still have no concrete ideas of how to combat all of the injustices on my own other than by speaking out as I am doing here and as I do within the communities. I learned the hard way in California that I could not fight the corrupt systems directly. Instead I had to educate the public relative to their rights and to their need to stand up against injustices. The lack of means relative to defending themselves legally has to account for the fact that so-called minorities are so over represented within every existing criminal system. However, the problem with many low income families is that they do not have either the know-how or the means to take a stand needed to protect and guarantee their rights. People within the African American communities are much more likely to speak up and out about injustices. On the other hand many Hispanic American families are often afraid to do so because of their cultural beliefs and customs of not challenging authority figures. Furthermore, people in general who are considered to be lower class citizens are afraid of retaliation from authority figures, especially law enforcement, if they do take a stand. The only way I can see is for large numbers of people to join forces and begin to demand the quality of services they deserve. There is a great deal of truth in the strength-in-numbers philosophy. This seems to be the only force big institutions and organizations understand and regard.

The emphases of funding provided to serve and assist low income, high risk, troubled kids need to be focused on providing the most appropriate and efficient services possible. These services must include educational programs which inform and empower low income families about their rights in all arenas. Determination of what these services and programs would include must be decided initially by examining the ineffectiveness and inappropriateness of existing programs. It would be important to look at what works and keep those components, while taking care to eliminate ineffective programs which exist only because of their ability to sustain themselves because of political issues and connections. The key to the success of any programs and the appropriate use of funding depends on the concept of collaboration. No one entity can possibly meet every need for kids within this population and it is foolishly arrogant for them to even try to justify their isolated existence. Programs for this population must be comprehensive and contributors must be patient relative to measurable outcomes.

There is no doubt in my mind that the right use of funding will prove in the long run to be very cost effective relative to reducing the numbers of adult offenders and the numbers of recipients of public assistance. So much money is being mismanaged and misspent that it wouldn't take very much for people to weed out the useful from the ridiculous. During the transition period toward the reductions in the need for large prison systems and outrageous law enforcement efforts, professionals could be retrained to put their skills to work preventing problems rather than only punishing offenders. For many this would take away opportunities to satisfy their childish need to play cops and robbers. I am not sure how easy it would be to get people with these kinds of personalities and approaches to populations in need to let go of their control issues and need for competition. These egotistical needs would have to be replaced with such altruistic notions as being of service to others without any secondary gains to service providers being the goals. Based on those I know working within the systems which are the most useless, I am not even sure if such a transformation is possible with many of these individuals. After all, they have been given unchecked power and authority, all protected by a veil of secrecy under Homeland Security and the US Patriot Act. There is no doubt in my mind that the recent rise in violent crimes is the responsibility of those who have been federally sanctioned with the opportunity to abuse their power and authority. The competition set up in the streets between themselves and groups, including kids they now treat like terrorists is culminating in what will likely become a national backlash against law enforcement by those they target with their unchecked abuses of power and authority. Even if or when conditions improve, we as a society need to learn from the injustices being perpetrated at this point in history.

Successful programs will need to be very comprehensive in and of themselves. Each program and program professionals will need to have a strong commitment both to this population and to the time it will take to serve these kids and facilitate their success. Evaluation of outcome results will need to extend out as much as three to five years beyond program completion in order to adequately prove program effectiveness. Every program must be scrutinized and monitored relative to responsibility and accountability on all levels. There is no doubt that efforts to assist and redirect the lives of troubled kids are time consuming and expensive. However, nothing is more time consuming and expensive that the current means and efforts being implemented and enforced which have proven to be useless relative to desirable positive changes and outcomes. As I stated earlier, the hurricane season of 2005 exposed to the world the scam being perpetuated within this country relative to the inhumane treatment of low income groups. Even though the storms revealed the injustices and inequalities present in the South, there is no doubt that these same conditions exist throughout the entire country.

While there are no quick fixes or easy solutions I am doing my part to at least start with what I know. As of August 25, 2005 I have incorporated a nonprofit youth center under the name of Liberating Youth, Inc. We had our first board meeting on September 19, 2005 and filed our application that same week with IRS for 501(c)3 status. Liberating Youth, Inc. (LYI) is a comprehensive program with a structured format, all of which has been copyrighted as of July 2005. I will be both the executive director and the clinical director, and we will carefully evaluate outcome results once the program is implemented. Our 501(c)3 status was granted in August 2006. While waiting for this process to mature, and while waiting to secure startup funding, I have set up my own private practice under the corporate name of ProKids, Inc., using law enforcements' criticism of my work with the kids in California as the banner under which I will practice and franchise the LYI model. All of this will be carefully studied and documented as we progress. When the time is right I will make every effort I can to publish, publicize, and franchise the LYI concept around the country. All work under the name of ProKids, Inc. will roll over into LYI once we having funding to get the LYI project started. In the meantime we will be applying for local, sate and federal funding to make LYI in Alabama a reality as the first of many LYI locations to come. Watch for us under the internet heading of LIBERATINGYOUTHINC.org in the very near future.

In California I frequently told the kids with whom I worked that my goal was to someday completely shut down the juvenile justice systems as we know them today around the country. The kids would laugh, but would agree that if they would stop getting into trouble there would be no juvenile court, juvenile hall, juvenile placement facilities, or juvenile probation. While this is somewhat of a lofty goal, it is not a bad goal to have. With the LYI concept and the ProKids, Inc. format I plan to work toward the realization of some form of this goal before I die. Talk about a collaborative effort! However, rather than underestimate me, wish me luck and join me in my efforts. One such approach I referred to earlier is my F.A.T.E. Stops the H.A.T.E. and equalizes the R.A.C.E. campaign. If every likeminded individual and organization would join forces with me in this effort we could literally change and improve the futures of millions of low income, disadvantaged kids. This will only happen when people in this country begin to altruistically focus on concepts related to pure, non-religious Spirituality, rather than dogma and doctrine associated with present day forms of organized religion emphasizing money and numbers. Please help me help those in need!

12

Psyche-Soul-ology

R ecently I was having a conversation with a friend of mine. He asked me about the work I do with troubled kids, and specifically how I conceptualize my work and why it is so important to me. Personally I love this kind of question because it opens up what I consider to be a philosophical discussion regarding my own personal philosophies which motivate and inspire me. Our discussion culminated in the title of this chapter, a phrase which seemed to capture all of my philosophies under one heading – *Psyche-Soul-ology*. Initially we both laughed about it, but after some 'philosophical' consideration we both agreed that my new term seemed to sum up everything I believe and practice relative to high risk, troubled kids. It is also the Spiritual Philosophy through which I live every moment of my life. Let me explain.

According to The American Century Dictionary, 1995, the word psyche is defined as "the soul, spirit, or mind." However, every derivative of the word psychology refers basically to all things mental or of the mind. The above referenced dictionary defines soul as "the spiritual part of a person, also regarded as immortal." And, finally, the suffix "-ology" refers to a discipline, or a branch of study, or a field of knowledge relative to various subjects and interests. What was initially something amusing to my friend and me suddenly seemed to embody a more accurate label for the profession I claim given the fact that I refer to myself as a spiritual psychologist.

To me there is no way to separate or ignore the connection between the mind (psyche) and the heart (soul) within the field of psychology. No one has yet figured out where the soul resides within the human body – assuming there is such a thing as a soul. However, many people seem to refer to issues related to the heart as being almost synonymous with the concept of soul. My tendency is to associate the soul with the heart, and the mind as being the connection between that part of us which is human and that part of us which is spirit(ual). This stems from my belief that we are spiritual beings having a human experience, rather than human beings searching for a spiritual experience. I have heard a quote (origins unknown to me) suggesting "the longest 18 inches in the world is the distance between the heart and the mind." It seems that all too often people tend to be more grounded in one at the exclusion of the other. Many clients in therapy are considered to be "stuck in their heads" suggesting they try to rationalize and over analyze everything within their realm of realities. However, the mind is associated with thinking and reason, while the heart is associated with emotions. In reality there is no way to deny the connection between the two since the two different entities drastically interact with each other, quite often over-interacting. The process of interaction between the heart and the mind can either be conscious or unconscious relative to our overt awareness of the connection between the two. But, there is no denying that emotions drive thoughts and thoughts drive emotions. The key is to develop the art of allowing them to work in unison and in harmony with each other. After all both are more compatible than competitive if we would only allow them to be.

This is no less true with high risk, troubled kids. Consider all of the complicating factors I listed in my first book, At the Mercy of Externals: Righting Wrongs and Protecting Kids, 2nd Edition. (If you haven't read my first book you cannot get the maximum benefit offered by this current book!) Complicating factors generate both thoughts and ideas about realities present in kids' lives. Because they are *complicating* factors they also generate emotions – emotions which in many cases are quite strong. My RFLAGS Model – explained fully in my first book - graphically depicts how intense negative emotions result from abuse and victimization, even if the abuse and victimization result from environmental or situational factors. As we know many environmental factors represent the "external" factors to which I refer and are quite often beyond the ability of individuals, especially kids, to control or even influence. The RFLAGS Model further depicts how people of all ages are usually cut off from and thereby unaware of these intense negative emotions which emerge as depression and anxiety. These emotional states which we experience physically then lead to hopelessness and helplessness. From there the emotionally-based states of mind or belief systems then lead to various acting out behaviors which unfortunately become counterproductive attempts to cope with damaging external factors. These failed attempts to cope – which are the origins of adult personality disorders - create a vicious cycle of maladaptive behaviors and only increase the emotions because of the futility of these actions. This scenario coupled with the difficulty of making connections between the emotions and the past get lived out in the present and perpetuated into the future. These conditions continue until the issues are identified and the emotions are faced and resolved to whatever extent possible. The goal is to leave the past, and the emotions it generated behind, thereby learning to break the destructive cycle of acting out. This redirecting of energy allows the individual to learn and utilize effective coping skills which will lead to productive, rather than destructive, outcomes.

The above outlined process is basically a process of recovery from the past which unites psyche (mind) and soul (emotions or heart) in a symphony of harmony rather than discord. My approach of attempting to redirect an individual's use of their energy allows them to write a new "score" which they can then "conduct" and "orchestrate" toward more favorable and controllable outcomes. This takes them to an internal reality that everything we need in order to survive and thrive can only be found within ourselves – within our psyche and within our soul as they merge into a force of one which works for, rather than against each individual. Therefore, my strongest belief is summed up by my statement, "The Energy that *is* Us is God *in* us." My statement is based in another of my very strong beliefs that there is no heaven or hell, no good or evil, only the misuse or right use of our Energy which is God.

When I work with high risk, troubled kids I do not ask them to change into someone else. I simply ask them to work differently with who they already are by redirecting their use of the Energy which defines them and their potential. In order to do this every professional must be able to look beyond everything negative manifested externally – manner of dress, language, criminal activity, substance use, defiance, anger/rage, etc. – and see the Soul or higher Self within every child we meet, even into their early adulthood. This can only be done if we learn to make observations rather than judgments about what we see. At the same time we must be able and willing to look beyond what we see on the outside and look for the goodness which is present within the Soul of every child. The best last chance we have is to reach out especially to those kids who have reached or are approaching late adolescence and early adulthood. Recent scientific evidence relative to brain development suggests that adolescence continues into the mid 20's for each individual. Think back to how much you thought you knew at 20 compared to all you learned even by 25 and beyond, and tell me this observation is not accurate.

I also firmly believe that present day religions have failed miserably in their responsibility of helping us find God within our core nature. Religious people across the board all believe that God is somewhere "out there", whether in or at church, temple, synagogue, or mosque; or on the other side of this life in whatever manner that gets depicted. Unfortunately the so-called other side is usually described as a place of paradise which can only be attained by the strict adherence to specific religious rituals and practices – and nowadays, as in the past, even acts of violence as sanctioned by religious extremists.

Religious followers are generally taught that many things within our worldly existence are grounded in evil and in some concept of the devil or Satan. The confession printed in the liturgical text of one of the many Christian sects requires that penitents "bewail and bemoan their manifold sins and wickedness." We are cautioned to be ever watchful and on guard from the likelihood of assault from all sides and within every context except our places of worship. No one within today's organized religions is taught to find refuge within by simply acknowledging the God who already lives within us and who seeks not to be worshipped, but to be celebrated and honored through our lives. The only way to honor God is through the right use of the Energy within Us which is God in us. As a practicing "Psyche-Soul-ologist" I believe it is my spiritual responsibility to introduce society's underdogs to the Divine which already exists within them. I can do this without introducing them to counterproductive religious dogma which represents rigid and authoritarian beliefs. This increases the likelihood they will be able to stop being "at the mercy of externals" by realizing that everything they need is already at their disposal internally.

Since I have now returned to the 'deep south' and am living again in "LA" (Lower Alabama) I find myself being somewhat apprehensive and reluctant to share my spiritual beliefs even within the context of this book. Because this text is written primarily for professionals working with kids within in various fields of study and contexts, I almost feel that I have to go with the dominant thinking of the region if this book is to be accepted at all. Because of the so-believed "blasphemous" nature of my beliefs, many people within this region and other extremely conservative regions of the country would reject this book outright after reading this, the last chapter in the book. That is how narrow minded religious conservatives are when it comes to "defending their faith".

It took me many years to even begin to think as I do now, given my strict religious upbringing within a very conservative Christian religion. My need to look beyond what I had been taught grew out of numerous experiences in my life where religion either failed me or directly opposed an area of enlightenment I chose to pursue. Just reading The Celestine Prophecy series, published in the late 1990's by James Redfield, or using The Book of Runes, by Ralph Blum as sources of guidance took a great deal of courage on my part. I know firsthand how damaging extreme religious dogma can be as applied to the teaching of spiritual concepts which should be user friendly and adaptable with time and according to individual needs. Over time I have learned to appreciate many sources of inspiration beyond traditional religious texts. I no longer seek out writings which only support a set of beliefs I was told were the embodiment of Truth.

The most helpful realization I ever gained was the reality that any beliefs related to anything "spiritual" or to God are all "faith-based". This clearly means that *nothing* we believe about God can be proven. Therefore it is impossible and foolish to state with certainty that any spiritual beliefs are "THE TRUTH". Faith-based beliefs truly mean that the believers or espousers of such beliefs believe in something they *cannot* prove, but choose to believe in anyway. While there is nothing inherently wrong with this reality there is a great deal of room within this way of thinking for abuse and victimization. This is especially true when people are taught to believe in something by making them afraid to believe in anything else.

One of my next projects will be to study more about the psychology connected to religious beliefs and institutions. With everything going on in the world today it becomes more obvious all the time that the Christians, Jews and Muslims are all fighting to gain the top position. They treat this as some cause worth dying for without realizing they could all be wrong! I will not believe that any form of God is truly backing their unholy causes. Nor will I ever believe that strict adherence to their externally imposed and outwardly exercised rituals of prayers, fasting, rites of worship, confession, and penance make them any better or more deserving of God than "the others". The concept of evil is a powerful tool relative to instilling fear in the "hearts" (souls) of the faithful. I recently heard in a documentary about religions that the Hebrew word for Satan simply refers to the one who opposes God. It seems to me to be absolutely absurd for people to engage in this battle between good and evil, when both of these concepts are based in nothing more than faith. To be completely honest, as I gained more awareness of alternatives to the beliefs I was taught as a child I became enraged with the fear tactics used against me to insure my adherence to what I was taught. Well, believe me, I am no longer afraid, but seem to become only more outraged with all I see relative to the constant misuse by political and religious figures of the Energy which is God. None of this would bother me so much if not for the potential destruction of the world and humanity literally connected to this way of thinking and believing.

All of that having been said, let me now tell you how this ties into the work I do with high risk, troubled kids. Over the years I have had many opportunities to work with troubled kids who were incarcerated within in various juvenile justice contexts. Because of this I know all about the so-called "ministries of outreach" provided within these settings by religious groups. Kids within these settings will usually attend these services only because they offer the kids some diversion from their otherwise monotonous and boring daily routines. However, after the true nature of these presentations becomes obvious to the kids they will choose not to attend future meetings. Only a very few of the kids buy into what they are being told and then only for a short period of time.

Keep in mind that many of these kids already feel like they are worthless lost causes. These religious groups then come in and tell them they are indeed worthless lost causes because the Devil lives in them and dominates their lives. They are told that the only way to "save" themselves is to renounce Satan as the devil and the evils of sin by acknowledging their shameful nature. They are then told they must confess their sins and ask for forgiveness before they can invite Jesus into their hearts, and he will then save them from eternal damnation. The presentations are often made by those who state, "We were just like you before we found Jesus". The kids look at these people and see them as no better off than they were before their "conversion" into a "new person". In reality all these people have done is trade in one lifestyle of dependence on external factors for another lifestyle of dependence on a different set of external factors. Only this time the kids see their new existence as being far less appealing than what they reportedly left behind. After all, the last thing these kids want is to take on beliefs which require a strict and continuing adherence to rituals and other "acts of faith" as a means of guaranteeing their salvation and protection from eternal damnation. It is interesting to me that different religious sects differ in their view and interpretation of the permanence of salvation, with some believing literally in a "once-saved-always-saved" approach.

The thing that gets to me the worst about all of this is the fact that none of this focuses on the concept of the God within or the innate goodness within each of us. While I believe there are some who are inexplicably flawed toward the deviant side of violence and self-destruction, I believe these to be very few in number. I also believe these people have very serious brain disorders which rob them of access to the inherent goodness present in each of us. I am talking here about people like serial killers and serial sex offenders who seemingly have no conscience or self-control. Even here, though, I look at this as their inability to "act right" due to abnormal brain functioning which blocks their right use of their energy, rather than as a manifestation of pure evil as some would say. Think about the countless numbers of people throughout history who were killed in some rather gruesome and inhumane ways because they were thought to be either possessed, or witches and warlocks.

I am not here to take anything away from people. Nor do I believe that religion in and of itself is always bad. However, I do believe that my way of looking at God and the world makes more sense. If nothing else it is certainly less threatening relative to the possible annihilation of the world. It requires nothing more or less than simply celebrating and honoring the God within us through right living which includes altruistic service to others. This is drastically opposed to the historical need and competition between organized religions to be right relative to the claim that their God is the only "true God", and their founders were the only "true Prophets" or "Sons of God". No one has the right to force their religious beliefs upon anyone else. The only thing which matters should be that everyone finds some path to God through which they can base their faith as being the right path for them. Add to that whatever you need in order to make it meaningful, but remain fully mindful that no one knows the "truth" about anything related to God and spirituality.

Troubled kids respond very well to the fact that any belief in God is an act of faith and is by nature then improvable. Most kids believe religious people to be nothing more than hypocrites anyway. Many times the most dysfunctional people in their lives are also very religious, allowing kids to see how foolish religion can be when it is misused and misunderstood. Kids are very open to the idea that nothing more is needed than to see God as an integral part of who we already are. It is very easy to get them to imagine the path God might want them to follow compared to the path they are beginning to choose. They are relieved to learn that they do not have to change into someone else in order to change the way they use their energy and skills. And, kids are really interested in Spiritual alternatives to religion which are much more interesting than traditional religious approaches.

Many kids are fascinated by fantasy and mysticism. They are intrigued by the idea of reincarnation as a possibility and are very interested in psychic phenomena. One of the most amazing experiences to give a kid is the use of guided imagery through hypnosis which I am trained to do. They like the idea of out-of-body experiences and the possibility that we stay connected spiritually to those who have died. They are also intrigued by the concept of meditation which leads to an altered state of consciousness. These are things I can talk about with them openly and knowledgeably because of my interest in these spiritual approaches as well. Initially I sometimes have to help a kid get around their fear of looking outside of biblical teachings for other spiritual experiences and other pathways to God. This is true mainly for kids who have a background in traditional religious teachings. Once I get them over that hurdle the sky is the limit in terms of what they can discover for themselves relative to limitless faith in the infinite possibilities of the Energy in Us which is God in us.

As I stated earlier I am not trying to take anything away from anyone. However, I feel that all of what I have learned and revised especially within the last 18 plus years, and actually starting in 1983, has only enhanced my belief in the existence of a Higher Being. I discarded everything I was taught to be the "Truth" as a child as I faced my own sets of traumatic life experiences and found that nothing I had been taught was useful because it made no sense to me. There is no doubt in my mind that my spiritual life is now based in celebrating and honoring God by being true to my concept of the God within, to my concept of myself as being called according to His purpose, and to my concept of actively living my life in the here and now in service to others. It took a lot of courage to make these changes because I firmly believed I risked the so-called "wrath of

God and eternal damnation" for turning my back on what I had been taught. But there is no doubt in my mind that I am stronger on all levels because of my willingness to make these changes. My spiritual experiences since these changes have served to reinforce my faith-based belief that I am on my *own* right path.

I share with kids the prayer I quoted in my first book, from Ralph Blum's The Book of Runes, which states that with all that I am "I will to will THY WILL". In other words from the core of my being I want to want what You want, or I desire to desire what You desire. This statement is uttered not only as a prayer, but as an ongoing commitment to seek out and actively live out each individual's role in the overall Plan of God. Recently I realized that the more spiritually mature version of this prayer is simply "I will Thy Will"; "I want what You want"; and "I desire what You desire". Rather than simply wanting or desiring to do so, this is an active statement of commitment to the Will of the Divine, based in the belief this is really all that matters if there truly is a God in charge of all which exists. This is in opposition to the religious perspective of living to die with the only things worth looking forward to being found on the other side, and then only if you say all the right things, practice all the right rituals, and believe only what you have been told to be the truth. The tragedy of religion is that religious leaders teach blind acceptance of what they espouse, equating doubt with sin. Doubt in a religious connotation includes any thinking or pondering which is contrary to what is being taught from the pulpit as the "Truth". This is nothing short of brainwashing with fear tactics being used to insure compliance with interpretations of religious doctrine and dogma. Believe me when I say that I know what I am talking about given the fact this is the way I was raised!

Individual uniqueness is a central theme to what I believe. When I tell a kid they are so unique that there are things in this life which they and only they can do, they are amazed at this perspective. By helping them see that because there is one and only one of them, they begin to understand their importance in a sense of some overall possible Plan which is bigger than each of us. They can understand that even if I could completely clone them physically, their clone could never be exactly like the person they already are. I explain that their clone would literally have to experience all of the exact same things in life they had experienced in order to be exactly like them. Kids understand this would be a phenomenological impossibility and can appreciate the likelihood that what I am saying is probably the truth. Individual uniqueness is the place to start with every troubled kid you meet. This is what gets their attention and ignites their willingness to consider other ways of looking at and experiencing life into their future which they will create either consciously and deliberately, or unconsciously and passively.

I wholeheartedly believe each of us possesses a very strong intuitive, psychic side to our overall nature and personal capabilities. However, very few people are taught to recognize this skill and nurture it into a conscious life tool which will guide us through every phase of our existence. It is interesting to me that many people openly admit they believe in psychic phenomenon, with many stating they have experienced something which they can only explain as being supernatural. There is a strong interest in the ability to connect with those who have died as evidenced by a large volume of literature and several television shows and movies which present these phenomena as realities. Many people also believe in near death experiences which transform lives for the better in most cases. People are interested in the prospect of miracles and the connection between the mind and the body when it comes to healing. To me all of these misunderstood and underutilized phenomena are very real parts of the Energy in Us which is God in us. If God is all knowing and possesses all of these kinds of powers, why would we be any less capable if we are truly created in the image of and by God?

This is no less true for troubled kids. All of this serves as a way to get their attention relative to looking differently at themselves and at life in general. This kind of thinking and questioning opens up infinite possibilities for kids who have very little, if any hope for their future. Since no one knows what the "Truth" really is anyway, why not at least give kids the opportunity to consider these possibilities along with other possibilities to which they have likely been exposed. Believe me, these kinds of subjects will open up some rather incredible discussions with kids who are open to such considerations. Not all kids are, and it is very important to acknowledge and respect the beliefs of every individual unless those beliefs are harmful to them in some way. However, a vast majority of troubled kids are desperately seeking knowledge and possibilities which will serve them better than the realities they have been exposed to so far in their lives.

My exposure to hypnosis started with my own therapist who worked with me for about five years in Los Angeles. At first I was very skeptical about allowing him to "put me under", but I finally agreed to at least experience the process of relaxing in preparation for hypnosis. This was all it took for me to be hooked on the entire experience. He only used hypnosis with me five times and each time was focused on a specific issue. In addition to the office sessions which he recorded for me, I practiced the experience of hypnosis at home using his tapes. Within no time I was able to induce my own hypnotic state without the guidance of a tape or a hypnotherapist. What an incredible skill to have! I have learned to use it as I meditate and pray, especially at times when I need to work through things in my life which are confusing or even baffling to me at the time. Hypnosis simply takes you inward and away from distractions so you can work on the things stuck in your subconscious mind.

After using the skill for my own enhancement, I eventually took a weeklong class with a well-known hypnotherapist while I was still in California. From these experiences I would use hypnosis in my classes at the local community college as just an interesting experience for psychology students who wanted to either participate or simply observe. I also used hypnosis very selectively over the years with some of my troubled kids I served as their psychologist – or Psyche-Soul-ologist. I would strongly encourage everyone to take a class in hypnosis, if for no other reason than to dispel the myths associated with the art as it is portrayed for entertainment and amusement purposes. No one will do anything under hypnosis they would not be willing to do under other circumstances. I believe that hypnosis can easily be misused in ways which could traumatize people, especially if it was used as a means to put people in touch with traumatic experiences they have had. I also believe it is useless in the recovery of suppressed memories given the fact that people in general are very suggestible. However, I do believe it is very useful with troubled kids only as a way of getting them to literally look at themselves in the imaginary mirror to see who they are becoming compared to who they are meant to be. This is the only way I have ever used hypnosis with anyone outside of my own meditation experiences.

While this is not a book about hypnosis, I do want to clarify how I use this with kids. After I explain to them that hypnosis has nothing to do with mind control or humiliation, and is only a state of deep relaxation, they are usually interested in at least trying the relaxation exercise. Hypnosis is actually used very frequently in various settings under the guise of "guided imagery". No one should use a guided imagery technique without the awareness that you have no way of knowing or controlling how your individual group members will experience even something related to grief recovery. Any form of hypnosis has the power to unleash strong and often unpleasant emotions; therefore, the use of hypnosis must be carefully implemented for a very specific purpose. Never take on any more than you are trained to handle. This is my reason for only using hypnosis with troubled kids as a means of getting them to see themselves differently. I would never try to get into their emotions, have them relive traumatic, or otherwise abusive experiences, or take them back into their past. Even in my classes I only used the imagery to help students see themselves as successful now and on into their future as they graduate, pursue additional education goals, and explore career options. I never do anything I think could traumatize anyone.

Because many troubled kids drink and at the very least smoke marijuana, I find it easy to get them to relax by having them think of hypnosis as the ultimate natural high. This also gets them to be aware that there are other ways, besides substance use, to help them feel good about themselves and their lives. This approach even works really well with hardcore gang members. Once I have a kid in the altered state of consciousness as achieved through the deepest level of relaxation possible, I take them into a room which they create in their minds. They can put anything in this room which makes them feel safe and comfortable. The only specific request I make is that the room include a large full-length mirror which is either attached to a wall or is supported by a frame and sits on the floor as with a dressing mirror.

After giving them some time to acclimate themselves to the room they have created in their mind, I ask them to stand in front of the mirror they have also created. While in front of the mirror I have them visualize themselves wearing the clothing and displaying the personae they literally wear out in the streets with their friends. After some time and some additional requests, I have them visualize their twin standing beside them to their left. This twin is to be dressed in the style and with the personae as the kid I have come to know and respect. I get them to spend a great deal of time carefully observing the stark difference between the two figures reflected in the mirror. My constant comment is that these twins represent different sides of the same person and are not two different people. They get this.

At some point I suggest they merge the two figures into one person, with the image of the kid as I know them superimposed over the kid I have never really known. This gives them the opportunity to see that their true nature can become their dominant nature if they would allow that process to begin. As they look at the kid I know superimposed over the kid on the streets I ask them to watch as the kid from the streets begins to fade, leaving only the kid I know as the unified self. I tell them that both sides of their nature still exist and that it is up to them as to which one dominates their choices for the future. I have them imagine the loss of the kid I know if they fail to make this transition as they learn to use their energy differently in more productive ways. I then have them imagine the kinds of positive things in life which would make them feel like they were successful in leaving the negatives parts of their past behind. I have them imagine things like graduating from high school, possibly pursing job training or education beyond high school, and then successfully selecting and starting a career. I also have them imagine how their lives will likely turn out if they continue making the wrong choices.

This is a very powerful experience for each kid. I have them look at the clock before we start and when I bring them back into full consciousness. Generally I keep them under for about 40 to 45 minutes. They are always amazed at the fact time has passed without their awareness of it doing so. I can get them to see that the negative images they imagined will be the way life is for them if they do not learn to take control over their destiny and make the decisions which will give them the future they deserve. After a little passes time for them to re-acclimate themselves to their surroundings I have them describe to me the details of what they literally created in their minds. This experience of recalling the details helps to make it stick and always gives me the chance to know what their mind did with my suggestions. This is fun for them and at the same time offers them insights it would be hard for them to attain just by talking about these issues. There is no way they will ever forget the experience. It is very important to watch every aspect of their body as they experience the hypnotic state. This is the only way to make sure they are experiencing everything as you desire it to be for them and is the only way to know how deep they go into the subconscious state. The kids find it hard to believe how incredible the experience was for them. They find it even harder to believe they were able to let it happen so successfully.

Another amazing experience is helping kids talk about friends and other loved ones who have died. The next step is to help them understand their grief experience as an adjustment to the fact these relationships changed, but did not end. This eliminates the pressure they may feel to forget and move on as though there is no lasting connection, at least not until after they have also died. One of the most significant factors in my own spiritual growth and development has been my work with a psychic who is also my strongest and most reliable spiritual advisor. I met her in January 1994 and have continued having regular readings at least two or three times a year. The most remarkable thing she did for me was to make me aware of my connections to several very special people in my life who have died. There is no doubt she was able to connect with them as evidenced by information revealed to her which could have only come from the individuals who made their presence known. It was within these moments that I learned my relationships with these souls did not end. Our relationships simply changed into something even more meaningful than what I had known on earth with them given the added dimension of a sense of eternal connection. I was given the assurance that we do continue beyond this existence. These experiences also gave me the assurance that there is a life after this one and also let me know it is not like anything I had been taught through any religious institution or frame of reference. Through the guidance of my spiritual advisor I learned that my intuitions relative to many things in life were my own spiritual abilities. She taught me to embrace these skills as the spiritual gifts they are.

My psychic, who wishes to remain anonymous, taught me that I have psychic abilities as well, something traditional religions disapprove of and denounce as heresy. She also stated that each of us has the skill, but very few ever work to consciously develop it due primarily to religious opposition and media portrayal of such skills as spooky. I already knew that I had a strong ability to "read" the kids with whom I worked. Quite often I have shocked them with questions regarding very specific issues about which no one else knew any details. Early in my career I just dismissed these readings as lucky guesses, but they clearly made an impact on my kids. Over time I nurtured these skills and eventually began to have the experiences as a medium with the kids I serve. This seems to happen only with kids who are open to the discussion of such possibilities. Only those kids who were comfortable talking about and learning about what is referred to in recent decades as "New Age Spirituality" were able to bring these kinds of encounters into the session. I never did anything to cause this. Nor is it something I can conjure up or do on demand. It always happens naturally as I discuss issues of death and grief with kids, and with other more informal acquaintances who have also experienced losses of friends and family members. Furthermore, there is no way for me to predict when or if these incidents will occur.

There is nothing magical about this. It just happens and is a very humbling experience for me. However, I believe it happens because I opened myself up to the desire to experience as much as I could relative to psychic and other spiritual phenomena. I pray openly for the abilities to heal, to see, to prophesy, to know, and to convey, all as what I consider to be the building blocks of deeper wisdom. How ridiculous for some people to think that I have opened myself up to the devil relative to things which are so sacred in nature. My awareness of the presence of another soul begins as a feeling of tension or tightness seated deeply in my chest. I have learned with time to pay very close attention to this when I am working with a kid. It feels like an intense level of energy and it seems that the souls somehow think themselves into my head. I do not see them as much as I see pictures of them and receive messages from them which seem like shared thoughts sent to me from them. Even if a kid is not open to such experiences, it will still happen occasionally. When it does I will find an indirect way to use the information I am being given to question the kid and help them deal with whatever comes up. It makes sense to me that anyone who works as a therapist would, or at least should have a very strong intuitive nature. I believe that intuition and psychic abilities are one in the same and should be pursued and developed as very useful clinical skills. I do not support anything bordering on witchcraft, black magic, voodoo or Ouija board/séance types of activities. While I do not believe in evil I do believe in the existence of negative energy which we cannot explain and do not need or want to encounter.

Each of these kinds of experiences has always been helpful to the kids with whom I have had the experiences. The detailed information revealed to me is undeniable by the kid. Every kid is absolutely astounded, intrigued, and transformed by the experience, including hardcore gang members who are at first alarmed that I can see and know such things about them and their past. My psychic tells people that I am "the only psychic for the gangsters". I tread very carefully into this with kids who are suspicious of people in general. If I sense any kind of resistance I back off, but still find some way to address some degree of what is happening within me. As a result I have never had a kid regret the experience. Because of the somewhat controversial nature of the experience I have to ask kids to not discuss what happened with other people who might not understand or appreciate what we shared. There is nothing unethical or immoral about what I do with any kid, but some people would accuse me of exposing kids to things which are evil in nature. This could not be any further from the truth. If this happens with a kid who knows other kids who have the same experiences with me I will ask permission from the kid to tell the others. If the other kids feel comfortable doing so, they can then discuss every aspect of what happened. I find this only reinforces the reality of what happened, even though this reality is ironically mystical in nature.

There is no doubt in my mind that the so-called "gifts of the spirit" listed in biblical texts are nothing less than the same psychic phenomena I am addressing here. Think about people who go into trancelike states who are said to be "filled with the spirit". Taken out of context they would be thought by many to be either psychotic or possessed. The same is true for people who possess the gifts of healing and prophecy. There are even biblical accounts of people who encounter the souls of people who have died. If God truly lives within us, and if the Energy which is Us is God in us, then it would make sense that we have more skills available to us than we allow ourselves to explore. The ability to develop these skills on our own reduce our dependency on religious institutions which do little more than foster dependency in order to keep their money and numbers factors strong. Organized religion is one of the biggest money and numbers games around.

With all of this said, I now close out the writings of this text, feeling and believing that everything expressed herein is Divinely Inspired. It is my hope that all who read this text will learn to utilize the approaches put forth in this and my first book. By doing so we can truly begin to help low income, disadvantaged, troubled kids successfully redirect the use of their Energy which is God within them. There is truly nothing magical about any of this. However, I believe very strongly that it is impossible for anyone to inspire others, especially kids, if we are not truly inspired spiritually. Therefore I urge each reader to think outside the traditional boxes, looking deeply within your own soul to find who you are truly meant to be. Failure to do so will completely undermine your efforts to successfully reach out to those within our society who are the most vulnerable. Please do not make the mistake of being one of those with the best of intentions who does the most harm. Learn to see and experience the world of troubled kids through their eyes and by understanding their realities. Only then can you be both compassionate and passionate in your work and dealings with this group of kids. Openly practice the concepts and approaches associated with Psyche-Soul-ology for yourself and for those you serve. Read the Oath toward the end of Chapter 6 in At the Mercy of Externals: Righting Wrongs and Protecting Kids, 2nd Edition, and truly take it to heart relative to all roles you play in the lives of kids. Be good to yourself and to the kids under your charge. And, may The Source be with you!

Printed in the United States
By Bookmasters